LAND AND CASTE IN SOUTH INDIA

Land and Caste in South India

AGRICULTURAL LABOUR
IN THE MADRAS PRESIDENCY
DURING THE NINETEENTH CENTURY

DHARMA KUMAR

MANOHAR
2026

First published by Cambridge University Press 1965
Reprinted with a new Introduction 1992, 2022, 2023
Reprinted 2026

ISBN 978-81-7304-005-4

Published by
Ajay Kumar Jain for
Manohar Publishers & Distributors
4753/23 Ansari Road, Daryaganj
New Delhi 110 002

Printed and bound in India

TO MY PARENTS

CONTENTS

LIST OF TABLES AND FIGURES

ACKNOWLEDGEMENTS

I am grateful for their help to Professor D. R. Gadgil, Professor J. A. Gallagher, Dr E. R. Leach, Dr Dharm Narain, Professor M. M. Postan, Mr V. K. Ramaswami and Professor M. N. Srinivas, and to Mr Haruray for preparing the graphs on prices and wages.

An article based on Chapters III and IV has appeared in *Comparative Studies in Society and History*, March 1962, and one based on Chapter X in *Contributions to Indian Economic History*, 1963.

A NOTE ON CERTAIN CONVENTIONS

No single system of spelling Indian words has been followed. In the case of place names, the old usage is adopted because it occurs so frequently in the quotations: for example, 'Trichinopoly' and not 'Tiruchirapalli'. For other words, such as the Tamil, Telugu and Malayalam agrarian terms, I have generally followed modern usage, but I have not thought it necessary to reach the point of precision of diacritical marks and so forth.

Indian words are italicized, except for names of coins, and for caste names, which are treated like other proper names.

Figures in rupees have been given in crores (1 crore = 10,000,000) and lakhs (1 lakh = 100,000), but figures of acreage are in millions.

ABBREVIATIONS

East India Papers	*Selections of Papers from the Records at the East India House, Relating to the Revenue, Police and Civil and Criminal Justice Under the Company's Governments in India*, 2 vols. (London, 1820).
Fifth Report	*Parliamentary Paper*, 1812, VII (377), *Fifth Report of the Select Committee on the Affairs of the East India Company*.
G.O.	Government Order.
I.O.	Despatches from the India Office to Madras, preserved in the Madras Record Office.
Moral and Material Progress Report	*Statement Exhibiting the Moral and Material Progress and Condition of India*.
P.B.R.	Proceedings of the Madras Board of Revenue, preserved in the Madras Record Office.
P.P.	*Parliamentary Paper*.
R.D.	Revenue Despatches from Madras to the India Office, preserved in the Madras Record Office.
Report on Slavery, 1841	*Report of the Indian Law Commissioners on Slavery*, 1841, *P.P.* 1841, XXVIII (262).
Select Committee Report, 1831–32	*Report of the Select Committee on the Affairs of the East India Company*, *P.P.* 1831–2, XI and XII.
Slavery Papers, 1828	*Slavery in India: Correspondence and Abstracts of Regulations and Proceedings P.P.* 1828, XXIV (125).
Slavery Papers, 1838	*Slave Trade: Correspondence, Orders and Regulations and Proceedings taken thereon, 1829–36*, *P.P.* 1837–8, LI (697).

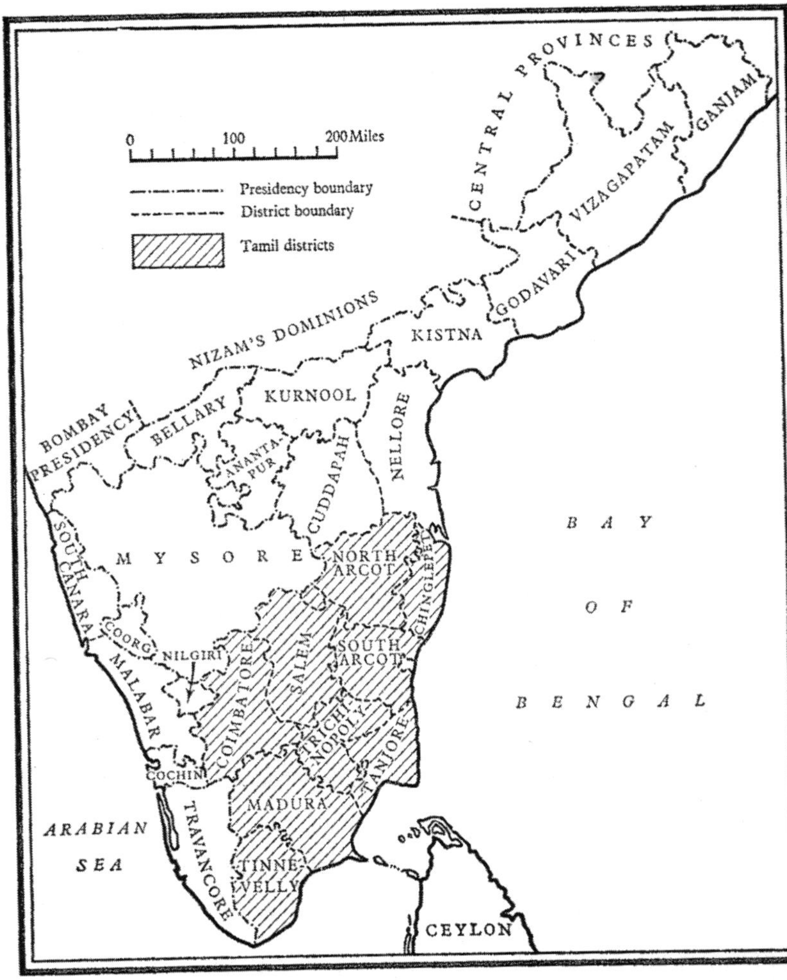

Madras Presidency in the late nineteenth century

INTRODUCTION TO REPRINT*

Land and Caste in South India (hereafter L & C)[1] was published in 1965. Twenty-five years later I would naturally write a very different book. There was no point in making minor changes to the original text; the choice before me was wholesale revision or the original version, and I took the easier course.

I have let the original version stand, but use this introduction to clarify some points and modify others, partly in the light of work that appeared after the manuscript of L & C was sent to press in 1963. This introduction does not set out to review the literature, nor does it cover all the subjects dealt with in L & C. So I do not refer to recent work, however excellent, if it is not substantially germane to the specific issues I am concentrating on. Three topics are discussed in subsequent sections: sources and the use of data; institutional issues, including definitions of status categories; and finally, estimates of the numbers of agricultural labourers at the beginning of the nineteenth century, and the connection between caste and occupation, the two points on which I have been most frequently quoted, and misunderstood.

Perhaps readers should be reminded at the outset of the intellectual climate of the 1950s and 1960s. The dominant view amongst Indian historians, many though not all of whom were Marxists, was that the class of landless labourers was created by imperialist rule, itself an inevitable part of the expansion of capitalism. S.J. Patel was the most frequently cited exponent of this view: "In pre-nineteenth century India there were domestic and menial servants; but their numbers were small, and they did not form a definite group that emerged during the late nineteenth and early twentieth centuries in India."[2] It was this view that I sought to question, by estimating the numbers of agricultural

*For helpful comments on this introduction and information, I thank Alan Heston, Ramachandra Guha, David Ludden, M. Atchi Reddy and Sanjay Subrahmanyam.

[1] The following additional abbreviations are used in the introduction:
IESHR: Indian Economic and Social History Review
L & C: *Land and Caste in South India* (1st printing)
MAS: Modern Asian Studies.

[2] S.J. Patel, *Agricultural Labourers in Modern India and Pakistan,* p. 32.

labourers around 1800 in Madras Presidency, an area singled out by Patel, and also one where landless labour was disproportionately large even in the 1950s.

Nor is this issue even now a dead horse - why it has lasted so long is a good subject for intellectual historians. Indian historians are not unique in their ability to believe in universal, "scientific" laws of history, despite the evidence, and Smethurst analysing Japanese historiography, has identified one intellectual habit also found in India: "The belief in the trend towards polarisation is based on the acceptance of a mode of analysis which precedes the accumulation of evidence, and this seems to make it very difficult to abandon."[3] A good Indian example is provided by the following defence of S.J. Patel, now elevated to a "classic":[4]. ".. while it is factually incorrect, such a statement [Patel's] is not to be contradicted with validity by making the counter-assertion (as Dharma Kumar does) that the class of agricultural labourers was not affected by colonial rule and was a pre-existing entity."[5] This is of course very far from what I said; a large part of L & C in fact discussed the various changes in the conditions of agricultural labour during the nineteenth century, including famines and population, wages and emigration. I was cautious about class formation, stating merely that "it was not the case that the class of landless labourers was *wholly* created during the British period by the impoverishment of the peasant proprietor and village craftsman" (L & C p. 193; emphasis added).

[3] R.J. Smethurst, *Agricultural Development and Tenancy Disputes in Japan, 1870-1940,* Princeton, 1986, p. 29.

[4] Cf. Irfan Habib, "Writing Colonial History Without Perceiving Colonialism," *Modern Asian Studies,* Vol. 19, No.3, 1985. Also see my reply in the same issue, "The Dangers of Manichaeism."

[5] Utsa Patnaik, introduction to Utsa Patnaik and Manjari Dingwaney ed, *Chains of Servitude,* Madras, 1985, p.27. Typically, Patnaik writing in 1985, cites Patel's inference that there was a huge increase in agricultural labour between the 1871 and 1931 Censuses even though Krishnamurty pointed out in 1972 the numerous errors Patel made in using the Censuses. Krishnamurty also showed that the Census data for undivided India for 1871-1931, and for the Indian Union in 1901-1961, "suggest no upward trend in the share of agricultural labour in the agricultural working force." J. Krishnamurty, "The Growth of Agricultural labour in India, *IESHR,* 1972, Vol. 9, p. 332.

DATA PROBLEMS

L & C was typical of its time in its complete reliance on official records. Also, while I did discuss the need to interpret early official writings with care, reflecting as they often did misunderstanding of Indian society and the drawing of inappropriate analogies with feudal Europe, later work has shown that I did not question my sources sharply enough, nor look for others.

Our most abundant source of information for the outset of British rule, and the decades preceding it, is still the official reports and correspondence of the first half of the nineteenth century. But early British officials were very unclear about South Indian laws, customs and social institutions; they confused caste with civil status and used European feudal terms to describe Indian land tenures. When using their writings we must always be aware of the errors they were particularly prone to. While difficult, this constant vigilance is not impossible. One may sometimes be able to judge whether a particular official was reliable or not,[6] but one's own judgement can be questioned too, and it is best to consider general issues as well as particular cases. There may be reasons to expect a particular bias; for instance, in the earlier colonial period, officials often wished to denigrate their native predecessors, to give themselves legitimacy. In later years, the desire to save money was a powerful motive; for instance officials became chary of reporting famine conditions when government expenditure on famine relief became obligatory.[7] There is also the problem, which Frykenberg pointed out, that British officials often relied on subordinate native officials who had their own axe to grind.[8]

Self-interest apart, native informants were (and are) imperfectly informed about the customs of other groups than their own. Scholars have stressed the errors the British fell into because of their over-

[6] This is the procedure followed by Benedicte Hjejle, "Slavery and Agricultural Bondage in South India in the Nineteenth Century," *Scandinavian Economic History Review*, Vol. XV, Nos.1 and 2, 1967, hereafter Hjejle, "Slavery and Agricultural Bondage."

[7] This is discussed in the context of the Orissa famines in Bidyut Mohanty, "Famine and its impact on the agrarian and demographic structure with special reference to Orissa, 1866-1921," Delhi University Ph. D. dissertation, 1989.

[8] R.E. Frykenburg, *Guntur*, Oxford, 1965.

dependence on pandits and mullahs for information on native laws; and British officials themselves occasionally recognised this problem.[9] Yet another error is to assume that native informants are reliable on historical issues, and that the further back one goes, the more reliable they get. It is certainly true that weight should be attached to the testimony of contemporary witnesses of events, but why should an early nineteenth century native know more about say, the origins of bondage in South India, than a late twentieth century historian, whatever his or her nationality? The chances are, on the contrary, that he will know less.

There are yet other problems with official documents that have not been mentioned at all, as far as I am aware, in the literature on India. Writing on Africa, Vansina points out that "It is a time-honoured custom in administrations to plagiarize earlier reports. Thus the case of an administrator publishing a study in which he incorporated crucial data and interpretations culled from an earlier manuscript written by a colleague is not uncommon. Forgery is rarer, but has occurred, at least forgery in the sense that the author falsely claimed that his information came from personal observation and direct oral inquiry."[10] Certainly official plagiarism is exceedingly common now, and not just of other official writing, but of academic books and articles; and forgery, in Vansina's sense, also occurs in India. Perhaps these were less common in the colonial era, but we should be aware of these possibilities of unreliability in official sources nonetheless. Plagiarism is particularly dangerous - one may take the fact that one report agrees with another as a sign of consistency, and hence of the strength of the findings, when it may merely be a sign of plagiarism. There is another serious problem, that of omission - the officials may simply have failed to record facts which we now see as important but which they were uninterested in, such as kinship relations, or were simply blind to, such as the means of legitimation or socialisation of relations of dominance. We can go a little way by speculating on the nature of the omissions, perhaps by using comparative data from other societies, but only a little way. Independent evidence on the way institutions actually functioned is essential.

9 Nelson is a notable South Indian example: J.D.M. Derrett,"J.H. Nelson: A forgotten administrator-historian of India," in J.D.M. Derrett, *Essays in Classical and Modern Hindu Law,* 3 vols, Leiden: 1977, vol. 3.

10 Jan Vansina, *Paths in the Rainforests,* London, 1990, p.17.

L & C relied too heavily on revenue records, and other official records should have been tapped. Thus court records may throw light on certain aspects of master-servant relations, though they have to be used with special care, because of the high probability of exaggeration and outright falsification. Nevertheless, it is unfortunate that these records have not yet been mined by the historians of South India, though David Ludden does refer to them.[11]

L & C was poor in the use of fairly easily available unofficial records, such as newspapers, and literature, especially autobiographies and memoirs.

Finally, there are the accounts of farmers themselves, a source which it is generally assumed does not exist in India. But Atchi Reddy, in his pioneering work on Nellore, has found a mass of private farm accounts and registers going well back into the nineteenth century. These are invaluable for economic historians; for instance the private farm accounts record actual wage payments, rather than the estimates of minor officials enshrined in the official series.[12] Imaginatively used, they can reveal information on questions almost totally neglected in the literature, as we shall see.

[11] David Ludden, *Peasant History in South India,* Princeton, 1985.

[12] M. Atchi Reddy, "Wages Data from the Private Agricultural Accounts, Nellore District, 1893-1974," *IESHR*, 16, 3, 1979. In addition, he has unearthed a large number of tenancy agreements, one aspect of which has been described in "Rich Lands and Poor Lords: Temple Lands and Tenancy in Nellore District, 1860-1986," *IESHR*, 24, 1, 1987. They are exhaustively analysed in a forthcoming book.

II. DESCRIBING INSTITUTIONS

L & C was rightly criticised for its unsatisfactory treatment of the institutions of bondage in Chapter III, but the reasons for this failure were not correctly identified. The first, shared by many of my critics, was simply my ignorance of the general literature. This ignorance was perhaps not as serious then as it would be now. Since L & C was written there has been an explosion of work on the institutions of bondage in anthropology, economics, sociology, and history. Western Europe is still pre-eminent, but work on other areas is growing fast, especially on Africa. But grave problems remain in defining, identifying and describing institutions. Bondage has many dimensions, and the social sciences differ in which dimensions they isolate for analysis. Thus neo-classical economists define bondage in terms of property rights in man, while sociologists concentrate on power (of which property rights are an aspect). The economist generally considers only formal law and takes its efficacy for granted, though the range of issues economists analyse is fast increasing. The sociologist considers not only types of law, but to what extent legal rights are in fact secured, and such issues as membership of society, and the role of the shame and honour.[13] For all theorists, slavery is the extreme form of bondage; what further distinctions one makes depends partly on one's general framework, but for historians, also on the data available.

The historian of South India is on the horns of a dilemma. Should she use English words like "slave", or words in native languages, like the Tamil *adimai*? Each course has its own advantages, but both suffer from the same defect. The advantages of using English words are manifest - they are understood by the general reader and they facilitate comparative studies. But they can also suggest inappropriate connotations - this is particularly true of "serf", which leads one straight into the confusions of "feudalism" and "semi-feudalism". Vernacular words do not have these disadvantages, but they do not have the advantages of English words either. There is no question, of course, that all vernacular terms should be listed and discussed, but English

[13] To the sociologist Orlando Patterson, *"Slavery is the permanent, violent domination of natally alienated and generally dishonoured persons"*, *Slavery and Social Death*, Cambridge (Mass), 1982, p.13. Emphasis in the original.

words also need to be used - in particular "chattel slave", "debt peon", and "bondsman". The former two have reasonably precise meanings, but the vagueness of the last term is useful too. It shows that some form of bondage is implied, but allows the historian to fill in the particular forms of bondage she is discussing.

But the really knotty problem is that the main sources are British officials, and to a lesser extent European travellers, whose use of both European and local terms is problematic; it is sometimes clear that they have made an error, but not always, nor can one be sure of how to correct the error. L & C met this problem by putting English words into quotation marks, but this is only an interim solution. No real progress can be made until we know more about how institutions actually functioned at various points of time.

INSTITUTIONAL QUESTIONS

Pre-colonial Regimes

Most of Madras Presidency, with the notable exception of Tanjore, was acquired from Muslim rulers - Tipu Sultan, the Nizam of Hyderabad or the Nawab of Arcot. But the length of time different regions had been under Muslim rule varied greatly, and I attempted to link this with the variation in the extent and harshness of agrestic servitude observed by the early British officials.

However, the nature of the connections between Muslim rule and agrestic bondage is still very obscure. Before one looks to it for an explanation of regional variations one must eliminate the possibility that these differences preceded Muslim rule, that, for example, bondage was less strong in the Telugu areas even before Muslim rule, perhaps for ecological reasons, such as the greater extent of dry lands. Agrestic bondage was certainly not unknown in the Vijayanagar empire,[14] for example, but no accounts are available of its extent or intensity.

The advent of Islamic regimes may have brought about other complex changes. For instance, when the low castes converted to Islam, they may have become less willing to accept old conditions of de facto bondage, even without any legal change in their status; for this very reason, their Hindu masters would have tried to prevent their conversion. It is possible that the Hindu masters' powers even over low caste Hindus weakened because they could only be maintained with state support,

[14] T.V. Mahalingam, *Administration and Social Life Under Vijayanagara*, Part II, *Social Life*, Madras, 1975, p. 10.

while Muslim rulers were not as active as their Hindu predecessors in maintaining the caste system, though it should be noted that they did recognise and occasionally enforce caste restrictions. Moreover, the ideological influence could work the other way. Political considerations apart, Muslims may have been influenced by Hindu notions of hierarchy and stratification, and this would affect, for example, the degree to which Muslims of low caste origins could be integrated into Muslim society.[15] It is well-known that even those formally converted did not change all their old ways, and it is also possible that the unconverted were influenced ideologically by Islam. What effect changes in ideology had on actual bondage is unknown.

Moreover, the impact of Islamic conquest may reflect political rather than ideological considerations, especially since chattel slavery was well-established in the Islamic societies of the Middle East.[16] For instance, Buchanan reports that Haider freed certain low caste "slaves" in Mysore.[17] But this is the kind of policy any invader might follow who wanted to break local big men, rather than win or buy them over. It is indeed possible that Hindu rulers also followed this policy when they invaded new territories. This suggests the hypothesis that the more frequent the changes of regime in any area, the weaker the ties of bondage; this is worth testing. However, political considerations would be modified by economic needs, especially by the scarcity or abundance of labour.

Formal and Customary Law

The second problem is that in pre-British India there were two separate categories of bondage; one implicit in the caste system, and the other in the separate categories of the legal systems. I occasionally refer to the latter as "civil status"; this is not an entirely satisfactory term,

[15] Cf: "The more rigid social stratification in the Western Sudan, where social status was determined by occupation, is one factor which might explain differences between the Western and central Sudan in the way slaves were incorporated with the society." Nehemia Levtzion, "Slavery and Islamization in Africa: A comparative study," in John Ralph Willis, ed., *Slaves and Slavery in Muslim Africa*, London, 2 vols. vol 1, 1985, p.195.

[16] The literature on African slavery and on Islamic jurisprudence extensively discusses the legal distinctions between slaves of different religions, but this important subject has been neglected in India.

[17] Francis Buchanan, *A Journey From Madras through the Countires of Mysore, Canara and Malabar*, 2nd edn. Madras, 1870, 2 vols: vol I, p. 13.

but I use it for want of a better. "Civil" has many meanings, one of which is "legal" as opposed to "natural".[18] However, the classical legal literature also covers caste; nevertheless the use of "civil" here, as meaning non-caste legal status should not lead to conceptual ambiguity. Under both Hindu and Muslim law there are specific categories of unfree status, including chattel slavery. Thus, the *dharma sastras*, or classical Hindu legal texts, enumerate several categories of *dasas*, often loosely translates as "slaves". *A dasa* could belong to any caste, with the possible exception of Brahmins, and a member of even the lowest castes was not necessarily a *dasa*. But though they were not completely congruent caste and civil status were closely linked: the high castes were much less likely to become *dasas* than the low castes, and in some texts no one could be held as a slave by someone of a lower order (*varna*) than himself.[19]

Caste is treated separately in the classical texts. For instance punishments for the same crime varied according to the caste of the criminal.

Here again, the historian must seek the help of the social anthropologist. The following quotation sets out beautifully the distinctions between caste status and legal status (here law refers to customary tribal law):

> "Paradoxically, even house-slaves, who are the absolute property of their owners and have strictly speaking no legal rights, appear much less as a 'depressed' class than many of the untouchable castes of India. They participate in the social life of the upper stratum of tribal society to a far greater extent than the members of any inferior Hindu caste can take part in that of the higher castes. The attitude of patrician masters to their slaves, moreover, is far less overbearing than the usual behaviour of high-caste Hindus vis-a-vis their untouchable employees or dependants. Whereas the under-privileged in traditional Hindu society thus enjoy personal freedom

[18] Cf. Anthony Pagden, *The Fall of Natural Man*, Cambridge, 1987.

[19] Two authors, Katyayana (c. 800 B.C. to 400 B.C.) and Narada (c. 100 B.C. to 100 A.D.) prescribe that a man can be a slave to a master only in the proper order of varnas, i.e. "the three varnas next to a brahmana may be slaves to a brahmana, a vaisya or a sudra may be a slave to a ksatriya, but a ksatriya cannot be the slave of a vaisya or a sudra, nor a vaisya of a sudra," P.V. Kane, *History of Dharmsastra*, 5 vols, Poona, vol II, part I, p.185-6. Katyana also states that a brahmin cannot be a slave even to another brahmin. Kane also discusses the treatment of slavery in other classical legal texts.

without being ever allowed to forget that they are members of an out-group despised by, and polluting to, the rest of society, Apa Tani slaves lack freedom but are accorded recognition as fellow-tribesmen and as such feel part of Apa Tani society."[20]

When we turn from legal texts to actual practice our knowledge is both limited and unclear. Many historians talk of the labourer's "rights", but this is meaningless unless one describes how they were recognised and enforced. Before the British, how, if at all, did kings support or enforce the powers of private masters over servants? Both Muslim and Hindu legal texts recognized outright sale of certain categories of human beings, and contracts of sale of human beings were presumably as enforceable as other contracts. And in fact some pre-British rulers seized slaves, along with other goods and chattels, against arrears of land revenue. Did they ever recognise and enforce any rights of *dasas*, such as the right to certain kinds of property, or not to be subjected to excessive punishment? Practically nothing is known on this subject,[21] which is not surprising, since the degree of organisation and extent of power of South Indian kingdoms is still so uncertain. The colonial period may yield some clues regarding its predecessors. For instance, landowners in the early nineteenth century expected official help in recovering runaway labourers and this expectation may well have been based on precedent.

In any case, local customs governed practice much more than formal texts, and this is true of the colonial period too. The vast majority of cases of infringement of the customary rules governing relations between masters and servants would be settled locally, often by the general village panchayat or council, or by the caste panchayats of the disputants. The caste panchayat formulated codes governing the behaviour of members of the caste, settled disputes between them, and could also act in inter-caste disputes. The way caste organisations functioned is therefore a crucial aspect of institutions of bondage. Unfortunately, for medieval South India most of the information relates to upper caste assemblies; the panchayats of the lowest castes are

[20] Christoph von Furer-Haimendorf, *The Apa Tanis and Their Neighbours - A Primitive Civilization of the Eastern Himalayas*, London, 1962, pp.90-91.

[21] Whether the king intervened or not would depend partly on the nature of the dispute. Thus Gune cites two cases, both of 1755 A.D., relating to property rights of "slaves"; V.T. Gune, *Judicial System of the Marathas*, Poona, 1953, pp.71 & 72.

described almost exclusively by twentieth century social anthropologists. Colonial or post-colonial accounts are admittedly an unreliable guide to pre-British conditions, but one can hazard the guess that the strength and power of panchayats were stronger in earlier times.

These accounts show that caste panchayats governed master-servant relations at several levels. One was to enforce customary norms. On the master's side, this would include the payment of customary wages; both over- and under-payment would be discouraged. On the side of the labourers, norms would include working customary hours in the customary manner. If the caste panchayat found one of its people guilty either of breaking a norm or a contract, it could prescribe a variety of punishments. The extreme punishment was to be outcasted[22] - the transgressor could not then use the caste well or the common grinding stone; the barber, the potter, the dhobi, and the merchant would all refuse to serve him. In the early twentieth century, if a Mala transgressor still refused to conform, he had to leave the district, according to one account.[23] On the other hand, Thurston wrote of the Paraiyan. "The punishment of excommunication, i.e. cutting off from fire and water, is sometimes the fate of the recalcitrant, either before the council or the Desayi Chetti, but it is seldom effective for more than a short time."[24]

Disputes between two masters or two labourers would be dealt with by the relevant caste panchayat. Disputes could still arise between individual masters and labourers; and either or both their caste panchayats might be involved.

Caste panchayats could act collectively, against each other, to protect what each saw as its traditional rights or to bring about a change in custom.

Occasionally there might be a higher level tribunal too. Thus, in

[22] In a U.P. village if a Thakur patron wanted to change a low caste leather worker working for his family, he could only do so with the consent of the latter's caste council. A Chamar who took the job without the council's appoval could be outcasted Bermard Cohn, 1954, "The Chamar of Senapur," Ph.D. dissertation, Cornell University 1954; p. 29. cited by Michael Moffat, *An untouchable community in South India,* Princeton: 1979.

[23] Sydney Nicholson, "Social Organization of the Malas - An Outcaste Indian People", *Journal of the Royal Anthropological Institute of Great Britain and Ireland,* Vol. VI, 1926, p. 98.

[24] E. Thurston, *Castes and Tribes of South India,* 7 vols, Madras. Government Press, 1909; vol. VI, p.91. Thurston points out that the efficacy of punishments varied with each district.

the Mysore village studied by Harper, "There existed a tribunal, heavily weighted in favour of the employer, where both master and servant could express their grievances and where disputes could be arbitrated".[25]

Punishments of the lower castes were often administered by the caste headman, who also acted as an intermediary in dealing with the higher castes; in the twentieth century this include bargaining over wage rates.

Sometimes a low caste could accept adjudication by an individual of a higher caste, particularly a merchant or Brahmin, or by a landlord, also likely to be of a higher caste.[26] Incidentally, corporal punishment was an essential part of the master's powers, and we badly need an account of the types of punishment in use.[27]

The untouchables had one potent weapon, the refusal to do degrading but necessary work. Moreover, their numbers and their readiness to use force made them useful supporters in factional disputes. The upper castes also feared "the powers of the sorcery of the very low," and frequently even Brahmins worshipped low caste deities.[28]

Needless to say, the masters were generally much stronger, especially

[25] Harper, *op. cit.*, p.50.

[26] Saraswathi Menon reports that the descendants of the Palayakaran of Thanjavur are important landlords "still retaining their ancient feudal privileges, of adjudicating caste and other social disputes in villages under their sway", and mentions one landlord in particular - V.N. Swaminathan, the Member of Parliament from Pattukottai. She has another significant example of landlord power. Labour continued to be impressed for pulling temple chariots in festivals in the twentieth century. Menon was informed that on one occasion early in the twentieth century, when a particular festival got delayed and so clashed with the beginning of the agricultural season, an influential landlord who was also a temple trustee, got official permission to requisition the workers of the Nagapattinam Rail Works to pull the chariot, Saraswati Menon, "Social Characteristics of Land Control in Thanjavur District during the Nineteenth century. A sociological study", Ph.D. dissertation Jawaharlal Nehru University, 1983, pp. 440; 499-500.

[27] For an analysis of the costs and benefits of various forms of labour control, and their suitability to differnent forms of production, see S. Fenoltea, "Slavery and Supervision in Comparative Perspective " *Journal of Economic History*, Vol XLIV, No.3, 1984.

[28] On Tamil Nadu, see Moffat op. cit., p.44. Gyan Prakash shows the complexity of spirit cults in South Bihar, including even the purchase and sale of ghosts; Gyan Prakash, *Bonded Histories; Genealogies of Labour Servitude in Colonial India*, Cambridge, 1990. Ch.5.

if they could enlist the aid of the police. And young labourers were particularly at risk.[29]

Colonial Laws

The colonial period is apparently marked by greater legal clarity, uniformity and efficiency in enforcement. But how the new laws and courts actually affected master-servant relationships is still an untold story. It is a complex one, where laws have indirect, often unexpected effects, and in a welter of misperceptions, government officials, masters and labourers change their strategies. Debt bondage and the use of contracts provide a good example.

Debt bondage has been found all over the world and from ancient times. In India the institution was not confined to agriculture, but was, and indeed still is, found in many traditional industries.[30] Sometimes the origin is clear - people have sold themselves and their relations after famines for centuries in India, exchanging liberty for security. The company records of the seventeenth and eighteenth centuries mention "flourishing slave markets" and international traffic in slaves from the Coromandel coast.[31]

While famine could reduce a person to bondage, it is not clear what could or did release him. Thus, a French observer in Karaikal around 1825 describes how many Indian "called slaves" sold themselves to mirasdars during famines for very small sums; if they repaid these sums they could regain their liberty but the "indolence of the Indian" was so great that they rarely did so.[32] Another observer wrote that

[29] M.N. Srinivas gives a graphic description of conditions in one Mysore village in 1948 in *The Remembered Village*, New Delhi : OUP, 1976 (South Asian edition), pp. 59-63.

[30] The Royal Commission of Labour found in 1930 that children, some only five years old, were bonded to pay off their parents' loans in artisanal industries, particularly carpet weaving and the making of cheap cigarettes, notorious employers of child labour to this day. The children worked very long hours, in wretched conditions, and under very harsh discipline *(Report of the Royal Commission on Labour*, Government of India, 1930, Vol. II, Part 2, p.92). One current study for South India is R. Vidyasagar, "Debt Bondage in South Arcot District: A case study of Agricultural Labourers and Handloom Weavers", in Utsa Patnaik and Manjari Dingwaney, ed., *Chains of Servitude*, Madras, 1985.

[31] S. Arasaratnam, *Dutch Power in Ceylon, 1658-1687*, Amsterdam, 1958, pp.130-131.

[32] F. Gros, ed: Le Capitain de Vaisseau Cordier, *Historique et Statistique de Karikal (*1825), Pondicherry, Institut Francais d' Indologie, 1971, vol. I, 1971, p.200.

during famines all castes but Brahmins sold themselves as slaves, but they were never resold (so the term "chattel slave" would not apply), even if the master became poor. In that case he "lent" them to someone who could feed and clothe them.[33]

But in other cases the debt was not the cause of bondedness, but part of a relationship with other, non-monetary causes, and this traditional relationship was sometimes transformed in the colonial period to a formal contract enforceable in the courts. There were different forces at work. Sometimes the traditional relationship continued unchanged, especially for the servant, but the master represented it to officials as a contractual creditor-debtor relationship to avoid coming under the purview of anti-slavery legislation, and with the additional benefit of being able to use the courts and the police.[34]

Debt was part of traditional bondage in South India too but perhaps only certain forms of bondage, and, yet again, with regional variations. To take Tamil Nadu, the Collector of South Arcot remarked in 1819 that amongst Hindus, "the lower castes are always looked upon as natural slaves, the property of any person who contributes to defray their marriage expenses, which is the ordinary way at present of constituting hereditary slaves."[35] More generally, Moffat states that "debt was part of the older *adimai* relationship, which in addition had some contractual features from the patron's and the client's point of view."[36] Moffat is referring here to the acceptance of mutual if unequal obligations,

[33] A. Walker, "Statistical Report on the Circar of Warangal", *Madras Journal of Literature and Science,* No.35, Jan-June, 1849, pp. 258-259.

[34] The best analysis is the study of the *kamiauti* system in South Bihar by Gyan Prakash, *Bonded Histories.*

[35] Collector, South Arcot to Madras Board of Revenue, 12/9/1819, in Proceedings of the Board of Revenue, 20/9/1819.

[36] Michael Moffat, *An Untouchable Community in South India,* p.45. Moffat cites Ludden, but Ludden in a personal communication to me stated that he was referring to "court cases in which Palla headmen were challenged by Mirasidars. I interpreted them to mean (with the addition of the *Mukkudal Pallu*) that headmen were faced with certain Mirasidar expectations that had to be met to keep the headman post. It also seemed likely to me that court cases arose from faction feuds in which headmen were allied to one set of Mirasidars, again implying some kind of reciprocity to maintain the alliance. 'Contractual' elements may or may not be inferred from all this, depending on how literal one is about what a contract is. I have no evidence of "real" contracts."

implicit in patron-client relationships, rather than explicit contracts.

The use of written contracts spread in Madras, sometimes perhaps to ward off official disapproval of a traditional relationship, and get official help in enforcing the master's power over the labourer, as in Bihar. But sometimes the contract was a recognition of a real change, namely of the opening up of new options for the labourer. Thus, a Madras official noted in 1906 that employers made labourers enter into contracts because they could emigrate without repaying the advances of the grain and money they had taken[37] – it is not clear how much protection this gave the employer.

Several service agreements have survived from the late nineteenth century onwards, and some of them specifically refer to liabilities under British Indian law, particularly the Workmen's Breach of Contract Act of 1859. Here is one example of 1916:

> Padiyal Advance (Loan) Bond executed on June 23, 1916, to Mr. Reddiar, son of Mr. Reddiar of Eruvelliipet, Tirukoilur Taluq on the personal security of Eruvellipet by (1) son of - and (2) son of - both of Alankuppam.
>
> Received cash this day towards marriage expenses by No. 2 of ourselves; Rs. 21.11.0; due already from No. 1 as per acknowledgement; Rs. 4.5.0. Altogether due to yourself by both of us Nos. 1 & 2, Rs. 26.
>
> It is hereby agreed that in lieu of payment of interest on this sum of Rs. 26, No. 2 of ourselves will serve as padiyal under yourself receiving the customary dues of kalam, kalavasam, and lakkapanam.
>
> If any inconvenience is felt by No. 2 which prevents his discharging his duty as a padiyal, No. 1 will discharge that duty without fail. If both of us stay away from work, it shall be the duty of the person standing surety for us to produce both of us before you. If both of us do not agree to work, we shall, besides being liable to punishment under Act 13 of 1859 make good any loss in the crops incurred thereby".[38]

Under the Workman's Breach of Contract Act of 1859, if a workman obtained an advance of money from his employer, and then refused to work, the employer could complain to the magistrate, and if the

[37] G.O. No. 468, Judicial, 11/3/1906, p.5.

[38] P.J. Thomas and K.C. Ramakrishan, *Some South Indian Villages: A Resurvey*, Madras, 1940, p.181.

magistrate was convinced that his complaint was justified he could order the workman to work. If the workman still refused to work, he could be ordered to repay the money, or be sentenced to not more than three months' hard labour. The Act was originally meant to apply to Presidency Towns, but it was extended to other areas. There is disappointingly little discussion of the Act in the historical literature. There are to my knowledge no detailed studies of the working of this Act. How many complaints were actually lodged under the Act? How many workmen were punished under the Act? Was the knowledge that these sanctions were available to employers a sufficient deterrent to workmen wishing to break the terms of the loan? It is certainly possible that the mere existence of the Act, and other similar regulations, did in fact reinforce the powers of the masters in the unequal struggle between masters and labourers.[39] The promissory notes from Madras also suggest that labourers felt that they could be punished under law for breach of their "contracts".

The law was repealed in 1926, and the general trend of legislation in the twentieth century was to move away from support of the masters. In Bihar, the government tried to regulate debt "contracts" by the Bihar and Orissa Kamiauti Act of 1920 but did not succeed in doing so. Specific laws of this kind were not enacted in Madras Presidency perhaps because the problem was less glaring there. In any case legal measures are generally insufficient in themselves, as shown by the frequent attempts of post-1947 governments to abolish bondedness by fiat.

The law apart, Government support to the masters declined in the course of the nineteenth century on such matters as bringing back runaway servants. Also the power of the lower officials, often related to or of the same caste as the landlords, weakened as the bureaucracy became centralized, as Breman has pointed out for Gujarat.[40] Perhaps too the official pronouncements against slavery had some effect, imperfectly obeyed though they may have been.

[39] This has been asserted, for example, to have been the case in part of Bihar, Detlef Schwerin, "The Control of Land and Labour in Chota Nagpur, 1858-1908", in Dietmar Rothermund and D.C. Wadhwa, ed. *Zamindars, Mines and Peasants,* New Delhi, 1978. The Act was also used by masters in Assam, R.P. Behl, "Some aspects of the growth of the tea plantation labour force and labour movements in Assam valley districts (Lakhimpur, Sibsagar and Dawang, 1900-1947)", JNU, Ph.D. dissertation, 1983. Nothing has been written on the working of the Act in Madras Presidency.

[40] Jan Breman, *Patronage and Exploitation,* Berkeley, 1974, p.77.

Communal Landholdings and Labour Management

Bondage was also connected with systems of land tenure, and the point has sometimes been made that "serfs" on communally held lands were better treated than "slaves" of individual owners, and that with the destruction or weakening of communal institutions in the colonial period, their status was automatically altered, presumably for the worse.

There was in fact a variety of communal tenures, and a greater variety of systems of labour management, both briefly described in L & C (pp. 15-18). In the simplest situation each plot was held and managed by an individual landowner (the plots might be periodically redistributed), and he dealt directly with his labourer or labourers. If his holding was very large, he might employ a supervisor, in particular the caste headman. Where the communal element was strongest, the land was jointly held and managed, and in the extreme case one can think of the landowners as a group dealing with labourers as a group, though either or both sides could have a representative.

One frequently quoted account was given by A.D. Campbell, who had once served in Tanjore, and asserted that those he termed "agrestic slaves" were largely held by the village community (in effect,the landowners) or temples, and that they were better off than slaves held by individual masters in Kerala and Kanara. The reason for this was apparently the difference in supervision:

> "The agrestic slaves work in bodies together, the village accountant registering the work executed by them which he inspects, but they are not personally superintended by any one nor placed under any driver. They usually work from about sunrise until sunset with the intermission of a couple of hours for their meal, during the middle of the day. They are not exempted from work on any particular day of the week, but obtain holiday on all the great native festivals, such as on those fixed for consecrating implements, the new year and other great days. No particular work is assigned to them daily; it is sufficient that the slaves of each master execute the work necessary for the cultivation and irrigation. . ."[41]

But it seems unlikely that there was no supervision or direction of group labour. It is of course possible that the degree of supervision was less rigorous than that exercised by individual owners, and also

[41] PP. 1834, XLIV, pp. 30-36.

that after field work was done there were fewer calls on the labourer's time.

Ludden has the best description of the variety and flexibility of labour organisation, though he too is constrained by the sources - a few accounts by British officials in the early nineteenth century.

> "A variety of labour relations organised the performance of these varied jobs. Though the mix of mirasidar collective and individual labour management would have varied according to the distribution of land among shareholders and the degree of village cooperation, in general it seems that agricultural labour operations were organised through dyadic contracts between mirasidars, either as families or as a community, and various client labouring households. Some client cultivators would have had their own stock and sufficient labour to cultivate as sharecroppers. Some would have worked for a daily grain wage, paid seasonally or by the task. Some would have worked for only one household and other families for the village as a whole. Gang labour, however, would be demanded by mirasidars of labouring caste groups as a whole."[42]

As L & C noted, communally held villages were reported in the early nineteenth century but the extent of joint cultivation is not known. By the middle of the nineteenth century the system had practically disappeared, though historical vestiges were left in a few villages,and indeed are occasionally reported even today. All things considered, too much importance should not be given to the dissolution of communal institutions; it affected the condition of labourers only in a few parts of the Presidency, and even there it was only one among several factors.

[42] David Ludden, *Peasant History in South India*, p.92.

ESTIMATING THE NUMBERS

L & C is best known for its estimate of agricultural labourers in Madras Presidency at the outset of British rule (for which we shall use the symbolic year 1800). Since this estimate has often been misunderstood or misrepresented it may be useful to summarise the argument briefly, reminding ourselves that statements about the de-industrialisation and polarisation alleged to have occurred in the course of British rule depend heavily on the implicit or explicit assumption that landless agricultural labour was insignificant in 1800. The novelty of my approach was to stress the connection between caste and occupation, and to extrapolate backwards the Census data on caste for the early twentieth century, to obtain an estimate for 1800, for which neither caste nor occupational data is available.

The rather simple argument, in its starkest form, ran thus:

In 1900 the agricultural labour castes, i.e. those whose traditional occupation was said to be agricultural labour, formed x% of the population.

Assuming that in 1800 (a) the agricultural labour castes formed the same proportion of the population as in 1900, and (b) all members of these castes were agricultural labourers, and no-one else, then agricultural labourers formed x% of the population in 1800.

I then went on to examine these assumptions.

The first is that the agricultural labour castes grew at the same rate as the rest of the population. Let us consider the usual demographic factors first, i.e. birth, death and migration. Nothing is known about caste differential birth rates, and there is little basis even for guessing. One can however guess that the death rates of the lowest castes are likely to have been higher than average, especially in famines. And finally, it is very likely that the lowest castes were disproportionately represented amongst the stream of migrants abroad and to other parts of India swelling towards the end of the nineteenth century. Thus the actual rate of growth of the agricultural labour castes may have been below the Presidency average.

There is also the probability that a large proportion of Christian converts were drawn from these castes. Converts were generally not included in these castes in the Censuses but were separately classified as Native Christians. In 1901, Native Christians amounted to a little under 4 per cent of the total population of the Presidency, and if most of these were from the agricultural labour castes, which seems likely, this would mean that estimates for 1801 based on 1901 caste figures would have to be revised upwards.[43] The balance of probabilities therefore is that agricultural labour castes formed a *larger* proportion of the population in 1800 than in 1900, but there is so much guesswork involved that it is best to ignore this consideration, especially since it supports our conclusion that these castes were significantly large in 1800.

The second assumption was the close link between caste and occupation. The official reports of the early nineteenth century suggested that in many areas members of certain castes were, by and large, agricultural labourers, and indeed bonded labourers. So close was the connection that some officials used caste names, such as Paraiyan, Palli and Cheruman, as synonymous with "agrestic slave". This usage covered confusions about the nature of both caste and servitude in South India; nevertheless it did point to an important feature of agrarian relations. Moreover, the censuses of 1901, 1911, and 1921 not only gave good caste data but also figures of those who actually followed their "traditional occupation" of agricultural labour, which was significantly high for all the six "agricultural labourer castes" (L & C, p.61). These castes formed 12-20 per cent of the total population (depending on whether the Palla were included or not), and 65-75 per cent of them were in fact agricultural labourers even in the early decades of the twentieth century. This of course was not proof that most members of these castes were agricultural labourers at the beginning of the nineteenth century, but, as we have seen, there is ample contemporary evidence to this effect. This suggests that there was a sizeable group, say 8-15% of the total population, of landless labourers belonging to the agricultural labour castes. Moreover, this estimate provides a floor, since agricultural labour was also drawn from other castes, and sometimes in considerable numbers, as again contemporary evidence shows.

This chain of inference was supported by scattered evidence on agrarian conditions in the first half of the nineteenth century which

[43] There were many reasons (apart from conviction of the truth of Christianity) for conversion, and as Kooiman has pointed out people could simultaneously hold two religious identities and even revert to their original faith in times of stress; Dick Kooiman, "Mass Movement, Famine and Epidemic: A Study in Interrelationship", *MAS*, 25/2, May 1991. This intrinsically fascinating issue is of relevance here only in connection with the reliability of census data.

showed significant inequality in landholdings; a considerable part of the area was covered by farms which could not be cultivated by family labour alone. Later analysis of patta data showed that land was very unequally held at the end of the first half of the nineteenth century, and there is no reason to expect a very different position around 1800. In fact, the distribution of land may have been somewhat less unequal in 1947 than in 1800, for a variety of reasons. The most obvious is the growth in population, coupled with equal inheritance amongst sons.[44] But there are less obvious reasons too, including deliberate government policies. The government introduced special rules under which a person who cultivated a piece of land for 5 years could make a claim to legal ownership, and made specific allocations of land to depressed castes and agricultural labourers, either directly or through Christian missionaries. By 1931 about 1% of the total cultivated land had been allocated in this manner,[45] though it was land of relatively poor quality; better land may have been occupied already.

Perhaps what was more important was the opening up of opportunities outside the village - on public works, tea and coffee plantations in the South Indian hills and above all, by emigration abroad. Many of the emigrants were agricultural labourers and of low caste. This mobility had two effects. First, the reduction in the amount of local labour available permitted wages to rise, or at least prevented them from falling. Secondly, those migrants who returned could buy land. Moffat shows that Tamil untouchables continued to acquire land from the 1860's onward, and by 1961 over 30% of the untouchable caste population owned land, as against over 50% for the general population - a striking statistic when one considers the very low level they started from. There was great variation between the districts, with the dry district of Ramanathapuram showing a very high proportion of land owned by the untouchables, and Tanjore and Coimbatore showing very low percentages. In general the more concentrated the land ownership to begin with, the worse the untouchables fared.[46] Unfortunately similar data is not readily available for earlier years for other regions, and so

[44] These facts are further analysed in Dharma Kumar, "Landownership and Inequality, 1853-54 to 1946-47," *IESHR*, Vol. XII, No.3, p.259.

[45] *Ibid.*, p.259.

[46] Moffat, op.cit., pp.48-50. In a detailed analysis of settlement registers for one taluk in Tiruchirapalli district Yanagisawa found that low caste agricultural labourers and tenants, - as well as merchants, had acquired lands from high caste landowners between 1895 and 1925, H. Yanagisawa, "Mixed trends in landholding in Lalgudi taluk: 1895-1925," *IESHR*, 26 (4), 1989.

many different factors accounted for land purchases and sales by untouchables that no reasonable guesses are possible. The proportion of land held by untouchables was clearly lower in the Tamil districts in 1900 than in, say, 1961, but we do not know how much lower.[47] There is no reason to expect different trends in other parts of the Presidency.[48]

This long chain of inference obviously does not constitute proof of the existence of a large group of landless labourers at the beginning of the nineteenth century. It is useful only in the absence of actual evidence, but none of the works published after my book contradicts the thrust of my argument, so far as I am aware.

However, my treatment was unsatisfactory in several ways. In the first place, the term "agricultural labour castes" suggests too strong a connection between caste and occupation. In fact, as I did recognise even then, the strength of the connection varied from caste to caste and region to region. The connection was closest in the case of the Cheruman,[49] most of whom were agricultural labourers, and throughout the nineteenth century; but they were also general labourers, or coolies; and had other, perhaps parttime, work, such as making mats and baskets. The connection was probably weakest, as noted in L & C (p.58) in the case of the Palli or Vanniyan, the only caste in the group who were not untouchables. But the other agricultural labour castes also had traditional non-agricultural occupations; for instance the Paraiyan were often village servants and part-time drummers, and the Mala were

[47] Moffat mentions that since the reservations of government jobs for untouchables from the 1930's, part of their salaries went to purchase land (p.48). But there was large scale net immigration in the 1930's. Again, the volume of land sales went up sharply during the depression and it is not clear how these factors affected the lower castes.

[48] For the dry Telugu districts Washbrook has argued for polarisation (in my view on insufficient evidence) and Bruce Robert against it; David Washbrook, "Economic Development and Social Stratification in Rural Madras: The Dry Region, 1878-1929", in C. Dewey and A.G. Hopkins, ed. *The Imperial Impact*, London, 1978; Bruce Robert, "Economic Change and Agrarian Organisation on 'Dry South India', 1890-1940. A Reinterpretation," *MAS*, 17(1), 1983, and "Structural Change in Indian Agriculture: Land and Labour in Bellary District, 1890-1980," *IESHR*, 22 (No. 3) 1985.

[49] Plural forms are now considered the polite term for a caste, i.e. Cherumar rather than Cheruman (singular). I continue the L & C use of the singular form to stand for the caste, and mean no disrespect thereby. Similarly the term "untouchable" is used in a purely technical sense.

leather workers. Also, members of each caste were priests to their caste fellows, and the numbers of such priests may not have been inconsiderable, since many villages may have had separate temples and priests for the different castes.[50]

Another mistake I made was to assume implicitly that there was a undirectional change, however slow, in bonded status in the British period. This is because I overlooked the conversion of tribals into untouchables and bonded labourers. This process not only has a very long history,[51] but continued throughout the British period and may even be taking place in backward parts of India today. Ludden refers to this process, citing an oral tradition regarding the Pallas.[52] His discussion is important but he attaches too much importance to the suspect etymology of caste histories[53] and suggests that field labour was ritually polluting, which was not the case.

For South India, Dirks has a brief but suggestive description of the way the Valaiyan, who once made their living by hunting and trapping, became agricultural labourers during the extension of agriculture in Pudukkottai from the seventeenth to the nineteenth centuries.[54] Other tribes suffering similar fates include the Yanadi, mentioned by many authors. But not all tribals became untouchables or low caste. The Gonds and Coorgs used military success to achieve Kshatriya status, a route also used by peasant warriors and others, and some tribal priests even became Brahmins.[55]

It is possible that the conversion of forest dwellers into field labourers quickened during the colonial period for many reasons. These include the use of timber for the railways, the forest laws and administrative

[50] On the diversity of occupations ca 1800, see Dharma Kumar, "The forgotten sector; services in Madras Presidency in the first half of the nineteenth century", *IESHR*, vol. 24, 1987.

[51] With increasing interest in subaltern groups and in ecological change, the conversion of tribals into agricultural labourers and peasants is also being studied. On ancient India the work of Vivekananda Jha is particularly important, in particular, "From Tribe to Untouchable: The Case of Nisadas," in R.S. Sharma and V. Jha ed., *Indian Society : Historical Probings*, Delhi, 1974, and "Candala and the Origin of Untouchability", *The Indian Historical Review*, 1986-87, Vol. XIII.

[52] Ludden, *Peasant History in South India*, p. 91.

[53] A useful corrective is provided by K. Hanumanthan, *Untouchability*, Madurai, 1979.

[54] Nicholas Dirks, *The Hollow Crown*, Cambridge, 1987, pp. 270-271.

[55] Pauline Kolenda, *Caste in Contemporary India*, Jaipur, 1984, p. 96.

rules outlawing swidden cultivation by tribals, increased mobility and hence the penetration of Hindu castes into tribal areas, besides the general growth of population and cultivation, and hence of deforestation. The dispossession of tribals, and their conversion into agricultural labourers, aroused official alarm, and led to laws forbidding the alienation of land to outsiders, such as the Agency Tracts Interest and Land Transfer Act (Act 1 of 1917), but these laws were not always successful.[56] Since these tribal groups were not included in the agricultural labour castes, the estimate for the beginning of the nineteenth century is not affected, but the numbers of agricultural labourers may well have increased over the colonial period, and after it.

How much weight should one give the tribal factor in Madras Presidency? Undoubtedly, tribals were converted to agricultural labourers, but the process may have been greatly quickened in the twentieth century. Moreover, "the jungle tribes now found scattered over Southern India in small groups can never have been very numerous and it was only the first efforts at production in the form of agriculture that paved the way to a settled life and resulted in a gradual increase in the population."[57] This small tribal population was very unevenly distributed, being much more extensive in the Telugu districts than in the Tamil regions or Malabar.[58] While of great interest in itself, and as a clue to the early history of agricultural labour castes in the plains, the tribal factor does not seem to affect the broad estimates of agricultural labourers in Madras Presidency for the beginning and end of the nineteenth century, though it may be important for particular districts.

There are great regional variations in the proportions of agricultural labourers to total or agrarian population, in the castes they belonged to, and in the severity of restrictions on them, points which were perfunctorily dealt with in L & C. The greatest source of difference was intensity of cultivation, which in turn was chiefly dependent on

[56] Thus Mala traders from the plains called themselves Konda Malas, listed as a hill-tribe, and hence transfers of land to them were not forbidden, C. von Furer-Haimendorf, *The Reddis of the Bison Hills*, London, 1945, p. 289. On general British policy towards tribals, including the designation of "scheduled tracts" for special administration, under the Scheduled Districts Act (Act XIV of 1874), see G.S. Ghurye, *The Scheduled Tribes*, Bombay: 3rd edn, 1963, Chs. IV & V. Apart from deliberate cheating, there are problems in the definition of tribes, including hill tribes; Ghurye, *op.cit.*, p.23.

[57] C. von Furer - Haimendorf, *op.cit.* p.4.

[58] Of all the districts in Madras Presidency, it was only in Ganjam, Godavari and Vishakhapatnam, that certain areas were listed under the Scheduled Districts Act of 1874; Ghurye, *op.cit*, p.78.

irrigation. Agricultural labourers were found in the greatest numbers in the "wet" or irrigated districts, and were subjected there to the greatest disabilities; in the "dry" tracts they were more mobile and freer, as Ludden's description of the dry regions of Tirunelveli district shows.[59] Apart from differences in physical conditions and in technology, political history and culture in the widest sense also led to regional differences. The fact that the worst conditions of servitude and of untouchability occurred in Kerala cannot be attributed solely to ecology,and ecological conditions are manifestly incapable of explaining why the greatest advances in the political and social status of labourers have taken place in modern Kerala. The fact of regional variation again cries out for detailed local studies.

Despite these various errors and omissions, I still feel that my main conclusions hold. Members of certain castes were by and large agricultural labourers at the outset of British rule; this connection enables us to estimate the minimum strength of agricultural labourers then, and the estimate shows that the group was sizeable so that it cannot be held that landless labour was virtually created by British rule.

However, we are interested not so much in the absolute numbers of agricultural labourers, but in their place in the agrarian economy, one indication being the proportion of agricultural labourers to the agricultural population. While we have some rough figures of population totals for some years even in the early nineteenth century, we have none for the total agricultural or even rural population, so for the present at least we have to fall back on inference.

Let us look first at the broad question of whether the proportion of work force in agriculture tó the total workforce was less in 1800 than in 1900. This is in fact a fundamental assertion of the "nationalist-Marxist" school, partly on the ground that massive deindustrialisation occurred, driving artisans into the agricultural proletariat. If this could be established, it would be a very powerful argument against my estimates, showing either that even members of the so-called agricultural labour castes were not in fact agricultural workers in 1800, or that large numbers of other castes, especially the artisan and weaver castes, became agricultural labourers by 1900. And we do in fact know that there were Mala leather workers and even some Paraiyan weavers around 1800.[60]

[59] David Ludden, *Peasant History in South India,* p.82.

[60] Buchanan for example mentions a few Paraiyan weavers near Coimbatore; Frances Buchanan, *A Journey from Madras through Mysore, Canara and Malabar,* 1881, 2nd edn. Madras, 1871, Vol. I. p.471.

It is worth looking at weavers in particular, since the destruction of handlooms is the core of the de-industrialisation thesis. We do not know how many weavers there were in 1800, but it is very unlikely that the numbers fell sharply in the first half of the nineteenth century,[61] and the evidence is also dubious for the second half. There is some support for this statement in the caste and occupation figures for 1901 and 1911. Actual occupations are given for the 3 main traditional weaver castes in selected districts; the Devanga, Kaikolan, and the Sale. 84% of the Devangas were still weavers in 1901, and 74% in 1911; the figures for the Kaikolan were 59% and 54%, and for the Sale 69% and 64%;[62] thus the majority of all three castes still followed their traditional occupation of weaving at the end of the nineteenth century. Of those that did not, a minority were field labourers. Moreover these three castes formed only a little over 2% of the total population of the Presidency in 1911, another reason for discounting the importance of the conversion of weavers into agricultural labourers.

Deindustrialisation apart, agriculture may well have been less important in 1800 than in 1900, as suggested by the great increase in exports of agriculture products over the nineteenth century, with complex effects on the occupational structure. There are other factors too. Lardinois has argued that during the prolonged crisis of 1780-1830, there was extensive depopulation, much land was available for cultivation and irrigation was badly neglected.[63] We do not know the sectoral incidence of the depopulation - weavers, village officials and priests may have suffered as badly as cultivators. Nor do we know the effects on labourers and the low castes - Lardinois does mention the shortage of labour in some districts. But was this merely a reflection of the general depopulation or did agricultural labourers suffer particularly, as we know they

[61] A broad argument to this effect is presented in Dharma Kumar, "The Regional Economy of South India", in Kumar ed. *The Cambridge Economic History of India,* Vol. II. This also mentioned the decline in the quality of cloth and hence in weavers' earnings. A later detailed study shows that the number of looms actually increased between 1820 and 1870, though there were wide regional variations and periodic crises, and that specific high quality products suffered, K. Specker, "Madras handlooms in the nineteenth century", *IESHR*, 1989, vol. 26, pp. 131-166.

[62] *Census of India;* Madras Report, Part I, Table XVI, p.360, 1911, pp.245-6.

[63] R. Lardinois, "Deserted Villages and depopulation in rural Tamil Nadu, 1780-c.1830" in Tim Dyson, ed. *India's Historical Demography,* London:1989.

did in other crises.[64]

In passing, the rise of agriculture is not in itself proof of deindustrialisation since, very probably, there were far more people employed in services than in handicrafts in the early part of the nineteenth century.[65]

If the agricultural work force was smaller in 1800 than in 1900, it is possible that the assumption that all or nearly all members of the agricultural labour castes were in fact agricultural workers, was wrong. Agricultural labourers will then have been a smaller proportion of the total population in 1800 than I estimated, but it is not certain that they would have been a smaller proportion of the agricultural population, since both denominator and numerator would have been smaller than in my estimates, since agriculture would have been a smaller sector of the Presidency economy.

With so many unknowns, it is not worth refining further on my estimates. Instead of broad estimates based on backward extrapolation - always hazardous - we require detailed studies of localities, from which a more reliable picture of the early nineteenth century can be built up. It is not clear whether sufficient data is available, but I venture to guess that it will not destroy the thesis that agricultural labourers were a sizeable proportion of the agricultural work force, that a large proportion of them were drawn from the lowest castes, and that in some areas, particularly those where irrigation raised the labour-intensity of cultivation, many labourers were in servitude of one form or another.

Fresh research will undoubtedly fill in many gaps in L & C and correct its errors, above all its too narrow focus. For instance Ch. VIII on emigration dealt with a very important avenue of escape, and was able to draw a fair amount of significant information from the revenue records alone. But a much fuller picture can be drawn from other official records, and from various studies of South Indian labour abroad.

There is little excuse for the neglect of women in L & C, since

[64] Famines have a complex effect on labour, depending on death rates according to income and occupation, sex and age, and on whether agricultural capital is destroyed in the course of the famine. The short and long term consequences may be very different. For a general discussion, see Michelle Burge McAlpin, *Subject to Famine*, Princeton, 1983.On South India see R. Lardinois, "Famine, Epidemics and Mortality in South India," *EPW*, vol XX, March 16, 1985; D. Rajasekhar, "Famines and Peasant Mobility", Changing Agrarian Structure in Kurnool District of Andhra, 1870-1900," *IESHR*, 1991, No.2.

[65] Dharma Kumar, "The Forgotten Sector : Services in Madras Presidency in the First Half of the Nineteenth Century", *IESHR*, 1987.

women have been working in the fields of south India for centuries - weeding and transplanting, according to the Tamil classics, were feminine preserves, and they shared in the task of watching crops.[66] It is essential too to consider female rights over children and property when analysing institutions of bondage, and there are several references in the records which should be brought together. Fortunately work on women has already begun, on the organisation of female labourers, on woman as emigrants (for India as a whole), and on some peculiarities of the demography of South Indian women (but not labourers).[67]

L & C also took too narrow a view of standards of living, discussing only wages. But even in narrowly economic terms, leisure , and the intensity of work, should be considered too. Atchi Reddy has found that the length of the working day of the agricultural labourer declined after 1920, and particularly sharply after 1967.[68] The labourer undoubtedly prefers an eight or ten hour day to one which is twelve to fourteen hours long. Admittedly if he had the choice, he may have preferred to work longer hours for higher wages; nevertheless an increase in leisure should be included in any evaluation of the changing standard of life of labourers, but this was probably not a major consideration in the nineteenth century.

And, going deeper, one should look at literacy, health, and, above all, changes in consciousness. Jodha has shown that the labourer perceives freedom from bondage to creditor or landlord as an important constituent of his welfare.[69] How did the labourer perceive himself or herself in earlier periods, and when and why did perceptions and resignation to one's lot alter? The mental world of the agricultural labourer awaits its historian, with sensitivity, imagination, and far better linguistic skills than I possess.

[66] K.K. Pillay, *Social History of the Tamils,* Part I, Madras, 1969, pp. 190-191; also see the several references in Buchanan, *Journey*.

[67] There are important articles on these topics in J. Krishnamurty, ed. *Women in Colonial India,* New Delhi, 1989.

[68] M. Atchi Reddy, "Work and Leisure: Daily working hours of agricultural labourers, Nellore district, 1860-1989," *IESHR*, 1991.

[69] N.S. Jodha, "Poverty Debate in India: A Minority View," *EPW*, Special Number, November 1988.

PART I

I. INTRODUCTION

In 1961 there were 31½ million agricultural workers in India, that is to say, around one-fourth of the agricultural working force.[1] Some of these labourers may own some land themselves, but these minute holdings cannot afford even bare subsistence for a family, and the major part of the labourer's income is derived from working on land owned by others. In this sense these labourers are 'landless'. The exact definition of the term 'agricultural labourer' has been much debated in recent years, and what is more, has varied from one official enquiry to another, with the result that estimates of agricultural labourers in the same year, 1951, range from 18 per cent of the total agricultural population (the Census of 1951) to 38 per cent (the First Agricultural Labour Enquiry).[2] But for our purpose these differences of definition are not important. It is clear enough that there has been a large group of landless labourers throughout the twentieth century, and that they are among the poorest and most depressed sections of Indian society; what is not clear is how long this group has existed and how it came into being. But these are problems of significance and not merely for Indian history.

The fortunes of this group are a good index of changes in the entire agrarian economy; movements in the numbers of agricultural labourers and in their wages reflect the growth of population, the extension of cultivation, the rate of industrialization, and the effects of integration in the world economy. And changes in the size and nature of the agricultural labour group may also throw light on the wider question of the effect of imperialist rule on subject societies. Did British rule shatter the structure of Indian society? Did it destroy the balance of the agrarian economy and create a new rural proletariat? Or did Indian social institutions possess

[1] *Paper No. 1 of 1962*, Census of India, 1961.

[2] The Census figures are likely to be a considerable underestimate, because some of the agricultural labour families owning small plots of land may have returned themselves as cultivators (50 per cent of the agricultural labour families in the First Agricultural Labour Enquiry owned land). On the other hand, the First Agricultural Labour Enquiry may exaggerate the numbers of agricultural labourers for various reasons; that it is an overestimate is supported to some extent by the fact that in the Second Agricultural Labour Enquiry for 1956–7, where agricultural labour families are those deriving the major part of their *income* from agricultural labour, such families form 24·47 per cent of the total rural families, as against 30·39 per cent in the First Agricultural Labour Enquiry; Government of India, *Report on the Second Agricultural Labour Enquiry* (New Delhi, 1960), vol. I, p. 47.

enough resilience and vitality to absorb the changes brought about by foreign rule?

The study of agricultural labour attempted here covers a limited period and area. The period is the nineteenth century, during which British rule was consolidated, and one of the main tasks of the work is to estimate the size of the agricultural labour group at the beginning of the period. This estimate would gain greatly in firmness and interest if it could be compared with pre-British conditions, but for the earlier period almost no information on the numbers of agricultural labourers is available. From literature and inscriptions it is known that agricultural labourers did exist in ancient and medieval India, often in conditions of slavery or serfdom, but the data are not precise enough to permit inferences about the numbers involved. In spite of this early evidence about the existence of agrestic serfdom, many writers have contended that the class of landless labourers was created during the British period, and one reason why they have disregarded the earlier records may be the paucity of quantitative information which can be gleaned from them.

This study is also limited to the old Madras Presidency (for convenience, the administrative unit of Madras Presidency has been selected rather than the whole of South India). Madras is of special importance for several reasons. It was here that the *raiyatwari* system of collecting land revenue from the individual cultivator—a system said to be directly destructive of the old village community—was introduced in its full rigour. Also, the rates of revenue collected by the British were much higher in Madras than in any other part of India. In the third place, South India today has the highest proportion of landless labourers to total population in India.[1] *A priori* it may be expected that the processes by which this class has been created will have been most manifest here. And finally, it is in South India that the caste system was peculiarly rigid; so that the role of indigenous societies in resisting changes projected from outside is best seen here. In fact, the strength of the caste system provides one method of estimating the number of agricultural labourers.

Of the two parts of this work, the first deals with the agrarian situation in South India at the outset of British rule, and some of the institutional changes brought about by the new administration. First, the actual agrarian structure in the early years of the nineteenth century is analysed; from this analysis alone the presumption arises that even as early as 1800

[1] In both 1950–1 and 1956–7, the Southern Zone, consisting of Madras, Andhra Pradesh and Kerala, had the highest proportion of agricultural labour to total rural households of all the five zones of India; *Second Agricultural Labour Enquiry Report*, vol. 1, p. 47.

there must have been a demand for a labour force outside the family of the cultivator. The traditional institutional forms of this labour are next described, as well as the connection of these institutions with the caste structure. On the basis of this connection, the number of agricultural workers in 1800 has been deduced from the caste structure at the end of the nineteenth century as shown by the censuses. This is done in Chapter IV. Chapters V and VI contain an account of the various changes made by the British, including their changes in the land revenue and land tenure systems, and their attempts to abolish slavery and serfdom.

The second part of the work is concerned with the main economic factors which may have contributed to the growth of landlessness during the nineteenth century. The central issue is of course the pressure of population on land, and the figures of growth of population as well as of land under cultivation are examined in detail in Chapter VII. The role played by emigration in lessening the pressure on land is analysed in Chapter VIII. The evidence about the changes in the land-labour ratio is incomplete, so that movements in wage rates have also been examined in Chapter IX; the wages data also throw some light on the question of the monetization of the agrarian economy. Finally, in Chapter X the occupational figures of the census data are examined in order to determine the numbers and proportions of landless labourers at the end of the nineteenth century. This brings us to the concluding chapter where the growth of landless labour over the century has been put into historical perspective.

II. THE AGRARIAN BACKGROUND

South India is differentiated from the rest of India both by the importance of pre-Aryan elements in its social structure and by the fact that Muslim invasions came much later than in the North and did not leave so deep an impact. Mahmud of Ghazni invaded the Punjab early in the eleventh century, and there had been Arab invasions of Sind even earlier, but it was not till the end of the thirteenth century that a Muslim army invaded the South.

The Aryanization of the South may have started around 1000 B.C.;[1] little is known about the Dravidian society that existed before that date. The degree of contact between North and South India fluctuated; at some periods North Indian empires such as the Maurya spread to South India; at times South Indian rulers such as the Andhra dynasty, the Satavahanas, encroached into the North, but for large expanses of time there was little contact between the two areas. The Satavahanas, whose rule lasted for four and a half centuries till around 230 B.C., were followed by many warring dynasties, including the Cheras, the Chalukyas, the Pallavas, the Pandyas, the Rashtrakutas and the Cholas, who ruled from A.D. 850 to 1200, and traces of whose achievements in the fields of administration and irrigation still remain.

The decline of the Chola empire was followed by a century of warfare, which culminated in the first Khalji expedition to the Deccan in 1296. Many other Muslim incursions from Delhi followed, and at one stage in the early fourteenth century, Muslim historians claimed, the whole of South India was part of the empire of Delhi. Yet the Sultan's power in the South was almost everywhere weak, and it was overthrown by the rise in the fourteenth century of the Hindu empire of Vijaynagar which grew to cover almost the whole of South India. Throughout its history the Vijaynagar empire was threatened by a hostile power nearer at hand, the Bahmani Sultanate of the Deccan, and after the decisive victory of the Bahmanis in 1565, the empire disintegrated. In the anarchy that followed small chieftains called *naiks* or *poligars* seized local authority, but few of these established permanent rule, and in most of South India power gradually passed into the hands of the Sultans of Bijapur and Golkonda. The gradual breakdown of Mughal rule again changed the political balance in South India. On the one hand, with the growth of Mahratta

[1] Up to the end of the Vijaynagar empire, this description follows K. A. Nilakanta Sastri, *A History of South India* (Madras, 1955).

power, Tanjore became a Mahratta principality; on the other, the Muslim subordinates of the Mughal Emperor carved out kingdoms of their own. Hence by the middle of the eighteenth century the ruling powers consisted of the Nizam of the Deccan, whose chief subordinate in the south was the Nawab of the Carnatic (otherwise called the Nawab of Arcot); Haidar Ali, the ruler of Mysore; and the Mahrattas.

But several European powers had already started to fish in the troubled waters of South India. The Portuguese were the first to form a settlement, followed by the French, the Dutch and the Danes. The British founded their first settlements in 1611 at Vizagapatam and Masulipatam, and in 1639 obtained the land on which Fort St George in Madras now stands. Further, the Europeans took opposite sides in the wars between the Nizam, the Mahrattas and the Muslim rulers of Mysore, which racked South India during the eighteenth century. In this struggle French power was destroyed, and the British then turned against Tipu, Sultan of Mysore. In 1792 Tipu was forced to cede one half of his territories; seven years later he was killed and a representative of the old Hindu dynasty was placed upon the throne in Mysore. The rest of the territories were divided among the British and their allies, the British getting Canara, Coimbatore and the Wynaad. In the same year the Mahratta ruler of Tanjore sold his kingdom to the Company, and in 1800 the Nizam ceded to it large portions of his territory, including the present districts of Bellary, Anantapur, Cuddapah and part of Kurnool, known as the Ceded Districts. Thus, by the beginning of the nineteenth century, the Company had won the whole of the modern Madras Presidency, except for a part of Kurnool district, a small Danish settlement at Tranquebar, the French settlements at Pondicherry and elsewhere, and the territories of five small satellite states. In 1839 the remainder of Kurnool was annexed; Tranquebar was purchased from the Danes in 1845, and in 1862 the district of North Canara was transferred to Bombay Presidency.

After it had been rounded off by conquest and cession, and excluding North Canara, the Madras Presidency covered about 140,000 square miles of southern India, between 8° and 16° N., with an outlying spur (the districts of Godavari, Kistna, Vizagapatam and Ganjam) stretching to the north-east. The bulk of the Presidency fell into three physical groups: the strip of land between the Indian Ocean and the Western Ghats (the districts of South Canara and Malabar); the strip between the Bay of Bengal and the Eastern Ghats (the districts of Tinnevelly, Tanjore, South Arcot, Madura, Chinglepet and Nellore); and the territory between these two coastal belts (the districts of Coimbatore, the Nilgiris, Salem, North Arcot, Trichinopoly, Cuddapah, Kurnool, Anantapur and Bellary). Between these twenty-one districts there were important differences. On the West Coast the monsoon rainfall is so lavish that double and treble cropping are common in Malabar and the low lands of South Canara. But on the East Coast, only Tanjore has abundant rain, while in the centre it is both scanty and capricious. Far and away the most abundant crops grown in the Presidency were cereals (rice, *cholam*, *cambu*, and *ragi*) although there were vegetable gardens everywhere, and during the course of the nineteenth century there were to be experiments with such cash crops as cotton, indigo and cinchona. The great range of rainfall and the qualities of soils produced great disparities of productivity between the West Coast and Tanjore on the one hand, and the poor lands of the interior on the other, and these disparities affected the agrarian structure of the various districts.

For our purpose, however, it is more convenient to follow linguistic, rather than geographical, grouping, particularly since the two overlap to some extent. The division of the Presidency into the Telugu districts (Ganjam, Vizagapatam, Godavari, Kistna, Nellore, Kurnool, Cuddapah, Anantapur and Bellary), the Tamil areas (Chinglepet, North and South Arcot, Salem, Trichinopoly, Tanjore, Coimbatore, Madura and Tinnevelly) and Malabar and South Canara, coincides more or less exactly with social and historical lines of differentiation, though, of course, none of the lines of demarcation is sharp.[1]

Two centuries of war had preceded the establishment of British rule, and during the eighteenth century in particular there had been much dislocation while Hyder Ali and Tipu were struggling against resources which the British drew from world-wide trade. The first British administrator of Canara remarked of the rule of Mysore over the West Coast:

> 'Hyder ruined Canara, a highly improved country, filled with industrious inhabitants . . . more comfortable than those of any province under any native power in India . . . he regarded it as a fund from which he might draw without limit. . . . The same demands and worse management increased . . . at the beginning of Tippoo's reign . . . the amount of land left unoccupied, from the flight or death of its cultivators, became at last so great, [that] the collections before the end of his reign fell short of the assessment from ten to sixty per cent.'[2]

In Malabar, Hyder and Tipu had raised the tax rates so high that 'it is impossible to believe that they were rigorously exacted';[3] in Coimbatore the officials of Mysore had taxed at rates 'only endurable by the fraud

[1] The small polyglot Nilgiri district has been omitted.

[2] Munro, 'The condition and assessment of Canara 31 May 1800'; A. J. Arbuthnot, *Major General Sir Thomas Munro . . . Selections from his Minutes and other official Writings* (London, 1881), vol. I, pp. 68–9 (hereafter *Minutes of Sir Thomas Munro*); *Manual of South Canara District* (ed. 1894), pp. 95–6.

[3] *Gazetteer of the Malabar and Anjengo Districts* (ed. 1908), vol. I, p. 310.

practised';[1] at Chinglepet and Nellore on the east coast, benevolences and forced loans had been screwed out of the cultivators, in addition to the land taxes, and here again, only bribery and mismanagement had made the system bearable;[2] while in Godavari, part of the north-eastern spur, there were heavy rents, arbitrary assessments and much oppression.[3] Again, in this time of troubles when much of the land was fought over, villages were frequently abandoned and reoccupied, village registers and records of rights destroyed and falsified, and any adventurer who could guarantee some security could usurp old established rights to land or land revenue. These changes brought to the top new landholders who usurped both the rights and the titles of the old.

It was little wonder that in coping with the aftermath of this chaos the British administrators were so confused about the rights they had to confirm and administer. To make matters worse, the information available on earlier tenures was very scanty (as indeed it is today). They had to choose between several claimants to rights in tenure systems largely unknown to them and described in a multiplicity of terms in Tamil, Telugu, Malayalam and Canarese. Added to these were Persian and Arabic terms introduced by Muslim rulers, which often were only substitutes for local words. And the British added their own element of confusion in their natural tendency to look at 'everything from an English law, or "Lord-of-the-manor" point of view'.[4]

This tendency was sharpened by their primary need to identify the landholder responsible for payment of land revenue, and indeed, they classified tenures according to the method of settling the revenue. Under the *zamindari* system, the land revenue was fixed in perpetuity and the *zamindar* had all the residuary rights to wasteland and the like which were not held by the cultivator. In the *inamdari* system also, the landowner was granted relatively favourable rates of land revenue. Finally, under the *raiyatwari* system, the State collected the land revenue in full, the rate of revenue being adjusted periodically, supposedly from the *raiyat* or actual cultivator. The term *raiyatwari* thus conjures up pictures of small holdings cultivated by peasant proprietors, each of whom paid land revenue directly to the Government. But this was far from the case. In most districts there were holders of 'inferior' and 'superior' rights in land, and controversy over the rights of the various types of landholders was to con-

[1] *Manual of the Coimbatore District* (ed. 1887), pp. 124–5.

[2] *Manuel of the Chingleput District* (ed. 1879), pp. 229–32; *Manual of Nellore District* (ed. 1873), pp. 479–84.

[3] *Gazetteer of the Godavari District* (ed. 1907), vol. I, pp. 161–2.

[4] B. H. Baden-Powell, *The Land Systems of British India* (Oxford, 1892), vol. III, p. 153.

tinue, in Government correspondence and in the courts, throughout the nineteenth century. Here only the briefest description of the 'superior' landholders—*zamindars* and *inamdars*, then the *mirasdars*, *janmis* and *mulawargadars* of the *raiyatwari* areas—and of the main types of landholders under them, need be given.

The Zamindari System

Under the Mughals, the term *zamindar* (literally, 'landholder') connoted a chieftain whose claim to a share of the produce was already recognized by local custom or law; while recognizing his rights, the Mughals also claimed land revenue from him. The Mughals claimed as well the right to confiscate, create and grant *zamindaris*, a power used most frequently by Aurangzeb, in whose reign the term came increasingly to signify a revenue collector, a functionary created and supported by the State.[1] As far as the administration of land revenue was concerned, there was probably little difference between the two, in that both types of *zamindar* had to collect the land revenue for the State, keeping a certain share (generally 10 per cent) for themselves. Both types were found in the South; some *zamindars*, particularly in the hills where Muslim rule was difficult to establish, were the old rajas or chieftains whose claims were at least partially recognized; others were revenue officials rewarded by the Muslim rulers with *zamindaris*. And during the wars *zamindars* came to assume various new rights of revenue collection or of land ownership. As the British found when they took over the government of the country, the origins of the *zamindars* and the rights they claimed reflected the political instability of the preceding years. 'It is wonderful how much, in times such as the last century, the robber, the raja and the *zamindar* run into one another.'[2] Moreover the British themselves virtually created some *zamindaris* by auctioning lands and conferring tenurial rights.[3]

By 1829–39 there were some 49,607 square miles under *zamindari*,

[1] W. H. Moreland, *The Agrarian System of Moslem India* (Cambridge, 1929), and Irfan Habib, *The Agrarian System of Mughal India* (Bombay, 1963), ch. V.

[2] Sir George Campbell, 'Tenures of Land in India' in *Systems of Land Tenures in Various Countries*, published by the Cobden Club (London, 1870), p. 141. The preceding sentence reads: 'To our ideas there is a wide gulf between a robber and a landlord but not so in native view.' Munro describes the hostility of the chief *raiyats* (cultivators) to the petty shopkeepers, public servants out of a job and adventurers who became *zamindars*. They regarded the *zamindar* as their social inferior and banded together against him, and he in return extracted as much revenue as he could. (Minute of 31.12.1824); Arbuthnot, *Minutes of Sir Thomas Munro*, vol. I, p. 255.

[3] Government of Madras, *Guide to the Salem Records*, pp. 3–4; Government policy towards *zamindars* is discussed in Chapter VI, *infra*.

about 35 per cent of the whole area of the Presidency.[1] But some *zamindars* were handicapped by uncertainties of status, others by excessive assessments, while others again were spendthrift or inefficient. The result was that by 1900 the area under *zamindari* had declined to less than 25 per cent of the whole.[2] By then 98 per cent of the total area in Vizagapatam and considerable parts of Ganjam, Godavari, Kistna and Nellore were *zamindari* lands, but in the remaining Telugu districts of Kurnool, Bellary, Anantapur and Cuddapah, there were none. In each of three Tamil districts, North Arcot, Salem and Madura, there were well over a million acres under *zamindari*, in Tinnevelly nearly a million acres, and all the other Tamil districts, excluding Nilgiris, had some *zamindari* lands.[3] In Malabar and South Canara there were none. By the end of the century, there were probably fewer than 1,000 *zamindars* in the Presidency and the average *zamindari* was very large.[4] From the figures given in the Statistical Atlas for 1900–1, it appears that the average size of a *zamindari* in Ganjam was 20,843 acres, in Kistna, 10,217 acres and in Trichinopoly 14,637 acres; the average for Vizagapatam is misleading, because one *zamindari*, the Vizianagaram Estate, is enormous.

The *zamindar*'s main right over his estate was to a share of the produce; the cultivator's share generally amounted to around 50 per cent of the gross produce though the great variety in modes and rates of payment makes generalization difficult.[5] In addition, the *zamindar*, where his power was strong and custom was weak, would doubtless make other more or less illegal deductions from the produce, and might even extract forced labour. But he could not claim full rights of ownership.[6] Again, he himself cultivated little if any of the land in his *zamindari*; home farms were relatively insignificant. According to custom and usage, the cultivator was probably entitled to security of tenure, but here again the rights actually given varied.

[1] *Parliamentary Papers* 1831–2, XI–XII, *Report of the Select Committee on the Affairs of the East India Company*, p. 66 (hereafter *Select Committee Report, 1831–2*).

[2] 'The process of decay was both rapid and long continued so that we find the whole of the Guntur collectorate and much of the Masulipatam collectorate passing over from zamindari to ryotwari between 1835 and 1849 and now the system applies to less than one-fourth of the Presidency'; *Cambridge History of India* (new ed., New Delhi, 1958), vol. VI, p. 44.

[3] Government of Madras, *Statistical Atlas for Madras Presidency, 1900–1*.

[4] 'There are 859 zamindars with 19 million acres of land under them'; speech by Narasimheswara Sarma in Legislative Council in 1905; Government of Madras, *Extracts Relating to Tenancy Rights in Inam* (Madras, 1935), vol. I, p. 10.

[5] This question is discussed more fully in Chapter VI, *infra*.

[6] 'Zamindari, therefore, did not signify a proprietory right over land. It co-existed with other rights and claims on the produce of the soil'; Habib, *The Agrarian System of Mughal India*, p. 154.

In general, it would appear that the *raiyats* of the southern *zamindaris* had firmer occupancy rights than those in the northern *zamindaris*; this follows the general pattern of the weakening of traditional rights in the Telugu districts. If one wishes to calculate the demand for agricultural labour the average size of the cultivator's holding is more important than that of the *zamindari*, but here, as on most other economic issues, there is, for obvious reasons, far less information available for the *zamindari* areas than for those directly administered by the Government.

The Inamdari System

Inamdar is another Persian term though it refers to a form of land tenure of ancient origin in the South.[1] Literally an *inam* is a gift. In this context it generally meant a gift of land, or of part of the land revenue accruing from a particular piece of land. In pre-British days *inams* were granted by kings (though this was, as the *Inam* Commissioner remarked, comparatively rare in Madras),[2] by the local *zamindar*, or by the villagers themselves,[3] and they were granted sometimes for life,[4] sometimes in perpetuity. Gifts of this sort can be classified into several hundred categories,[5] but their underlying purpose may be broadly described under four heads. Some of them were intended for the maintenance of the families of rulers and other notables. Others were set aside for the support of such public utilities as schools, bridges and irrigation works. A third group went in payment for past or current services by officials and specialist workers. Lastly, *inams* might be granted to temples, mosques, Brahmins and the like, or to persons carrying out various offices in places of worship. In fact the Madras Government itself created some *inams* in the early years of its rule, and a comparatively small amount of land was even given in *inam* by the Collectors; but despatches from the Court of Directors in 1822 and 1829 which expressed a preference for money pensions put a stop to this practice.[6]

Although *inams* sometimes carried ownership rights, their main feature

[1] Previously the Sanskrit word *manyam* was widely used. For various forms of 'eleemosynary and service tenures' in the Chola period, see K. A. Nilakanta Sastri, *The Colas* (Madras, 1955), pp. 574–82.

[2] Government of Madras, *Report of the Inam Commissioner* (1859).

[3] See, for example, A. Appadorai, *Economic Conditions in South India, 1000–1500 A.D.* (Madras, 1936).

[4] *Altamgha inams*, which were granted by the Muslim rulers, were not only resumable in theory, but in fact were frequently resumed. Arbuthnot, *Minutes of Sir Thomas Munro*, vol. II, p. 151. There were also cases of grants for several lives.

[5] *Report of the Inam Commissioner*, Appendix B, 'A descriptive list of the Inam Tenures of Madras Presidency'

[6] *Ibid.*

was the alienation of land revenue; the grantee generally could not dispossess the actual cultivator, but he could collect the full revenue from him and pay land revenue (or quit-rent) to the Government at a favourable rate. In Tinnevelly there were certain *inams* not even assigned to a particular piece of land, but consisting of a payment out of the annual produce of the village.[1] But even traditionally the *inam* 'tenants' did not always have occupancy rights, though this was generally the case.[2] In pre-British days the quit-rent could be either a fixed sum in money or grain, or a proportion of the crops. After piecemeal attempts to deal with claims to these rights, the Government set up a special Inam Commission in 1858 to validate the claims for *inams* in lawful possession for over fifty years, to resume others or commute them for money pensions or to 'enfranchise' them, that is, to allow the *inamdar* to convert them into private property by payment of an annual or capital sum. The Commission was wound up as a separate department in 1869, but its work continued to be dealt with by a member of the Board of Revenue. The extent of *inamdari* was considerable. By the end of the century the Inam Commission (and later the Board) had dealt with nearly 445,000 titles, affecting more than 6½ million acres and some 2½ millions of grantees. Of these 6½ million acres, nearly 1½ million were assigned to religious institutions and 3½ millions to Brahmins and other religious persons.[3] *Inam* lands were found in all the districts. Unlike the average *zamindari*, the average *inam* was very small, although there were a number of large *inamdars* holding one or more villages. The average size was lowered by the enormous number of very small *inams*, generally those belonging to village officials and artisans, to small village temples, or to persons who had performed a specific service in the past (founding the village, marking the village boundaries and so forth). Large *inams* generally belonged to religious institutions, not to individuals. However, like the *zamindar*, the *inamdar* generally rented out his land, particularly in the early period. This was of course particularly true of the lands of the larger *inamdars*, but even the smaller *inams* were frequently leased out. Thus in 1817 the Collector of Trichinopoly wrote to the Board of Revenue: 'Generally inam lands are never cultivated by the inamdars and are cultivated by the ryots of the village.' He added that

[1] *Report of the Inam Commissioner*, Appendix B, 'A descriptive list of the Inam Tenures of Madras Presidency'.

[2] E.g., in Chola times the rights given to Brahmins included *kudimikki*, the right to evict old tenants; Sastri, *The Colas*, p. 578. See also the Government's reply to the *raiyats'* deputation in March 1934 where it is stated that the tenant does not always have occupancy rights in *inam* villages; Government of Madras, *Extracts from Papers Relating to Tenancy Rights in Inam*.

[3] Baden-Powell, *Land Systems of British India*, vol. III, pp. 81–3.

inams of village officials were cultivated by the *raiyats* of the village or by those of the neighbourhood, and sometimes by hired labour, while temple lands were rented out.[1]

Raiyatwari: the Mirasdari System

The *mirasdar* of the Tamil areas had more in common with a modern landlord than the *zamindar* or the *inamdar*. Here again the nature of his rights was obscured by the changes that took place during the instability of the eighteenth century. When the British started to settle the Tamil districts, the Settlement Officers had frequently to choose between conflicting claims to land. On the one hand they found the actual occupants, and on the other the 'ancient *mirasdars*'[2] who asserted that their hereditary rights were valid even though they had fled the village or had left the land uncultivated for a number of years. Nearly all administrators agreed that a favourable form of tenure, carrying with it heritable rights of sale and purchase, had obtained under the Hindu rulers in the Tamil areas, although there were differences of opinion regarding its origin and the scope of the rights involved. The popular account of the origin of the system was that when the ruler Tondaiman settled certain areas in Chinglepet and Arcot, in order to encourage the settlers he gave them land on a favourable tenure. Munro held that the system originated in local circumstances, from the need to construct tanks and water works at public expense. Since the Government could be recompensed for its investment only if the cultivation was regular, the cultivators were charged a moderate revenue and were given hereditary rights in the soil.[3]

> The uncertainty of the means from which the produce of the lands springs renders it impossible to know, before the season of rains and the freshes from the rivers have passed, what fields in the village can be cultivated and which of them must remain barren for want of water. Hence the ancient custom of the whole wet lands of many villages being held in common, and hence the usage to which this general but undefined right of property has led, of dividing the land that can be cultivated into lots and each proprietory ryot drawing out his lot for the year and being bound to cultivate that and that alone for the season.[4]

[1] Trichinopoly Records, vol. 3675, pp. 137–45.

[2] *Miras* is an Arabic word, and replaced the Tamil word *kaniatchi*. A *miras* is literally a hereditary right, and the word was used not only for land but also for village offices. In Bellary, for example, the term *mirasdar* in itself conveyed no meaning, and people had to be described as *karnam mirasdars*, barber *mirasdars*, and so on; Sundararaja Iyengar, *Land Tenures in Madras Presidency*(Madras, 1916), p. 43.

[3] Arbuthnot, *Minutes of Sir Thomas Munro*, vol. 1, p. 240.

[4] Proceedings of the Madras Board of Revenue (hereafter P.B.R.), 2.5.1831. Again, 'Even today when land is owned by separate patrilineal families the system of irrigation requires owners to be in frequent contact to arrange such matters as the

Again, apart from villages given for the cultivation of lands, the *agraharams* or Brahmin villages were also held jointly, particularly in the Chola and Pandya areas.[1] Whatever its origin, it seems almost certain that the *mirasi* system was, originally at least, a communal system.

But this communal system of landholding underwent a number of modifications. Its earliest and strongest form was *pasankarei* or *samudayam*, under which the lands were not only cultivated jointly but were also held jointly. There was a variation: lands could be held separately by each landowner, but the produce was pooled and then redivided according to the shares held by each of them. The only truly separately held lands were house gardens. Under the *kareiyedu* or *visabadi* system, which can be regarded as a modification of this, the lands were temporarily cultivated in separate shares by the co-sharers, being subject to periodic redistribution, so as to give good and bad lands to each in turn.[2] Under both these forms, the landowners were jointly liable for government revenue. But in either case a landlowner might mortgage, sell, or otherwise alienate his rights. In course of time the lands came to be held separately and in perpetuity, this third form of communal ownership being known as *arudikarei* in Tamil and as *phalabhogam* or *ardhachandrarkam* in Sanskrit.[3] Vestiges of the former joint ownership lingered on: the landholdings continued to be expressed in terms of 'shares', and shareholders had certain rights in common: they had claims on village waste lands and they sometimes claimed pre-emption rights. Finally, when one individual came to hold all the lands of the village, it was known as *ekabhogam* or *ejamana grama*.[4]

release of water from one set of channels to another during the ploughing and sowing season'; Kathleen Gough, 'Caste in a Tanjore Village' in E. R. Leach, ed., *Aspects of Caste in South India, Ceylon and North West Pakistan* (Cambridge, 1960), p. 36.

[1] B. H. Baden-Powell, *The Indian Village Community* (London 1896, reprinted New Haven, 1957), pp. 366–74.

[2] Inscriptions show that even in the eleventh century joint cultivation of communal property was uncommon and the *kareiyedu* system widespread; A. C. Burnell, *South Indian Paleography from the Fourth to the Seventeenth Century A.D.* (2nd edn., London 1878), p. 117. For evidence of communal ownership in the Chola period, see Sastri, *The Colas*, p. 567; A. Appadorai, *Economic Conditions in South India*, p. 110, *et seq.*

[3] According to Ellis, the Collector of Madras, in his reply to the Board of Revenue's questionnaire on *mirasi* rights, *mirasi* villages held by Brahmins were generally *arudikarei*; W. H. Bayley & W. Hudleston, ed. *Papers on Mirasi Right* (Madras, 1892), p. 295.

[4] S. Sundararaja Iyengar, *Land Tenures in Madras Presidency*, pp. 46–8. Ellis has a slightly different classification: (a) *Pasankarei*, where lands of all descriptions were held in common and periodically redistributed; (b) *Arudikarei*, where cultivated lands were permanently distributed, but all other rights, including rights to waste

That communal land tenures had existed in the Tamil areas is indisputable, but it is not at all clear how widespread they were at the beginning of the nineteenth century. At that time there were still joint villages in several Tamil districts. Since these villages were most commonly found in the wet areas, it was in Tanjore that the system was widespread. Here in 1805 it was reported that of the 4,783 villages, 1,774 were *pasankarei*, or jointly held and cultivated, 2,202 were *phalabhogam* or separately held, and 1,807 were *ekabhogam*, or held by one landowner.[1] The Collector of Madura reported in 1815 that the *mirasi* right existed in 870 villages, but he does not state how many of them were joint villages.[2] Ellis stated in 1816 that in the Collectorate of Madras there were fifteen villages in which some sort of *mirasi* right had always obtained, and eleven of them were originally *pasankarei*.[3] There was also a large number of joint villages in South[4] and North Arcot.[5] In 1818 in Tinnevelly a *phalabhogam* village was reported where the cultivators exchanged their shares every five or six years.[6] Chinglepet in particular was a stronghold of the system, and in 1799 Place found a very large number of *mirasi* villages. It is not clear how many of them were jointly held in fact, but there is evidence that the system was still alive. In 1787 and 1788 the Collector described three *pasankarei* villages: in one no share of the land could be sold without the consent of the inhabitants of the village. In another village, the principal inhabitants decided that land could not be sold to a particular purchaser, because one landholder objected; since the village was *pasankarei*, all the 'inhabitants' (i.e., landholders) had to consent to the

land, were held in common; and (c) *Ijamana gramam* (i.e., *ejamana grama*), where the cultivated lands were held in common but distributed under fixed rules by the *ejaman* or headman. This type, he added, was rare. Bayley & Hudleston, *Papers on Mirasi Right*, p. 253. See also Graeme, Report on North Arcot, 31.3.1818. *Selections of Papers from the Records at the East India House, Relating to the Revenue, Police and Civil and Criminal Justice under the Company's Governments in India* (London, 1820) (hereafter *East India Papers*), vol. I, pp. 966–7.

[1] Wallace, 'Report on the Settlement of Tanjore', Bayley & Hudleston, *Papers on Mirasi Right*, p. 94.

[2] Madura Records, vol. 1163, pp. 9–14.

[3] Bayley & Hudleston, *Papers on Mirasi Right*, p. 172. See also Francis Buchanan, *A Journey from Madras Through the Countries of Mysore, Canara and Malabar* (1801, second edn. Madras 1871) (hereafter *A Journey from Madras*), vol. II.

[4] In 1897 the Resident of Travancore said that the custom of redistributing the land periodically had existed when he was employed in South Arcot. J. F. Hewitt, 'Communal Origin of Land Tenures', *Journal of the Royal Asiatic Society*, vol. XXIX, pp. 628–41, 1897.

[5] Baden-Powell gives a few further references from District Manuals; Baden-Powell, *Land Systems of British India*, vol. III, pp. 114–15.

[6] Collector, Tinnevelly to Board of Revenue, 23.4.1818; Tinnevelly Records, vol. 3595, pp. 180–90.

sale of land.[1] The third village, Chumbakkam, was originally owned by the Raja who abandoned it during the wars, and the village had since become *pasankarei*.[2] If this is true, it is evidence of the vitality of the system. But by the middle of the nineteenth century there appear to have been few joint villages left, their breakdown having been hastened by the *raiyatwari* system of land revenue and registration. Yet the communal system did not disappear completely; even as late as 1921 there were still a few Tanjore villages in which the land was periodically redistributed, although long before 1890 these had become exceptions and individual ownership the rule.[3] Various forms of communal tenures existed in Chinglepet as late as 1878; in Chinglepet *taluk*,[4] out of 175 originally joint villages there were still nine where lands were held in common, although in the rest some 3,100 acres of common land had been divided by the settlement officers among 1,666 shareholders. In Trivellore *taluk* ten villages transferred from North Arcot were still held on the *visabadi* or *kareiyedu* system of the 'annual interchange of shares'; but in nearly all the other villages the joint lands had been divided, some 2,556 acres being split up between 1,071 shareholders.[5] Again in Madura, even at the beginning of the twentieth century, '... in a good many of the riverside villages a curious relic of the corporate unity of the village in former times remains in the common ownership of the village dry land by those of the ryots who hold any of the village wet land. The dry land is generally in a joint *patta*[6] entered in the joint names of several owners and is leased out to others, the produce being jointly enjoyed.'[7] On the other hand, in Tinnevelly it was the dry lands which were first separately assessed; the *mirasdars* were jointly assessed for the wet lands in 1813.[8]

Although very little information is available for the Telugu districts, they were not so different from the Tamil districts as was once believed; traces of *visabadi gramas*[9] or joint villages were found extensively in Cuddapah, and to a lesser extent in the other Telugu areas. But it was peculiar to the joint village system here that if a *raiyat* considered his field to be over-assessed and someone else's under-assessed, he could offer to take up

[1] Collector, Chinglepet to Board of Revenue, 2.8.1787; Chinglepet Records, vol. 443, pp. 173–4.

[2] Collector, Chinglepet to Board of Revenue, *ibid.*, pp. 211–13.

[3] Settlement Report on Tanjore, 1921, p. 6.

[4] A *taluk* is a sub-division of a district.

[5] P.B.R. 8.5.1878, No. 1228.

[6] A *patta* is a document, in this case issued by the Government, showing terms of payment of revenue, area held, etc.

[7] *Madura Gazetteer*, 1906, p. 151.

[8] Minute of the Board of Revenue, 5.8.1813; *East India Papers*, vol. I, p. 594.

[9] *Visabadi*: Village settlement [of assessment] by shares in ready money.

the latter's holding at a higher rate, and the latter had either to exchange holdings or pay a greater share of the assessment. In Nellore also there were vestiges of the joint village system. Here the *kadims* corresponded to the *mirasdars* of the Tamil districts; they were responsible to the Government for the land revenue and employed *payakaris* or tenants and crop-sharers to cultivate the land.[1]

The term *mirasdar* far outlived the communal system—indeed, it is still in use today; it has the long life of most names that confer status upon their bearers. Probably used initially for a descendant of one of the original shareholders of a village, the term was extended to cover any one who could claim hereditary rights in land, the most important being rights to buy and sell the land itself, and including rights over the common waste lands of the village. Only the latter continued to be a real matter for debate throughout the nineteenth century, since with the development of the *raiyatwari* system[2] any *raiyat* registered as an occupant of land came to have the same rights to buy and sell it as the *mirasdar*.

But an important question remains: was the *mirasdar* (or the holder of non-*mirasi* lands) the actual cultivator, or was he the landlord of the cultivators? In part the answer depended on the size of his holding; it was related to his caste as well. These factors can be studied most clearly in the Tamil and the West Coast areas.

Strikingly enough the Tamil district with the most unequal distribution of land ownership appears to have been Tanjore, one of the districts where communal tenures still obtained. In 1800 the Collector pointed out that the wealth of Tanjore was very unequally distributed and he believed that the chief landowner alone could control the grain market. Indeed, he recommended that there should be a ceiling of 202½ acres on individual holdings; 'there will be difficulties in the way of such a reform but they can be surmounted'.[3] Again, the Tanjore Committee reported in 1807:

'Every extensive property in land is held by the Mirassidars; many possess from three to four thousand acres, not always a separate and distinct property, in whole villages, but in various proportions of the Mirassi of different villages. But the property of a much greater number is very small, many of those whose property is extensive . . . are said to have acquired this property by means not always justifiable.'[4]

[1] The first British settlement in 1801–2 was with each village as a whole; *Guide to Nellore Records*, pp. 2–4.

[2] This is discussed in Chapter III *infra*.

[3] Collector, Tanjore to Board of Revenue, 3.8.1800; Tanjore Records, vol. 3200, pp. 121–36.

[4] Report of the Tanjore Committee, 1807; Bayley & Hudleston, *Papers on Mirasi Right*.

These large *mirasdars* were spread through the district: the Collector reported in 1827 that there was usually one *mirasdar* in every village who possessed a large extent of lands scattered over and outside the district.[1] And nearly all the *mirasdars* tilled their lands with the help of hired labourers or serfs.[2]

There are at least two other instances, by inference, of large holdings in other Tamil districts. Place gives the example of a landowner in Chingle-pet who had 400 slaves. Because of his father's improvidence he could employ only 100, while the rest were working for Europeans but would gladly have gone back to him.[3] In Tinnevelly it was reported in 1835–6 that a landholder had 500 slaves, for each of whom he received a fixed quantity of grain per day (apparently because he could not employ them and so allowed them to work for others).[4] But these must at best have been exceptional cases, since there is no other evidence of individual farms large enough to employ such numbers of 'slaves'.[5] In fact the data point the other way. Of 1,080 villages in Tinnevelly, the Collector reported in 1817 that there were 37,494 *mirasdars*, of whom 20,553 cultivated the land 'entirely by themselves'; 13,708 cultivated the lands 'entirely by *parakudis*; 2,514 used both *parakudis* as well as *pallans* [serfs], or let the land out; and 359 leased their lands out'.[6]

Coimbatore, like Tanjore, was relatively prosperous, but it had fewer

[1] Collector to Board of Revenue, 22.11.1827; Tanjore Records, vol. 4228, pp. 100–12.

[2] Settlement Report on Tanjore, 1805; Bayley & Hudleston, *Papers on Mirasi Right*, p. 99.

[3] L. Place, Report on the Jaghire, para. 79.

[4] *P.P.* 1841, XXVII, *Report of the Indian Law Commissioners on Slavery* (henceforth *Report on Slavery, 1841*), p. 20.

[5] A rough indication of the small size of the average holdings in Tinnevelly is that in 1832 it was reported that on an average 48,300 *pattas* (titles to *raiyatwari* lands) were issued; in addition in a number of villages the village lease system still obtained. Collector, Trichinopoly to Board of Revenue, 5.1.1832; Trichinopoly Records, vol. 4401, pp. 6–9.

In 1901 the area under *raiyatwari* in Tinnevelly was 2,278,572 acres. In 70 years a considerable expansion of cultivation must have taken place, so that the average in 1832 is likely to have been well below 47 acres (the ratio of 1901 *raiyatwari* area to number of landholders in 1832). In 1901 the average *raiyatwari* holding was 6·34 acres; *Statistical Atlas for Madras, 1901*.

[6] There were 40,000 *mirasdars* as well as 30,000 cultivators 'who cultivate their own lands', but it is not clear whether the figures are mutually exclusive or not. In either case, the figures given in the text are a large enough proportion of the total to be taken as representative. Some information is also given on the share of the produce accruing to the *mirasdar* under each system of cultivation, but this is hopelessly confused. Replies of the Collector, Tinnevelly to the Questionnaire on Mirasi Rights, 8.5.1817 and 23.4.1818; Tinnevelly Records, vol. 3594, pp. 115–21 and vol. 3595, pp. 180–90.

very large holdings. In Pollachi in South Coimbatore, according to Buchanan, there were a few farmers with holdings of 86 acres apiece, but the great majority had no more than about eight to nine acres each.[1] If the land was leased out to cropsharers, these might keep six-fifteenths of the gross produce, and the remainder would go to the land revenue, and to interest on the money, grain, cattle and implements advanced by the farmer.[2] In 1816 the Collector reported that the *raiyats* could be divided into three classes, the first of whom enjoyed a 'very respectable' income; these *raiyats* were graziers as well as farmers, and indeed only a minor part of their income came from cultivation.[3] Seven years later, the Collector announced a significant increase in the general prosperity of the district and in some individual holdings; he mentioned three landholders whose lands were assessed for Rs. 7,000/-, Rs. 14,000/- and Rs. 20,000/-.[4]

But in most other Tamil districts, both the average holdings and the larger holdings were probably much smaller than in Coimbatore and *a fortiori* than in Tanjore. In Salem five ploughs would make a farmer rich, and the majority of farms were cultivated by family labour alone, except at seed time and harvest.[5] In the fifteen villages of the Madras Collectorate there seem to have been few or no tenants in 1816, though this had not always been so:

> 'At present circumstances are so changed, that there are few, if any, inferior cultivators resident in the Madras villages. What remains of the village lands, not converted into gardens, is cultivated by hired labourers, sometimes engaged in one place and sometimes in another, and frequently more profitably employed as Coolies.'[6]

Munro's picture of the north of Salem probably describes the northern

[1] 'One plough is reckoned here adequate to cultivate . . . 8·569 acres. A few farmers possess 10 ploughs but by far the greater number have only one'; Buchanan, *A Journey from Madras*, vol. II, p. 32. Buchanan generally measures the wealth of farmers by the number of ploughs they possess. This is of course not synonymous with possession of land, and tenants may cultivate leased land with their own ploughs, or farmers borrow or hire each other's ploughs, but on the whole, the number of ploughs is probably a fairly good guide to land ownership, and particularly to the size of home farms.

[2] *Ibid.*, vol. II, pp. 32–3.

[3] Quoted by Nilmani Mukherjee, *The Ryotwari System in Madras* (Calcutta, 1962), p. 295.

[4] P.B.R., 15.5.1823, and *Asiatic Journal*, May-August 1830, pp. 73–8; quoted by Mukherjee, *op. cit.*, p. 309.

[5] Buchanan, *A Journey from Madras*, vol. II, p. 520. Each plough could cultivate 1¼ acres of rice land and 3¼ acres of dry. Buchanan admits that the *inam* lands were better cultivated than the *raiyatwari* lands since the *inamdars* let them at a lower rent than the Government's land revenue.

[6] *East India Papers*, vol. I, p. 820.

Tamil and the Telugu districts fairly well. Out of a total population of 600,000 in 1796, there were 45,000 to 50,000 'independent farmers', of whom not even ten had 150 acres of dry land or 40 acres of wet. The average holding was 10 acres of dry or 2½ acres of wet land, and the 'middling farmers' might own up to twice this amount. There was not a man among them worth £500 and, if cattle were excluded, nine-tenths of them would not have £5.[1]

So the availability of land for renting varied from one district to another. But the fact that there were well-established systems of leasing out the land, and that the distinctions between various types of tenancies were well developed, provides further support for the hypothesis that a fair amount was rented out in the Tamil areas. There were three systems by which the large estates were cultivated. Probably the most common was the *varam* (share) system, under which the land was let to tenants who paid as rent a fixed proportion of the gross yield. Occasionally the land was leased out for a rent fixed in absolute cash terms (*kuthugai*) or, more rarely, in kind (*pattam*).[2] This system was commonly known as the 'lease system' and was found generally in the dry areas,[3] or, particularly towards the end of the century, in those areas where the landlord lived away from his land.[4] Finally, there was the *pannai* or home farm, cultivated by labourers or *pannaiyals*. Although this was the least widespread method by the end of the nineteenth century, this may not have been the case a hundred years earlier.

There were several categories of tenants, the main distinction being between the *parakudi*, or tenant from outside the village, and the *ulkudi*, or resident of the village.[5] The *parakudi*'s lease usually ran for a year. The

[1] G. R. Gleig, *The Life of Sir Thomas Munro* (2nd ed. London, 1831), vol. 1, p. 208 and pp. 226–7. The acreage has been calculated from Munro's figures of revenue paid by the various classes of cultivators, and from his statement that the land revenue on dry land did not exceed one pagoda per acre, while the revenue on wet land was four times this amount.

[2] V. Krishnan, 'The Thambraparni Ryot', unpublished thesis for the Ph.D. degree of Madras University, 1931, p. 40.

[3] But in the twentieth century it spread to other areas; in fact, according to Dr Krishnan, *varam* gave the least incentive to the cultivator: 'Passing along the banks of the channel, one can point out which fields are under *varum* tenure, which under *pattam*, and which under the cultivation of owners', since the fields are in increasingly good condition; *idem*.

[4] In fact, according to the *Statistical Atlas* for 1908, the lease system was the worst of the three, since the landlord was generally an absentee and the tenant had no capital. *Statistical Atlas for Madras Presidency* (1908), p. 514.

[5] Other categories are described in Sundararaja Iyengar, *Land Tenures in Madras Presidency*. The Collector of Madura described in 1808 a system of *pattucattu raiyats* with hereditary rights, *vellaversey raiyats* with weaker rights and *yerwaddi* or 'non-resident' *raiyats*; Madura Records, vol. 1154.

ulkudi frequently inherited the right to occupy the land, and could occasionally mortgage his rights, but he could not sell them;[1] he had more secure rights of occupancy but paid a higher rent. His share of the crop was generally about 5 per cent less than the *parakudi*'s; that is to say, he would receive about 45–50 per cent of the crop, net of land revenue.[2] The percentage of the crop paid as rent depended on whether or not the landlord supplied the stock, seed, cash and so on; and it varied too with the fertility of the soil.

There were many ways in which the expenses of cultivation and the provision of capital were shared between landlord and tenant. Frequently the landlord bore all the expenses involved in the preliminary stages of cultivation: manuring, levelling the land, the clearance of channels and weeding. The *parakudi*'s responsibility began with the ploughing of the seed-bed and ended just before the harvest. Harvest expenses were met from the gross crop, before the division between landlord and tenant; they included the cost of extra labour, and the *parakudi* himself was frequently paid during the harvest like other hired labourers. The crop was then divided between landlord and *parakudi* according to the agreed shares, the landlord paying the land revenue out of his share. If the landlord supplied the seed, as well as the cattle, implements and the rest, the *parakudi*'s share naturally fell. For instance, in Tanjore in 1805 the *parakudi* got between 22 per cent and 30 per cent of the gross produce if he supplied all the capital: seed, cattle and implements.[3] In 1921, the settlement officer for Tanjore found that the rate of *varam* was rigidly fixed by custom in each village, and had been unchanged for at least a century. 'In only two villages out of nearly two hundred did I find any recent change; in one of these cases the *parakudis* had combined in a strike last year, and successfully increased their share from one-fifth to one-fourth.' The *parakudi*'s share varied from one-fifth of the crop to one-half; in the irrigated areas, the common rates were one-fourth if the tenant supplied the seed and incidental expenses, and one-fifth if not.[4] There is further evidence regarding the widespread practice of renting out land at the beginning of the nineteenth century and it is fairly precise. When the Collector of Tinnevelly examined the accounts of 1,080 villages, in 1817–18 he found a total of 37,494 *mirasdars*; 359 of them leased their lands out to 'renters',

[1] A. Sarada Raju, *Económic Conditions in the Madras Presidency, 1800–1850* (Madras, 1941), pp. 32–4. See also *East India Papers*, vol. I, p. 817; Bayley & Hudleston, *Papers on Mirasi Right*, p. 96.

[2] Report of Collector, Tanjore; *ibid.*, p. 88. The Collector tried to raise and fix the share given to the tenant.

[3] Settlement Report on Tanjore; *ibid.*, p. 97.

[4] Settlement Report for Tanjore, 1921, pp. 9–10.

getting as their share $4\frac{7}{8}$ per cent of the gross output; 13,708 let their lands out to *parakudis*, getting $12\frac{25}{32}$ per cent; and 20,553 cultivated the land themselves with the help of 'slaves', getting $12\frac{21}{64}$ per cent; while the remaining 2,514 used a combination of these three systems.[1] In another account, of the $43\frac{1}{8}$ per cent of the crop left after paying the land revenue, the allowance to the temple and similar charges, the *mirasdar* got one-third and the *parakudi* two-thirds.[2] So the renting of land to small tenants was well established in the Tamil areas by the early nineteenth century. How far was this the case on the West Coast?

Raiyatwari: The West Coast

The West Coast districts were marked by high rainfall and hilly lands, and they also differed from the rest of the Presidency in that their land revenue had traditionally been very low; in fact the landowners of Malabar claimed that they had paid no land tax at all before the Muslim invasion. The land revenue systems of Malabar and South Canara were very different from any others in the Presidency, and unfortunately even less is known about their early history.

One important reason is that from A.D. 825, when the ruler of Malabar became a Muslim and distributed his land among the main chiefs of the warrior caste, the Nairs, until its conquest by Mysore in 1776, Malabar appears to have had no central ruler. Each Nair chief had his estate, part of which may have been cultivated by agrestic serfs. The remaining land was either let out for rent to members of the cultivating castes, or granted to the less important Nairs on a special tenure known as *kanam*. Other land was also held free of tax by Brahmins, with the obligation to maintain the temples. Since the Brahmins could not cultivate their lands (and indeed probably could not even supervise the work of the 'slaves', who were not only untouchable but practically unseeable), they let it out in the same way as the chieftains. These superior landholders—rulers, Brahmins or upper members of the warrior caste—were called *janmis*. The *janmis* had a number of social privileges over their tenants which were extremely important in a hierarchical society. As late as 1881, tenants complained that the landlord made them use 'repugnant forms of address', prostrate themselves before him and refer to their own belongings only in abject terms; if the tenants did not comply with these requirements they were threatened with eviction.[3] Fortified by these wide customary

[1] Letters from Collector, Tinnevelly Records, 8.5.1817; vol. 3594, pp. 115–21, and 23.4.1818; vol. 3595, pp. 180–90.

[2] *Select Committee Report, 1831–32*, p. 402.

[3] Government of Madras, *Report of the Malabar Special Committee*, 1881–2, vol. III, Appendix XII (Register of Petitions), p. 371.

powers the holders of the land were traditionally more than mere landlords.

But in some ways they were also traditionally less.[1] This was particularly the case in their relations with the *kanamdars* or *kanakkars*, often members of their own caste, who held from them on the *kanam* tenure. At the outset of the contract the *kanamdar* gave the *janmi* a lump sum or *kanam* and thereafter paid lower rates of rent than other tenants, the level of the rent being related inversely to the lump sum payment. On the termination of the agreement the original lump sum was returnable to the *kanamdar*, or the agreement could be renewed.

The origin and significance of this type of tenure are matters of doubt. One explanation is that it was essentially feudal; the *kanam* was a fee given in token of allegiance, the subordinate chiefs retaining the right to demand the fee back, relinquish their lands, and transfer their allegiance.[2] According to Logan, who was Collector of Malabar for many years, the region had evolved into a corporate society, each class performing a special function and being allotted a particular share of the produce. The land itself belonged to no one landlord: the *janmam* was not a right to the soil, but a 'mere right to exercise authority over the persons of those who resided thereon'.[3]

The modern view is to regard the *kanam* as a form of usufructuary mortgage: the *kanamdar* is the mortgagee and deducts the interest on the *kanam* or loan from payments of rent. Originally the 'mortgage' could be redeemed neither at pleasure nor after a period fixed by contract; when either the *janmi* or the *kanakkar* died, the principal debt was scaled down, generally by about 13 per cent. Even after the debt had been completely worked off, the *kanakkar* could remain in occupation but would have to pay the full rent.[4] In course of time the agreement came to be renewed every twelve years, when the *kanam* was either repaid by the *janmi* or more frequently was renewed after scaling down. The *kanakkar* thus secured rights of occupation by custom.

There were many variations on the *kanam* tenure, two of the most important being the *kuzhikanam* and *otti* systems. Where waste lands had to be reclaimed, they were given on *kuzhikanam*: at first the cultivator

[1] Eric J. Miller, 'Caste and Territory in Malabar', *American Anthropologist*, June 1954.

[2] Note by Chief Commissioner, Coorg, in 1885, quoted in Baden-Powell, *Land Systems of British India*, vol. III, p. 162.

[3] *Malabar Manual*, vol. I, p. 491.

[4] *Ibid.*, vol. I, p. 605. Strictly speaking, 'rent' is not completely accurate, since the *janni* was not (particularly at this period) a complete landlord, but it is not as clumsy as such terms as 'produce-share' and is hardly more likely to confuse.

would pay no rent but paid a small fee or *kanam* for a particular term (which came to be fixed at twelve years); at the end of this period the *janmi* would pay the cultivator a certain sum and then take the normal rent; usually this sum was not treated as an advance with interest deducted from the rent, as in the ordinary *kanam* tenure. Since in many parts of Malabar the land is hilly and conditions of cultivation are difficult, this form of tenure was important. Where the interest on the advance was as large as the rent, so that the *janmi* received no annual payments, the tenure was called *otti*.

The position is further complicated by the fact that both *janmi* and *kanamdar* could lease the land out to tenants known as *pattamdars* or *verumpattamdars*. The *pattamdars* in their turn could lease the land out to sub-tenants for twelve years or less, or the *pattamdar* could be a tenant-at-will. Warden reported in 1815 that he had come across many cases in which the *janmi* and the *kanamdar* had paid the land revenue without getting a 'grain of rent' from their under-tenants; they could evict them but had to go to court to get their dues.[1]

By far the greater number of the *janmis* let their lands out; in 1815, 'It is stated that out of the total number of Jenmkars or Proprietors amounting to 44,378, not a twentieth part pay their own revenue, that is, the Circar [Government] revenue assessed upon their lands.'[2] In 1841 Sullivan reported that all the land in Malabar was the property of 45,000 individuals who leased it out to 166,000 'tenants'. Many of the proprietors received only nominal rents or lived too far from their lands to collect them, so that a large portion of the land was actually in the hands of the cultivators or *raiyats*.[3] Since the land revenue was considerably lower in Malabar (and Canara) than in the rest of the Presidency, the scope for renting out the land was greater:

> In Malabar and Canara the landlords paying the land-tax enjoy in many cases a clear rent, amounting to 40 or 50 per cent of the net produce or rent of their estate. The land is saleable property, and the landlords, so far from ever wishing to relinquish their estates, will on no account part with them, unless obliged by the most urgent necessity.[4]

The average assessment on holdings did not exceed Rs. 100, so that the average size of holding must have been fairly small. As Munro put it:

[1] T. Warden, *Report on the Land Tenures in Malabar 1815* (Calicut, 1916), p. 4.

[2] P.B.R., 6.2.1815.

[3] Sullivan, *Report on the Provinces of Malabar and Canara*, 29.1.1841 (Calicut, 1916), p. 19.

[4] Minute of Board of Revenue, 5.8.1813; *East India Papers*, vol. I, p. 587.

The assessment of Malabar is in general very moderate, but were it lowered one half, failures would still be frequent. They must always be expected among such a body as forty thousand petty landholders, a considerable share of whom are little above the rank of common cultivators.[1]

Buchanan remarked that in Palghat, South Malabar, a farmer with about 35 acres 'is reckoned a substantial man, and hires a servant to superintend his slaves'. For a farm of this size, he would require 5 ploughs and 10 oxen, and 5 families of slaves.[2] Here, as in the rest of Malabar, many of the landholders (or *janmis*), or the tenants (or *pattamdars*) leased their land out, in general for three years, for a fixed annual rent.[3] After paying the rent and every other kind of expense, the tenant was left with 40 per cent of the gross produce.

The proprietor of the land, therefore, were the land-tax to exhaust the whole rent, and were he in consequence reduced to the necessity of cultivating his estate on his own account, would be in a much better condition than farmers are in general in India; but they are by no means reduced to this state, although in general they now cultivate as much of their own lands as they can conveniently superintend.[4]

In Tellicherry, North Malabar, the cultivators were poorer and mostly worked with their own hands. They had very few slaves, but they employed hired labourers.[5] In another part of North Malabar there were a few 'great farmers' who had 10 ploughs, 20 oxen, 20 male and female slaves, and 10 male and female hired labourers apiece. There were no more than 10 or 12 such farmers in the whole district, most farmers having only 1 or 2 ploughs, but almost all of them had slaves: 'they are a few only that are reduced to the necessity of labouring with their own hands'.[6]

South Canara had a history somewhat similar to that of Malabar and hence a somewhat similar land tenure system. Here the *mulawargadar* (from *mulawarga*, original or hereditary estate) corresponded to the *janmi*, both in his origin in a military ruling caste and in most of his rights. The *mulawargadar*'s rights were saleable, but even when they were sold the land continued to be registered in his name and the land revenue to be paid through him. There was no such elaborate system of mortgages as in

[1] Munro's Report on Malabar, 4.7.1817; *ibid.*, vol. I, p. 856.

[2] Here, as in Bengal, a plough would cultivate about $7\frac{1}{2}$ acres of rice land. The superintendent was hired by the year and was not required to do any manual labour. Buchanan, *A Journey from Madras*, vol. II, pp. 68–9.

[3] Frequently Buchanan uses 'rent' as synonymous with land revenue, but in Malabar he always makes a distinction between them, since it was accepted by the Company that in Malabar the land belonged to the *janmi* and not to the Government.

[4] Buchanan, *A Journey from Madras*, vol. II, p. 66.

[5] *Ibid.*, vol. II, p. 173.

[6] *Ibid.*, vol. II, p. 153.

Malabar.[1] However, there were *mulgeni* tenants[2] whose rights resembled those of the *kanamdar* in that they had a permanent lease; in addition, the rent was permanently fixed. In fact, the word 'tenant' is misleading, for the *mulgenidar* was really a kind of subordinate landlord or sub-proprietor. There were also *chaligeni* tenants, or tenants-at-will, and *vaidageni* tenants, or lessees for terms of years.

Canara had as much rainfall as in Malabar—and too much for cattle—but the conditions of cultivation were harder, the land being rocky and uneven, and the soil poor. In Canara, again as in Malabar, the land revenue was lower than in the rest of the Presidency, which was one reason for the relatively high value of land ownership. In 1800 Munro wrote of Canara, 'In the Baramahal [*sic*] not one complaint in a hundred was about property in land—here nine in ten are on that subject.'[3] The land was freely saleable: between 1800–1 and 1812–13, there had been 2,573 sales or transfers, apart from sales for arrears of land revenue or in satisfaction of court decrees.[4] The Settlement Report for 1812–13 also points out that there were very few tenants, and that almost all of these were tenants-at-will. Few new *mulgenis*, or permanent leases, were being created, since the landlords preferred to cultivate the lands themselves or to let them out to *chalgenidars* or tenants-at-will. The *mulgenidar* paid 50 per cent of the gross produce as rent, the *chalgenidars* paid 50–60 per cent. But by 1841 Sullivan noted the increasing tendency for land to be purchased by merchants who could not cultivate it themselves[5]—another point of resemblance with Malabar, where the first half of the nineteenth century saw a very large number of land transfers from the original landowner to merchants.[6] Sullivan estimated that about 45 per cent of the lands in Canara were occupied by tenants, and in the low-lying areas about 60 per cent. This argues a sharp change since 1812–13.

In Canara as in Malabar, the average holding was not very large, but the cultivators of South Canara were better off than those of the neighbouring

[1] Buchanan does mention that the *aduvacaras* or mortgagees paid the land tax to the landowner for transmission to the Government, keeping the rest of the output to cover the interest on the mortgage. But the land could be resumed whenever the landowner could redeem the mortgage; *ibid.*, vol. II, pp. 31–3.

[2] There were two kinds of *mulgeni* tenures: *mulgeni* and *shudhmulgeni* (obtained by simple purchase) of which the former, being the more ancient, was the more secure; Sundararaja Iyengar, *Land Tenures in Madras Presidency*, pp. 229–30.

[3] Letter to Cockburn, 7.10.1800; Gleig, *Life of Munro*, vol. I, p. 321.

[4] Collector's Report on Settlement of Canara for 1812–13; P.B.R., 1814.

[5] Sullivan, *Report on the Provinces of Malabar and Canara*, p. 19.

[6] The fact that the original *janmis* were Hindus and the merchants Muslims was a source of communal troubles; Government of Madras, *Correspondence on the Moplah Outrages in Malabar* (Madras, 1863), vol. I, pp. 429–30.

district. According to Buchanan, a rich farmer would have 20 to 25 ploughs (or 140 to 175 acres),[1] and there were many with 2, 3 or 4 ploughs, although the majority had only one. But even with only 4 ploughs, the *raiyat* would require the full time services of 6 men, 4 women and 8 oxen, as well as the part-time services of women for transplanting rice. The proprietors (*mulawargadars*) were generally Brahmins; most of them cultivated the land on their own account (with labourers), but some let it out on leases of four to ten years, and for a grain rent. Land was both sold and mortgaged.[2] Munro also mentions the very large number of holdings in Canara; on the average holding the land revenue was about 20 to 25 pagodas (or Rs. 70/- to Rs. 87/8as.) and this would be around one-fourth of the gross produce, though on many estates the land revenue was less than one-sixth of the gross produce. There were a few estates on which the land revenue was as high as 1,000 pagodas. In general the district was prosperous and even the smaller farmers were comfortably off; one result of this was endless litigation.[3]

What conclusions about agrarian structure can be drawn from these fragmentary data? It is clear that the village was not always and everywhere a simple community of peasant proprietors; often it was far more differentiated and complex. The *zamindars* and larger *inamdars* leased out their lands and not merely to tenants-at-will. In fact there were cases of *mirasdars* holding lands under *zamindars*,[4] and some of them may well have leased out their lands again. In the *raiyatwari* areas also there were elaborate gradations of tenancy: the *mirasdar* of the Tamil districts leased to the *parakudi* or *ulkudi*; the *janmi* and *kanamdar* of Malabar leased to the *pattadar*; the *mulawargadar* of Canara leased to the *mulgeni* or *chaligeni* tenant. Moreover the size of the units of cultivation also varied. Admittedly, although in a few districts such as Tanjore there were some very large landholders, holdings in excess of a hundred acres or so were very rare. There are no recorded instances of *hacienda* type estates, and beyond a certain limit land would be leased out. But in very many villages there would be a few large holdings which could not be cultivated by family labour alone, and there was thus a demand for hired labour.

[1] There is some confusion about the extent of land cultivated by a plough here. Buchanan says that the figures supplied by the Collector would yield 21·13 acres per plough, but that this is obviously absurd and the allowance per plough should be six or seven acres; *A Journey from Madras*, vol. II, p. 227. This latter figure is certainly the more reasonable in view of the statistics for other districts.

[2] *Idem.*

[3] Letter dated 16.6.1801; Gleig, *Life of Munro*, vol. I, p. 348.

[4] Lawsuits arising out of this in 1859 and 1861 are described in Bayley & Hudleston, *Papers on Mirasi Right*, pp. 578, 589–90.

In reality, a *parakudi* or a tenant-at-will, who was generally a crop-sharer, can hardly be distinguished from an agricultural labourer. First, the crop-sharer's functions consisted almost entirely of agricultural labour. All the capital was provided by the landlord, who frequently advanced a loan even for the crop-sharer's living expenses. There were not many 'decisions' to be taken regarding the crop to be sown and the techniques of cultivation, since agriculture was stagnant; in fact, since the landowner's share of the crop was so large, he may frequently have supervised the work of the crop-sharer almost as closely as that of his agricultural labourers proper. The similarities go further. If the crop-sharer bore the risk of the crop turning out badly, the agricultural labourer too was paid his wages in the form of a share of the crop, though it is true that he generally got a daily wage as well. The incomes of the poorest crop-sharer and the agricultural labourer were frequently the same, and this seems to reflect the fact that there was no great difference in their economic functions. Indeed the same person might play both parts. As a case in point, the *pannaiyal*[1] or agricultural labourer was sometimes given a small plot of land to cultivate as a tenant. In this case the landlord seems to have allowed the *pannaiyal* a lower share of the crop than the *parakudi*, and he was more frequently given a small piece of land to cultivate free of rent. Again, as we have seen, the *parakudi* might receive daily wages during the harvest.

Understandably, the early writers (and some of their successors) frequently confused the terms *parakudi* (a tenant, however poor) and *pannaiyal* (a labourer); or they defined as a 'labourer' a crop-sharer who provided his own stock, and who should therefore have been classed as a tenant:

> 'Almost everywhere in Tanjore the labourers under a mirasdar have a proportionate share in the land. In every country and in every possession, it is usual for the master to find the stock, and for his servants to do the work, but in Tanjore, and in agriculture, the servants do the work and find the stock too.'[2]

All sorts of misinterpretations are possible from these confusions. But the point is that they would never have arisen if the tenant himself had not been so poor.

The fluidity of the society must also be noted, or more precisely, the fact that economic (but not social) categories were fluid. Land was abundant at the beginning of the nineteenth century. Any one who agreed to pay the land revenue could take up lands from the Government and

[1] For a discussion of the term *pannaiyal* see Chapter IV, *infra.*

[2] Harris, Report on Tanjore to the Fifth Committee, 9.5.1804; Bayley & Hudleston, *Papers on Mirasi Right*, p. 85.

(except at the very beginning of the century) could abandon them with equal ease. And this was in fact what often happened:

> Whenever a farmer's servant saves a few rupees he buys a pair of bullocks. His plough does not cost him a rupee; he rents a few acres from the Government and commences farming himself; if he is successful, he continues his business; and if he meets with an accident he sells his cattle to pay his rent, and returns to his former employment of common labourer. In such a state of things, it is almost impossible that great landed property can ever be obtained by any one man, unless by fraud or violence.[1]

Of course the most fertile lands had already been taken, and there seems to have been a fairly highly developed land market in some areas. Lands were bought, sold, mortgaged and leased out in a variety of ways. It is significant that it was in those areas where traditional tenures were most developed, or had disintegrated the least, that transactions in land were most frequently recorded. We have seen that in Malabar and Canara land was freely sold and mortgaged; and in some Tamil districts too, such as Tanjore and Trichinopoly,[2] the Collectors reported that such transactions took place. But they were infrequent in the Telugu districts; of Guntur it was reported that as a rule 'no lands of whatever description, were bought and sold'.[3]

Social rigidities set two brakes on these frequent economic transitions. At one end of the scale, Brahmins could not perform several types of manual labour. The strictness of the prohibition varied: the Haiga Brahmins of North Canara could do every kind of work on their own land but could not offer themselves for hire,[4] but in Malabar, where certain untouchables were also 'unseeables', even the supervision of labour was sometimes forbidden. Brahmins could either lease their lands out or employ labourers, but cultivation with labour was more frequent than one might have inferred from caste rigidities. For example, in Tamilnad, which in the matter of strictness of caste rules would probably fall between South Canara and Malabar, the Chinglepet Brahmins were reported in 1819 to hire labourers, either for a fixed daily wage or for a share of the produce; the non-Brahmin *mirasdars* were themselves cultivators, and

[1] Letter from Trichangoor, 21.9.1798; Gleig, *Life of Sir Thomas Munro*, vol. II, p. 227.

[2] For Trichinopoly see Trichinopoly Records, vol. 4397, pp. 72–5, and Government of Madras, *A Collection of Papers Regarding the Value of Land in the Early Nineteenth Century* (Madras, 1916), pp. 18–19.

[3] *Ibid.*, p. 19.

[4] Buchanan, *A Journey from Madras*, vol. II, pp. 345–59. See also p. 298 for a description of Haiga Brahmins on whose farms most of the labour was performed by the 'slaves'.

they also hired labour.[1] Since a large proportion of the land was held by Brahmins, particularly in such districts as Tanjore, this fact itself explains why it was necessary to hire labourers or lease lands out to tenants, even where there were not many very large holdings. At the other end of the social scale, the lowest castes were probably prevented by powerful social sanctions from owning or leasing land.

Thus the facts of social structure provide strong grounds for arguing that a class of landless labourers must have existed at the beginning of the century. What can be glimpsed of the economic structure points to the same conclusion. The available data show that there were several estates, whether in the Tamil and Telugu districts, or on the West Coast, where labourers working for fixed wages or a share of the crop must have been essential for their operation; farms employing one or two labourers were extremely common, particularly in the irrigated areas.[2]

These converging arguments establish *a priori* that there were agricultural labourers in South India at the outset of the British period. But they do not establish that these labourers were essentially of the same type as those of, let us say, the twentieth century. For all his disabilities, the labourer of 1800 may have enjoyed customary 'rights' and benefits of which his successors have been stripped as custom has declined.

There are two problems to be faced in dealing with early nineteenth-century Madras, and unfortunately neither of them is satisfactorily soluble. First, what was the ideal or traditional pattern of relations between the various groups who lived on the land? In what sense, if any, does the distinction between first, the *zamindars*, *mirasdars*, *janmis* and *mulawargardars*; second, the *kanakkars*, *payakaris*, *ulkudis* and *verum pattamdars*, and third, the *adimais*, *pannaiyals* and *padiyals*,[3] correspond to the distinction between landowner, tenant and labourer? Is there any point at all in trying to approximate to the Western terms? We have already seen some of the differences between, for example, the *zamindar* and the landlord; clearly the former had far more restricted rights. In fact relationships in the Indian village were generally far more restricted than in their English counterpart, and not merely by law and custom but also by the caste system, and, in the widest sense, by the lack of economic opportunity. The *zamindar* could not remove a hereditary 'tenant' and put another in his place; the

[1] Collector, Chinglepet to the Board of Revenue, 31.7.1819; Chinglepet Records, vol. 467, p. 110.

[2] In Travancore for instance, it was reported that while all wet labour was carried on by 'slaves', most landowners had not more than three 'slaves'; *Select Committee Report, 1831–32*, pp. 550 and 552.

[3] See Chapter III for definitions of these terms, the last three of which apply to agricultural labourers.

janmi could not dismiss the Cherumans[1] he had inherited; he could sell them if he found a buyer, but if not he had to maintain them. They in their turn could run away from a cruel master, but only to work for another master, and they could ideally never aspire to own land. Landowners were invariably Brahmins or members of the higher non-Brahmin castes, and at the lower end of the scale, only certain castes could be sold into bondage, and so on. These economic restrictions were matched by social restrictions, by prohibitions, taboos, measures of pollution, and so forth. Thus, if one takes a static view of the village one sees a system in which the castes stand in an unchanging relationship to each other; where caste determines each man's social and economic role; where all the roles are interdependent in an architectonic whole; where, for example, the land provides a livelihood for those playing different parts, the rights and duties of each being strictly defined and none having absolute rights of ownership and possession. Such a view is an essential corrective to the old attempt to fit Indian conditions into English boxes. But it has its own dangers: first, just because it is an ideal view it is very important to discover exactly to what extent it obtained at any point of time. Clearly, in early nineteenth-century Madras some 'superior' rightholders claimed and actually exerted rights of dispossession. Also, even if two economic roles are interdependent, the degree of interdependence need not be the same; the *adimai*'s freedom to change his master may well have been rather different from the latter's freedom to change him, and certainly the master had much greater powers in altering the wages of the 'slave' than the latter had in altering his share. Looked at over a period of a hundred years, the tendency of the system to depart from the ideal becomes clearer, and so does the fact that some groups enjoyed much less social and economical mobility and a much narrower range of alternatives than others.

An equally important point is that in some respects there has been much less change than is imagined. It is very tempting to consider the ideal type of village economy, in which the labourer is as much a rightholder in relation to the land as the owner or tenant and enjoys security of employment and maintenance, and to contrast it with the modern system where the wage labourer has no rights and no security. But the actual differences are much less sharp than this, and each situation has contained elements of the other. Even in the Madras of 1951, 16 per cent of the agricultural labourers were still attached in some sense or other.[2] Already by 1880

[1] An agricultural labour caste; see Chapter III, *infra*.

[2] This figure is the average for the southern zone: Andhra Pradesh, Madras State and Kerala. In 1950–1, the percentage of attached labourers to total agricultural labour

some agricultural labourers were merely hired hands, and the 'rights' actually enjoyed by labourers attached to the land varied widely.

households was only 5·4 per cent, reflecting differences of definition; Government of India, *Report on the Second Agricultural Labour Enquiry, 1956–57*, vol. I, p. 53.

III. FORMS OF AGRESTIC SERVITUDE

The evidence that there were well-developed institutions of 'agricultural labour' and 'serfdom' points to some very important facts about the agrarian structure of early nineteenth-century Madras. The terms 'slavery' and 'serfdom' may be applied to it, in so far as some agricultural labourers were bought and sold, and others were born into a state where they owed service to the masters on their lands. But of course terms drawn from European experience do not fit Indian conditions perfectly. One of the most striking and important peculiarities of the Indian forms of servitude is their close connection with the caste system. Most types of servile status were hereditary, and in general the 'serfs' and 'slaves' belonged to the lowest castes. Although this group as a whole was at the bottom of the caste ladder, there were further gradations within it, each sub-group having its articulated rights and disabilities. In fact, the caste system not only confirmed the economic and social disadvantages of the agricultural labourer, but also gave him some rights, some economic, others of a social and ritual nature.

Most important among the serf's rights was that of working on a particular piece of land. If he was born into a family 'owned' by a particular landholder, the landholder had the obligation to employ him on the land and pay him the customary wages. In this sense it can be argued that the labourer was not landless. But two points are very relevant here. First, although the serf may have had some right to a share in the produce of 'his' land, he had far fewer economic rights than the *mirasdar* or tenant; his share of the produce was very much smaller, and he had moreover no right to sell the land. Secondly, as we shall see, the right to work on a particular plot of land was not always granted. In Malabar the agricultural labourer was in some respects treated like a commodity of production, and even in Tamilnad his rights were very circumscribed. In early nineteenth-century Madras there was a great variety of institutional forms, ranging from slavery to completely 'free' hired labour. And these covered not only agricultural labourers but also domestic servants[1] and even artisans.[2]

[1] Although domestic slavery did exist in South India at this time, particularly among the Muslims, it was not widespread. Domestic slavery was generally not hereditary; individuals became slaves because they were sold as children during famines or because they sold themselves in cancellation of a debt, and not because they were born into a particular caste. Also, since domestic servants could not be untouchables, they had to come from completely different social groups from the agricultural labourers.

[2] Thurston quotes an instance of smiths who were praedial slaves in Tinnevelly district; E. Thurston, *Ethnographical Notes on South India* (Madras, 1906), p. 456.

The main sources of information about the forms of servitude in the various regions consist of replies sent by the revenue and judicial officials to enquiries about the nature and extent of slavery and serfdom in their districts. The first enquiry was carried out in 1819 and was published as *Slavery in India: Correspondence and Abstracts of Regulations and Proceedings from 1772.*[1] Twelve years later the Commissioners for the Affairs of India circulated a number of questions on slavery in India, the answers to which are contained in Appendix K to the report of the Select Committee of 1831–2.[2] There was another enquiry in 1836, issued as *Slave Trade: Correspondence, Orders & Regulations, and Proceedings taken thereon, 1829–1838.*[3] But most of the administrators were baffled by the distinctions between the various classes of labourers. Faced with these groups, who were clearly in some or other degree of servitude, they fell back on ancient terms from the English land law, such as 'allodial slave of the soil', 'agricultural serf', 'villein' or '*adscriptus glebae*'. The result was a palimpsest of definitions, none of which fitted South Indian conditions. Because of the confusions inherent in these European terms, in what follows the local names will be used whenever there is a danger of ambiguity. This means that each of the three main linguistic regions must be described separately, but in any case this is convenient, since the forms and degrees of servitude were very different in all three of them. In descending order of the rigour of this servitude, we shall examine first, the West Coast districts (Malabar and South Canara), then the Tamil districts (Tinnevelly, Madura, Trichinopoly, Coimbatore, Salem, Chinglepet, Tanjore, North and South Arcot), and lastly the Telugu and northern districts (Bellary, Anantapur, Kurnool, Nellore, Cuddapah, Kistna, Godavari, Vizagapatam and Ganjam).

West Coast Districts

Almost every administrator who went to Malabar in the early nineteenth century remarked on the rigour of the slavery and the wretchedness of the slaves. Thus in 1801 Buchanan remarked that in South Malabar,

by far the greater part of the labour in the fields is performed by slaves, or *churmar*.

[1] *P.P.*, 1828, XXIV, *House of Commons, No. 125: Slavery in India: Correspondence and Abstracts of Regulations and Proceedings* (hereafter *Slavery Papers, 1828*).

[2] *P.P.*, 1831–2, XI, XII, *Report from the Select Committee on the Affairs of the East India Company* (hereafter *Select Committee Report, 1831–2*).

[3] *P.P.*, 1837–8, LI, *House of Commons, No. 697: Slave Trade: Correspondence, Orders and Regulations, and Proceedings taken thereon, 1829–38* (hereafter *Slavery Papers, 1838*). These were later summarized in *P.P.*, 1841, XXVIII, *Report of the Indian Law Commissioners on Slavery* (henceforth *Report on Slavery, 1841*).

These are the absolute property of their Devarus or lords and may be employed in any work that their master please. They are not attached to the soil but may be sold or transferred in any manner that the master thinks fit. Only husband and wife can be sold but children may be separated from their parents and brothers from their sisters.[1]

It is significant that Buchanan uses the caste name of Cheruman (i.e. 'Churmar') instead of the Malayalam word for slave, '*adima*'. This was very natural since by far the largest proportion of the *adimas* were Cherumans,[2] as they were known in South Malabar, or Pulaiyans or Pula Cherumans, as they were known in North Malabar, both being of the same caste. It is also significant that the word 'slave' is invariably used for describing Cherumans; in fact the term 'serf' hardly occurs in the literature on Malabar. Since there is little room for confusion here, we shall use 'slave' rather than *adima* in dealing with Malabar. Even within Malabar itself the incidence of servitude for the *adimas* was not uniform, but there were certainly places where they were treated almost exactly like other forms of property. For example, Buchanan mentions three modes of transferring slaves here: (i) *janmam* or sale, where the full value of the slave was given and the property entirely handed over; (ii) *kanam* or mortgage, where the proprietor got a loan and a quantity of rice, to show that his property in the slave was not extinguished, but could be resumed once the loan was repaid; (iii) *pattam* or rent, where the slave was hired out for an annual sum, the hirer paying the cost of maintenance.[3] Again in 1822, when Graeme was describing still more elaborate ways of transferring slaves, he stated that they could be mortgaged under *veerum pattom* (*verum pattam*) *paneyam*, *kanam*, *wottee* (i.e. *otti*) and *pair*.[4] Strikingly enough, both Buchanan's and Graeme's sets of terms are identical with those used for the transfer of land, either by sale or mortgage.[5] In many parts there were almost no restrictions on the master's rights: both Buchanan and Graeme concur that here slaves might be sold independently of the land. Buchanan adds that the only restriction on the master's powers of sale was that husband and wife might not be sold separately. The children belonged to the master of one or other of the

[1] Buchanan, *A Journey from Madras*, vol. II, p. 67.

[2] In fact according to Thackeray 'no other castes are bought and sold as slaves in Malabar' (Report on Malabar, Canara and the Ceded Districts, 8.9.1807), but Vaughan enumerates 20 'slave castes'; *Select Committee Report, 1831–32*, Appendix K, and a Judge in Malabar lists eighteen different castes, though of course several are only sub-castes; *Slavery Report*, 1841, p. 468.

[3] Buchanan, *A Journey from Madras*, vol. II, pp. 67–8.

[4] Graeme, Report on Malabar, 14.1.1822; *Slavery Papers, 1828*, pp. 914–15.

[5] Cf pp. 24–5 *supra*.

parents, depending on the marriage customs of the caste.[1] In some areas there was the further restriction that the slave could not be removed far from his village: Graeme says that a slave might be sold in another *taluk*, but it had to be contiguous with his own.[2] It was reported from North Malabar in 1812 that a Pulaiyan sold or transferred could not be removed out of the district in which he was born.[3] But if they obtained anywhere, it was precisely in North Malabar that such restrictions on the master's power of sale were most to be expected, for there the conditions of servitude were noticeably milder. Yet here again agricultural slavery was widespread, and once more it was closely connected with caste. Of Wynaad in the north, Graeme remarked that 'the landed proprietors . . . are torpid to a degree; all the field work is done by slaves called *Painers* who are held in higher estimation than the slaves of the lower districts. They are admitted to the threshold of their masters' houses, and they are even employed in grinding rice for the use of the temples.'[4] The caste referred to here is probably the Paniyans.[5] Baber has a fuller description of Wynaad: the four castes of 'agrestic slaves or more properly, conditional labourers' were the 'Koorcher' (i.e. Kurichans or Fowlers), the 'Kooramer' (probably Kurumbans, Shepherds), the 'Kadder' (some hill tribe possibly) and the 'Pannie' (Paniyans). The 'Koorchers' worked in the hills, the 'Kooramer' in both high lands and low lands and in the gold mines; the 'hill proprietors' claimed both types, but they were never sold. In fact they barely yielded obedience to their masters. The 'Kadders' were more submissive but were never sold, and deserted if they were beaten. The 'Pannies' alone were liable to be sold, but never out of the area.[6]

Witnesses quote the prices of slaves in various places, and this establishes a presumption that the market was fairly developed. According to Buchanan, a mature male slave cost the equivalent of £2 7s. 8d. in South Malabar; in North Malabar a male might sell at anything between 9s. 6½d. and £1 8s. 6d. and he might be hired out at just under 2s. per annum.[7] These discrepancies did not merely arise from differences of age and condition, as in other systems of slavery. Here the caste of the slave was

[1] Buchanan, *A Journey from Madras*, vol. II, p. 67.
[2] Graeme, Report on Malabar; *Slavery Papers, 1828*, pp. 914–15.
[3] Magistrate, North Malabar to Government, 31.3.1812; *ibid.*, p. 567.
[4] *Ibid.*, p. 924.
[5] 'In the fifties of the last century, when planters first began to settle in Wynaad, they purchased the land with the Paniyans living on it, who were practically the slaves of the landowners'; E. Thurston, *Castes and Tribes of South India* (Madras, 1909), vol. VI, p. 58.
[6] *Select Committee Report, 1831–2*, Appendix K, p. 557.
[7] Buchanan, *A Journey from Madras*, vol. II, pp. 68, 154. Rates for women and children are also given.

another determinant of the price. For example, Vaughan reported that the best male slaves were sold at £6 5s. and hired out at 3s. 9d. per annum, but that the corresponding rates for Cherumans were £1 4s. and 1s. 3d. The average sale price for all castes was £3 6s., and the average annual 'rent', that is hiring charges, was 2s. 6d.[1] Again, in 1836 it was stated that the average prices ranged from Rs. 20 to Rs. 28.[2] The Rev. J. Fenn, who had lived eight or nine years in the interior of Travancore, reported that there the price of a good male slave was £1 5s., which is nearly the rate for Cherumans in Malabar but much lower than the highest prices for other slaves. He added that the slaves were in an 'awful state of degradation'.[3] In 1841 again, a Judge reported that the price of a male child was about Rs. 3/8as. In terms of another currency, one pair of slaves was said to be equivalent to four pairs of buffaloes.

But though he might be bought and sold, the Cheruman had some rights which saved him from being a mere commodity. His daily wages were fixed by custom. Again, Cherumans could escape from a particular master who did not pay their daily wages or who otherwise treated them badly, but in the society of the time, they could not escape from their servile state. The only course open to them was to work as slaves for another master; if they were found, they were shared between the old and new master.[4] If the master was unable to pay them the customary rate he would sell or mortgage them, whereas a free-born labourer might not have found alternative employment. 'In some respects Churmas may be considered in more comfortable circumstances than any of the lower and poorer class of natives. An instance of a Churma being a beggar is unheard of.'[5]

In South Canara the caste system operated with much the same rigour as in Malabar. On the whole, agricultural labourers were a little freer, but they were still very far from being free. The term 'slave' was invariably used for them, and here again the general practice of the first administrators was to use a caste name, Dhed (spelt variously Dherd, Daird, etc.), almost as a synonym for agricultural slave. Typical of these is the report of the Collector of South Canara in 1801, that the Dhed fell into three groups. The first of these, the Mogare or Magor 'come nearest the description of slaves', but they fell short of it in the following respects: although

[1] *Select Committee Report, 1831–2*, p. 558.
[2] *Slavery Report, 1841*, Appendix X, p. 511.
[3] *Ibid.*, p. 550.
[4] Thackeray, Report on Malabar, Canara and the Ceded Districts, 8.9.1807.
[5] Collector, Malabar to Board of Revenue, 20.7.1819, *Slavery Papers, 1828*, pp. 845–6.

they could be bought and sold, their service was conditional upon their master's giving them the customary allowance of rice, cloth, and so on. Should he fail to do so, in principle they could recover the balance. Should they be sold to a new master, then 'if from any real cause they have a dread of the man, their old master will generally, on being asked, keep them till he can get another purchaser'. Should they be asked to leave the district of their birth, they could refuse, and they were in fact rarely taken more than twenty or thirty miles from their place of birth. For this status, the Collector of South Canara devised the ambiguous definition, 'conditional servants for ever'. The second group, the 'maurey dherd' were generally attached to the land; they had much the same privileges as the first group, but if the master did not give them their allowances, they had not the redress of leaving his service. Thirdly, there were the 'moondaul dherd', whose wedding expenses were paid by the master, in return for which the 'slave' and his wife had to serve him and his heirs during the lifetime of the male slave. On his death, his wife and children went to the wife's brother, and had to work for his master, if he had one. Never bought and sold, these Mundalas could be mortgaged by their owner. These the Collector defined as 'conditional servants on the male side for life'.[1] Occasionally, their service was supposed to end when the loan was repaid, though experience suggests that this right was purely theoretical. The description is clear enough about the fact of servitude, but clear about little else.

In addition to the usual confusion of caste and status, there also seems to be some confusion in caste names. Dhed is a caste more commonly found in the Deccan and North Canara; in fact the 1891 Census showed only 31 Dheds in South Canara. The agricultural caste there is the Holeya (cf. the Malayali Pulaiyan). The Holeyas are divided into three sub-groups: the Maris (cf. the Collector's 'maurey'), the Meras, and the Mundalas or Bakudas (cf. 'moondaul');[2] his third group, 'mogare', seems to be derived from Mogeru, a fisherman caste in Canara.[3] Moreover, it is very doubtful whether these sub-divisions correspond to the kind of economic differentiation the Collector describes. The Canarese terms for agricultural labourers include *huttalu*, *mannalu* and *salada*.[4]

In most of the hilly taluks each vargdar, or proprietor of a landed estate, owns a set

[1] This account has been compiled from Collector, South Canara to Board of Revenue, P.B.R., 3.8.1801; and from his letter of 7.8.1801; *Slavery Papers, 1828*, pp. 549–50.

[2] Thurston, *Castes and Tribes of South India*, vol. II, p. 329.

[3] Sir Athelstane Baines, *Ethnography* (*Castes and Tribes*) (Strasbourg, 1912).

[4] *Huttu*: birth; *mannu*: land; *alu*: man, servant; *sala*: loan.

of servants called Huttalu or Huttu-Alu and Mannalu or Manna-Alu. The former is the hereditary servitor of the family, born in servitude and performing agricultural work for the landlord, from father to son. The mannalu is a serf attached to the soil and changes with it. These are usually of the Holeya class but in some places men of the Hasalar race have been entertained.[1]

The *District Manual* for South Canara has a different classification of agricultural labourers: *mulada* Holeyas and *salada* Holeyas. The first were traditionally hereditary serfs attached to the *mulawargas*, the second were 'debt slaves', that is those working off a debt.[2] In any case it is clear that the Holeyas were generally saleable; the fact is mentioned even in folk songs, as in the Coorgi wedding song: 'Then with his wealth he bought a band of Holeyas to till his land.'[3] Some other castes may occasionally have been in a condition of servitude, including the Hasalas mentioned above. Buchanan states, for example, that the 'Corar or Corawar' (a hill tribe) of Canara were all slaves, though a few of them were permitted to rent land as tenants.[4]

Later references confirm that this position still held good for some decades of the nineteenth century. They also show the existence of a market for these labourers. In 1819 the Collector reported that slaves might be sold with the land or separately from it, that they might be mortgaged or hired out, and that the price of a strong male slave varied between Rs. 12 and Rs. 26.[5] The wife could be sold separately from her husband, but this was rare since the husband would then desert his master. Again, slaves were not sold to 'distant estates'. Ten years later the First Judge of the Court of Circuit mentioned 'a civil suit where a demand was made for twenty *moolumunishers* [slaves], value 50 pagodas; without individual specification, immediately followed by a like summary demand for brute animals'.[6] Even as late as 1844, the Collector reported that the purchase price of estates almost invariably included the value of the Dheds belonging to the estate.[7]

Thus South Canara resembles Malabar in several respects: a similar system of property in land, with the *mulawargadars* of South Canara corresponding to the *janmis* of Malabar; a system of transferring landless

[1] *Census Report for Mysore, 1901*, quoted in Thurston, *Castes and Tribes of South India*, vol. II, p. 335.

[2] *South Canara Manual*, vol. I, p. 173.

[3] Charles Gover, *Folk Songs of South India* (1871, reprinted Madras, 1959), p. 126.

[4] Buchanan, *A Journey from Madras*, vol. II, p. 271.

[5] Collector, South Canara to Board of Revenue, 10.7.1819; *Slavery Papers, 1828*, p. 843.

[6] *Report on Slavery, 1841*, p. 147.

[7] P.B.R., 11.1.1844.

labourers analogous with the system of transferring land; and several types of rigorously servile status.

Tamil Districts

In the Tamil districts, the status of the various agrarian groups was less rigorously defined, being in the same state of confusion as the land tenures, and for much the same reasons. Consequently, the first British Collectors had to deal with a social structure that was still changing, and changing at different rates, almost from village to village. The fact of agricultural bondage was palpable. But did it amount to slavery or did the residual rights of the labourers raise their status? Englishing these status groups was a task which strained the resources of the administrators' vocabulary. They defined the superior sort of dependent labourers as 'villeins' or 'serfs' (terms they never employed on the West Coast); but the right not to be sold off the land which such terms would normally connote was not granted in all villages, and indeed it was hardly ever acknowledged by the masters.

There were two Tamil terms which the administrators might have used: *pannaiyal*, or permanent farm servant (this term will be employed hereafter to cover all unfree labourers in the Tamil districts unless other writers are being quoted) and *padiyal*, or hired farm servant receiving wages in kind.[1] There is also the Tamil word for 'slave', *adimai*. It may well be that the word was originally used of those who could be transferred separately from the land (although the Tamil Lexicon defines *adimai* as 'a slave formerly attached to the land and transferable with it'), while *pannaiyal* was used of those permanently attached to the land. But if there had ever been such a distinction, by the nineteenth century it seems to have become blurred; the term *pannaiyal* is used far more frequently than *adimai*.[2] But here too the administrators preferred to use the names of the agricultural labour castes, Palli, Pallan and Paraiyan; further proof, if any be required, of the functional role of caste in these districts. The history of agrestic serfdom in the Tamil districts is as confused as that of the *mirasi* system, and this is consonant with, but does not necessarily confirm, the theory that the two had the same origin—a view expressed by some of the early native writers, for example, Ramaswami Naidu who ascribes the origin of both to the settlement of Tondaimandalam.[3] According to Prof.

[1] *Pannai*, a farm; *padi*, a fixed daily allowance of food; *al*, a labourer. The Malayalam equivalent of *padiyal* is *vallial*; see K. P. Padmanabha Menon, *History of Kerala* (Ernakulam, 1924), vol. III, pp. 477–8.

[2] The Collector of Chinglepet provides one of the rare examples of the use of *adimai* in his letter of 31.7.1819; Chinglepet Records, vol. 467, p. 113.

[3] According to this theory, when Ananda Chakra settled Tondaimandalam, he

Nilakanta Sastri, however, 'there is no clear evidence of the predial slavery [in the Cola period] though it is possible that most of the labourers of the "last classes" did not differ much from slaves in their status'.[1] Later on, however, he gives details of types of slaves and even some prices. Ramaswami Naidu also describes the elaborate system of sales prevailing in more recent times: most of these relate to the regulation sales of female slaves. The price of male slaves, he says, was formerly not more than half a pagoda; since a pagoda was Rs. 3/8as., this seems absurdly low. He goes on to state that female slaves sold for higher prices—up to 1 pagoda, which is contrary to most other evidence, but which can be explained by the fact that the children belonged to their mother's master.

In any case, whatever the origins of the system, it is clear that at the beginning of the nineteenth century the *pannaiyals* in some Tamil areas were in a condition of servitude. They were born into servitude, and they died in it. In South Arcot it was explicitly stated in 1819 that there was no possibility of enfranchisement except when the master's family died out. And even in this case the *pannaiyals* were forced by their poverty to consent to 'perpetual and hereditary' bondage for a marriage loan of 20 to 30 pagodas, and there was no known case of the labourer discharging his loan by manual labour.

They could not leave their master's land; this was so generally recognized that in the early years the Collectors would help to catch runaway labourers. As late as 1830, the Collector of Trichinopoly wrote to the Collector of Salem for help in bringing back ten Pallans who had absconded from their master (to whom they were not in debt): 'They are slaves of the soil and as such are not at liberty to leave the estate to which they belong. The owner of the estate, a Brahmin, is quite unable to cultivate the lands without their help, and if he be not assisted in recovering his rights over them, the land must lay waste and the Government be losers.'[2]

There is a wealth of evidence that *pannaiyals* were sold and mortgaged through all nine Tamil districts. In 1819 for example, a male labourer in Tinnevelly might fetch up to Rs. 32; in South Arcot (where labour was scarce) a slave family might cost between Rs. 35 and Rs. 175; in Coimbatore 'the highest price for a good slave is 50 rupees, the price however is seldom so high'.[3] And in 1836, a judge in the same district reported that

gave the first settlers proprietory (*mirasi*) rights in the soil, and also the rights to buy, sell and pledge the Paraiyans and certain other castes; Ramaswami Naidu, 'Remarks on the Revenue System and landed tenures of the Provinces under the Presidency of Fort St. George,' Part I, *Journal of the Royal Asiatic Society*, vol. 1, 1834.

[1] Sastri, *The Colas*, p. 87.

[2] P.B.R., 8.11.1830.

[3] Collector, Tinnevelly to Board of Revenue, 30.6.1819; *Slavery Papers, 1828*, p.

in one or two cases a certain number of slaves had been included in mortgages of land.[1] From such transfers the higher castes of *pannaiyals* were not exempt. Pallans in Trichinopoly might be sold at prices between Rs. 15/8as. and Rs. 35 and their services could be mortgaged as well; female Pallans, on the other hand, the Collector reported, were never sold.[2]

Whether or not a *pannaiyal* might be sold independently of the land he tilled was a convention which varied from district to district in the early decades of the nineteenth century. In South Arcot the 'slaves' could be sold to anyone and to an 'alien village', but this was rare.[3] In Coimbatore too the right to sell *pannaiyals* in this way was 'very seldom, if ever, exercised'; and in fact slavery was rare, apart from some debt slavery.[4] In 1836 it was reported that there were 'slaves' in two villages only.[5] *Padiyals* were more common than *pannaiyals*.[6] Pallans in Trichinopoly were usually sold with the land, and should they be sold away from it, they were never taken involuntarily from their villages.[7] In 1819 the Collector of Tinnevelly reported that it was usual for 'slaves to be sold or mortgaged either with the land or separately . . . there is no particular rule'; but seventeen years later it would seem that there was, and that now Pallans normally went only with the land.[8] There was a similar variation in Tanjore. In 1785 it was decided that as the *pannaiyals* employed in a village of Devacottah originally belonged to another area, Shiyali, belonging to the Rajah, they should be restored to the Shiyali landlord, their sale price, together with interest thereon, being returned to the inhabitants of Devacottah; here the *pannaiyals'* attachment to the soil was recognized.[9] In 1819 the Collector wrote that, 'I do not find that the system of slaves attached to the soil, and transferable by purchase, as an appendage to the land,

841; P.B.R., 25.11.1819; Collector, Coimbatore to Board of Revenue, P.B.R.' 24.1.1819.

[1] *Slavery Report, 1841*, p. 459.

[2] Collector, Trichinopoly to Board of Revenue, 1.7.1819; Trichinopoly Records, vol. 3677, p. 153.

[3] P.B.R., 12.9.1819.

[4] Collector, Coimbatore to Board of Revenue, 24.6.1819; *Slavery Papers, 1828*, pp. 836–7.

[5] *Slavery Report, 1841*, pp. 459–62.

[6] Buchanan, *A Journey from Madras*, vol. II, p. 217.

[7] Collector, Trichinopoly to Board of Revenue, 1.7.1819; Trichinopoly Records, vol. 3677, pp. 151–60. Reply of Magistrate, Trichinopoly, 5.1.1836; *Report on Slavery, 1841*, p. 460.

[8] Collector, Tinnevelly to Board of Revenue, 30.6.1819; *Slavery Papers, 1828*, p. 847. Replies of Assistant Judge, 15.5.1836, and Joint Magistrate, 21.12.1835; *Report on Slavery, 1841*, pp. 457–60.

[9] Letter from Sub-Secretary, Revenue Department to the Resident of Tanjore, 24.9.1785; Tanjore Records, Bundle 3443 (Resident's Correspondence, 1785), pp. 183–92.

obtains here'; Pallans and Paraiyans did enter into a contract of slavery, in return for maintenance throughout their lives; they could be sold, though not to distant parts of the country but actual sales were rare.[1] In 1836 a judge in that district could report that Pallans had been sued for as transferable both with and without the land.[2] In Madura slavery seemed to be 'gradually disappearing' as early as 1819; even under the Nawab's rule Pallans and Paraiyans were not so much born into slavery as sold (by themselves) into it. After British rule was established many of them left their masters, some enlisting as sepoys, and there had been no fresh contracts into servitude for some years; some Pallans even cultivated their own lands.[3] But the system had not vanished by 1836; some forms of 'slavery' were reported then, but they were comparatively mild; the 'slaves' formed an insignificant part of the total population,[4] and could only be sold with their own consent. But in Chinglepet in 1819 'these persons are not in any way attached to the land but are the property of the individual and may by him be called away . . .'.[5] Here too the system may have been losing some of its rigour by 1836, but even then the Vellala (non-Brahmin) cultivators kept 'slaves', and the masters could sell them or mortgage their services or hire them out (the earnings going to the master).[6]

There may well have been some connection between serfdom and communal landholding. In communal villages labourers were jointly held. As the Collector South Arcot, reported in 1819, '. . . in some villages it is known *mirasdars* have advanced pretensions to possess an equal property of the slaves with their share of the village'.[7] Where the *mirasdars* were Brahmins there were additional reasons for the survival of the *pannaiyal* system, as the Collector of Trichinopoly pointed out,[8] though others held that Brahmins did not employ slaves but hired labourers.[9] Another theory was that the Brahmins employed Pallis or 'villeins' and the non-Brahmins employed Pallans and Paraiyans or 'slaves', but this is almost certainly a

[1] *Slavery Papers, 1828*, p. 838.

[2] Tanjore Records, vol. 3284, pp. 73–6; Reply of Judge, Kumbakonam, 20.1.1836; *Report on Slavery, 1841*, p. 459.

[3] Letter from Sub-Secretary, Revenue Department to the Resident of Tanjore, 24.9.1785; Tanjore Records, Bundle 3443 (Resident's Correspondence, 1785), pp. 183–92.

[4] *Report on Slavery, 1841*, pp. 455–7, 459–60.

[5] Collector, Chinglepet to Board of Revenue, 1818; Chinglepet Records, vol. 467, p. 113; also printed in *Report on Slavery, 1841*, Appendix IX.

[6] *Ibid.*, pp. 448–50.

[7] *Slavery Papers, 1828*, pp. 871–2.

[8] Trichinopoly Records, vol. 3677, p. 151.

[9] Bayley & Hudleston, *Papers on Mirasi Right*, p. 225, 335. Letter from Collector of Chinglepet, 31.7.1819; *Slavery Papers, 1828*, pp. 868–9.

theoretical rather than an actual distinction;[1] there is at least one reference to an actual case where a Brahmin held Pallans as serfs.[2]

Labourers in whom the whole village held joint property could not be sold separately from the land; their duty was to work for each *mirasdar* in turn during a period proportionate to his share in the village lands.[3] Traces of this system lingered on long after communal tenures had died out: in 1864 it was reported of North Arcot that when family lands were subdivided the agricultural labourers were similarly shared out.[4] But where a labourer was held individually by a *mirasdar*, he could be sold without reference to the land.

Whatever their status in principle, liberty was relative for the free labourers too. These *padiyals* were hired for very long periods, and they could be enchained by debt to one master. Buchanan noted at Coimbatore that '. . . the hinds, or servants hired . . . by the farmers are here called *Puddial*. . . . They sometimes bind themselves for a number of years, in which case the master advances money for their marriage expenses, and deducts so much from their monthly pay, until he is repaid.'[5]

Probably they were often in debt. For instance, the Collector of Chinglepet stated in 1819 that the free labourers frequently borrowed money for house building, marriages, or other heavy expenditure.[6] Moreover, there were hereditary relationships between masters and men, and indeed it was not unknown for the descendants of labourers to claim work as a right from the descendants of former employers.[7] After all, there were certain advantages about servitude; from one point of view, an obligation to work could be construed as a right to employment. The resemblances between the actual social and economic conditions of the free and the unfree were doubtless reinforced by the fact that they frequently came from the same caste. Although the agrarian structure of Tamilnad was still in transition, and this had already changed many things, the connection between occupational status and caste was still firm.

Telugu Districts

Since it was in the Telugu districts that Muslim overlordship had been

[1] Bayley & Hudleston, *Papers on Mirasi Right*, p. 335.
[2] Trichinopoly Records, vol. 4399, p. 361. For more details see Chapter V, *infra*, pp. 52–3.
[3] Bayley & Hudleston, *Papers on Mirasi Right*, pp. 334–6.
[4] P.B.R., 29.1.1864.
[5] Buchanan, *A Journey from Madras*, vol. I, p. 441–2.
[6] Chinglepet Records, vol. 467, p. 111.
[7] Place, Report on the Jaghire, para. 75.

firmest, it is to be expected that those forms of servitude closely connected with caste would be milder here than in other parts of South India. Domestic slavery was more common than elsewhere,[1] and a slave trade was fairly brisk in the early nineteenth century (in the northern districts slaves were certainly being bought for export; this was mentioned in a warning proclamation by the Governor General),[2] but agrarian slavery or serfdom seems to have been rare. Indeed, the Board of Revenue went so far as saying in 1818 that here the agricultural labourers were free. But this was putting it too strongly, for they frequently worked on contract and were bound to the village until their time was up, and moreover they generally stayed in these villages, their descendants remaining attached to the same families.[3] In any case the information sent in by the Collectors in 1819 and by the judges and magistrates in 1836 did something to quench the Board's optimism. It was true that the conditions of Tamilnad did not obtain, except perhaps in Masulipatam, but there were references in 1836 to slavery of the 'mildest nature' in Ganjam, and to servants of the *zamindars* being near slaves in Guntur.[4] In Masulipatam, 'the far greater proportion of the more substantial ryots have slaves, or rather they have men whose families have been in the employment of their ancestors from time immemorial, and whose services they have a right to enforce'.[5] In 1839 this description became more precise. It was then reported that while 'slavery in the usual acceptation of the word' did not exist, there were three categories of dependants who were usually called slaves: the servants of the *zamindars* or *kasalu* ('personal servants' in Telugu), the servants of the Muslims or *goolam* ('slave' or 'servant' in Urdu) and finally the *palalu* (in Telugu, 'hired labourers') who were Paraiyans attached to the *raiyats* or cultivators. These *palalu* were not saleable, but when the land was sold they went with it. They might not desert their master, or if they did, he could claim them back. 'To these persons, however, although they live in a state of perpetual servitude to their masters, the term of "hereditary servants" might be more properly applied, as they are neither saleable nor is the authority of the master legally recognized.'[6] There were reports of 'voluntary servitude' in Rajahmundry as well. As the Law Commissioner on slavery pointed out, it was very likely that in the neighbouring parts of

[1] Replies of judicial officers in Telugu districts; *Report on Slavery, 1841*, Apppuəix IX, pp. 445–6.

[2] Godavari Records, vol. 918, pp. 15–18.

[3] Minute of Board of Revenue, 5.1.1818, para. 13; *East India Papers*, vol. 1, p. 887.

[4] *Report on Slavery, 1841*, pp. 445–6.

[5] Collector, Masulipatam to Board of Revenue, 20.3.1819; *Select Committee Report, 1831–32*, Appendix LXXXIX, pp. 511–12.

[6] *Report on Slavery, 1841*, Appendix IX, pp. 444–5.

Rajahmundry and Guntur at least, and probably more widely, cultivation was carried on by labourers who were in the same condition as those called 'slaves' in Masulipatam.[1] As late as 1892, the term *goti* was also used for serf in describing debt slavery in Vizagapatam.[2]

It is significant that in the early literature about the Telugu districts there appears to be no reference to agricultural labour castes; here caste restrictions may well have been weaker than in Malabar or Tamilnad. Even in the twentieth century the depressed castes of Andhra were socially much better off than in Malabar and South Canara. Although they were untouchable, their shadow did not pollute, as it did in Malabar, nor did the higher castes pass resolutions banning them from wearing gold or silver ornaments, owning land or bargaining for wages, as the Kallans did in Ramnad as late as 1938. But even in Andhra and even in 1952, they were subject to some restrictions: for instance, they could not walk well-dressed down the main street of the village.[3] And caste and occupation were still strongly connected, in the sense that the agricultural labourers were almost certainly recruited from the lowest castes, particularly from the untouchable castes of Mala and Madiga, although traditionally these castes had other occupations, such as weaving and tanning. In 1898 the Collector for Anantapur reported that most agricultural labourers in his district were Malas, Madigas and Boyas; the Malas and Madigas, he said, were 'attached' to the *raiyats* and were paid in kind, whereas the others were paid in cash.[4] And even now the bulk of the agricultural labourers are Malas and Madigas.

Thus modes of dependence in early nineteenth-century Madras spanned a wide range from near-freedom to near-slavery. Generally, servitude was less widespread and less rigorous in the Telugu districts than in Tamilnad and much less so than in Malabar and South Canara. Within each area there were wide variations, particularly in Tamilnad. Admittedly some of the confusions about South Indian slavery may be merely semantic, but many of them must surely spring from the evolution of the agrarian structure itself. Agricultural servitude was obviously deep-rooted in South Indian society. The complex dealings in human beings that Buchanan saw in 1800 must have developed over a long period of time.[5]

[1] *Ibid.*, p. 115.

[2] *Vizagapatam Gazetteer*, p. 109.

[3] N. S. Reddy, 'Transition in Caste Structure in Andhra Desh with particular reference to the Depressed Castes' (Unpublished Ph.D. thesis, Lucknow, 1952), pp. 22, 35–6. Also see J. H. Hutton, *Caste in India* (2nd ed. London, 1951), p. 205.

[4] Government of India, *Report of the Indian Famine Commission*, 1898, vol. II, p. 3.

[5] There are also references to servitude in temple inscriptions and in the accounts of early foreign travellers. For a description of early forms of agricultural labour,

And the social and economic disabilities actually involved in any particular status can be measured only in the context of social and economic structure of the time. Indeed, it may be argued that the 'slave' or 'serf' can also be regarded as a landholder, in the sense that he had the right, frequently though not invariably, to work on the land to which he was attached. In addition to the obligation to employ him, his master had also to maintain him and his family in sickness and in health. But whether attachment to the land was a constraint hindering advancement or a source of security would depend on the availability of land or other avenues of employment. In fact, even of the Cherumans the Collector of Madura said in 1819 that they were better off than 'any of the lower and poorer class of natives'; no Cheruman was a beggar.[1] 'Slavery', said a member of the Indian Law Commission on Slavery, 'may be regarded as the Indian Poor Law and preventive of infanticide.'[2]

The master's treatment of his labourers would again depend on the availability of surplus labour; when labour was scarce, it would be easy for the labourer to escape, though only to another master. The Collector of Trichinopoly pointed out that Pallans were generally well treated (and in fact were amongst the most 'athletic' classes in the district, unlike the agricultural labourers of Malabar), since their rights were so 'distinctly defined by custom and the interests of the *mirasdar* so substantially affected by the good conduct and health of the Pullars [Pallans]'.[3] This mutual dependence was ritually stressed once a year by the 'slave castes' of Tamil Nad, especially around Madras, who had the practice of striking work, complaining of various grievances and threatening desertion. On this occasion the agricultural labourers had to be given promises of better treatment and small presents by the masters.[4] The Paraiyans as a caste had certain other ritual privileges as well.[5]

All in all, it is difficult to separate caste from economic status at the beginning of the nineteenth century. For analytical purposes this is a great advantage, since the close connection between caste and servile status provides a method of estimating the size of the servile groups at this time.

including types of 'serfdom', in the Chola period (*flor*, first to thirteenth centuries A.D.) in the Tamil areas, see Sastri, *The Colas*, pp. 567–70. For Malabar see references in Menon, *History of Kerala*, and in Duarte Barbosa, *A Description of the Coasts of East Africa and Malabar* (English translation, London 1866).

[1] *Slavery Papers, 1828*, p. 846.

[2] Minute by Cameron, *Report on Slavery, 1841*.

[3] Letter to Board of Revenue, 1.7.1819; Trichinopoly Records, vol. 3677, p. 154.

[4] Ellis, in Bayley & Hudleston, *Papers on Mirasi Rights*, pp. 336–7.

[5] Thurston, *Ethnographical Notes on South India*, p. 456.

IV. THE IMPORTANCE OF AGRICULTURAL LABOUR IN THE FIRST HALF OF THE NINETEENTH CENTURY

In the light of this connection between caste and occupation it is possible from the censuses of 1871 and thereafter to estimate the numbers of agricultural labourers in the pre-census period. More precisely, such an estimate requires two assumptions. As we have seen, the agrarian 'serfs' and 'slaves' were drawn from a few castes such as the Cherumans, Pallans and Paraiyans, which may be termed the agricultural labour castes. The first assumption is that most members of these castes were in fact agricultural labourers, whether free or unfree. The second and less important assumption is that these castes did not grow at very different rates from the rest of the population. Thus, from the proportion of these castes to total population at the end of the century as given by the census returns, and from the figures of total population at the beginning of the century as given by contemporary estimates, one can derive the size of the agricultural labour castes and hence, on the first assumption, of the rough number of agricultural labourers at this date. There is the further possibility that agricultural labourers might have been drawn from other castes as well.

However, the argument is not sustained solely by this chain of inference; the evidence of contemporary documents also supports the presumption that slavery was widespread in the early nineteenth century. Figures of the 'slave' population at this time are available for certain districts. These figures, which were supplied by the Collectors to the Board of Revenue, have to be used with caution, since the Collectors did not distinguish clearly between the traditional occupation of the caste and the actual occupation. Whether they are referring to caste or occupation can sometimes, but not always, be inferred from the context; it is likely that most figures of 'slaves' refer not to those who were actually agricultural or other 'slaves' or serfs, but to the Cherumans, Pallans, Holeyas, etc. But the fact that caste and occupation were so easily confused is significant in itself.

As one would expect, the fullest data are available for Malabar and Canara where agricultural servitude took its harshest form. Figures are available from as early as 1800–1, when Buchanan quotes the estimates given to him by the Collectors of Malabar and Canara. The population data are defective, so that the following figures have a fairly wide margin of error, but even allowing for this, the proportion of 'slaves' to *total*, not merely agricultural, population, was significantly large in certain districts. In South Malabar the 'slaves' formed 13·4–17·3 per cent of the whole population.[1] In the three northern areas of Tellicherry, Mahe and Dharmapatnam, the 'slaves' formed only 3·9 per cent of the total population, but slavery was rare in North Malabar. Again, in the neighbouring areas of Cannanore and Chirakkal, the 'slaves' formed around 8 per cent of the total population.[2] In three other northern areas the 'slaves' formed 13 per cent of the population, but if, as Buchanan held, the population figures were underestimates, the true proportion would be lower.[3] In districts a little further south, the proportion of slaves was 25·1 per cent.[4] In Irnad in central Malabar the 'slaves' formed between 10 per cent and 13 per cent of the total population.[5] In 1806–7 the Principal Collector of Malabar estimated that there were 96,386 slaves out of a total population of 700,000 or 13·7 per cent. By 1815–16 he estimated that the numbers had dropped to 94,786; in 1819 there were about 100,000 'slaves',[6] excluding 3,000[7] in Wynaad. In 1827 the proportion of 'slaves' to total population had fallen as low as 9·5 per cent (95,696:1,003,466); but if 3,000 'slaves' for Wynaad are included, the proportion rises to 11·1 per cent.[8] The caste break-up of these figures was given: almost all the 95,696 'slaves' consisted of subcastes of the Cheruman, except for the 'Betwas or Wettowar' (i.e. Vettuvans) who numbered 3,347. It was pointed out that only a portion of the Vettuvans should be included since it was only in some districts of Malabar that they were claimed as slaves.

However, the number of 'slaves' rose again to 140,933 in 1833. This figure, based on the census of 1833, was supplied to the Board of Revenue

[1] The Collector supplied figures of the number of houses in his district. Using two different estimates of the number of persons per house—a common way of estimating population in the pre-census period—Buchanan arrived a estimates of population, excluding 'slaves', of 106,500 and 78,925. The number of 'slaves' was given separately as 16,574; Buchanan, *A Journey from Madras*, vol. II, p. 61.

[2] *Ibid.*, vol. II, p. 198. The total population has been calculated on the assumption of 5 people per house, as in Palghat.

[3] *Ibid.*, vol. II, p. 146.

[4] *Ibid.*, vol. II, p. 162.

[5] *Ibid.*, vol. II, p. 117.

[6] Collector, Malabar to Board of Revenue, 20.7.1819; *Slavery Papers, 1828*, p. 845.

[7] According to H. Bevan, a military officer, there were 100,000 slaves in Wynaad in 1832, but his evidence is probaby not as reliable as that of the administrators; *Select Committee Report, 1831–32*, Appendix K, p. 577.

[8] All figures from T. H. Baber's evidence in *Select Committee Report, 1831–32*. Mr Baber had served for 32 years in Bombay, Malabar and Canara.

by the Principal Collector in 1835. It was said to include 'slaves of all descriptions'.[1] The judge at Calicut pointed out in 1842 that the censuses of 1835 and 1842 showed the slaves increasing from 144,000 in 1835 to 159,000 in 1842, and he concluded from this that 'no gradual extinction of slavery is going on in Malabar'.[2] The census figures of that period generally contained caste data without occupation data, but if the judge were quoting caste figures his conclusion was obviously absurd. The figures of the censuses are not available, but taking population figures for the nearest years, which are for 1836 and 1838, the proportion of 'slaves' to total population would have been 12·9 per cent and 13·6 per cent, respectively. In 1838 the Principal Collector of Malabar estimated that the aggregate number of 'slaves' was a shade more than one-seventh of the total population.[3] Thus while the Collectors had concluded on the basis of the figures up to 1827 that in the Malabar area the 'slave' population seemed to have been diminishing, in subsequent years the proportion of 'slaves' to total population returned to the 1801 level of around 13 per cent.

In Canara, according to the Collector of the Southern Division,[4] the Dheds (i.e. Holeyas), who are defined as 'slaves employed in cultivation', alone amounted to 11·9 per cent of the population,[5] while if to these are added the three castes who are defined as 'cultivators and servants' or 'cultivators and labourers', and the eight castes defined as 'day labourers' alone or as combining day labour with other occupations such as traders or messengers, then the proportion of agricultural labour to total population rises to 15·4 per cent. Buchanan remarked that in North Canara there were very few slaves. In 1819 it was estimated that in the whole of Canara there were 82,000 'slaves', of whom 60,000 belonged to the agricultural castes.[6] Population figures are not available for that year, but on the assumption that the population increased steadily from 1801 to 1827, in

[1] This was disputed by Mr Brown, manager of the Randeterra plantation, who held that this figure related to caste and not actual occupation, and included men who cultivated their own land. He also said that the correct census figure was 146,202; *Report on Slavery, 1841*, p. 127.

[2] W. Logan, *Malabar Manual* (1906), vol. I, p. 151.

[3] Principal Collector of Malabar to the Board of Revenue, 24.4.1838, quoted in P.P. 1841, XXVIII (238), *Slavery Correspondence*, p. 93. Census figures are discussed in detail in ch. VII, *infra*.

[4] North Canara was separated from South Canara and added to Bombay Presidency in 1863, but unless otherwise noted, Canara stands for South Canara throughout this book.

[5] Buchanan, *A Journey from Madras*, vol. II, pp. 203–4.

[6] The remaining 22,000 were described by the Magistrate of Canara in 1819 as descendants of persons taken in battle, or Brahmin women who had lost caste; *Slavery Papers, 1828*, pp. 843–4.

1819 the proportion of slaves to total population in South Canara would have been around 10 per cent.[1]

As for the Tamil districts, the Law Commission Report on Slavery of 1841 contains some figures[2] of the numbers of 'slaves' or of Pallans or Paraiyans, but it is often difficult to relate those to the population figures. In South Arcot the 'slaves' who were 'mostly of the pulley and pariar castes and the majority of them are chiefly devoted to the pursuit of agriculture', were 17,000 in 1819, or less than 4 per cent of the population,[3] although in 1836 the Magistrate stated that agricultural slavery was considerable, particularly in the two *taluks* bordering on Tanjore.[4] For Tanjore the 'slave' population was stated to be 'very numerous' or 'many thousands'.[5] In Madura the Magistrate stated in 1843 that the 'slaves of all kinds' were 'a trifling proportion' to the whole population, but the Census of 1841 showed that the Paraiyans and Pallans were 16 per cent of the population. In Tinnevelly the Collector estimated in 1832 that the 'slaves' formed 38 per cent of the whole population, but this was so much higher than the proportion in the other Tamil districts that the 1841 Commission referred the question to his successor, who stated that the Censuses of 1821–2 showed the numbers of Pallans, Paraiyans, etc., to be about 16 per cent[6] of the total population. In other words, he assumed that 'slaves' were identical with members of these castes, or at least could not exceed them in number. In Trichinopoly the Collector estimated in 1819 that there were 10,000 Pallans in the wet districts and 600 in the dry lands.[7] This works out to about 2·2 per cent of the population of 1823; the proportion of Pallans to total population in the wet lands alone would probably be more significant, but the latter figure is not available. A census of Trichinopoly was taken in 1830, according to which Pallans, Paraiyans, etc., formed 20·8 per cent of the population.[8] Similar caste figures are

[1] The population of South Canara in 1800–1 was 396,672; the population of the whole of Canara was 576,640 in 1807 and 665,652 in 1827.

[2] Unless otherwise stated all the figures in this paragraph are from the *Report on Slavery, 1841*.

[3] Collector, South Arcot to the Board of Revenue, 12.9.1819; *Slavery Papers, 1828*, p. 871.

[4] *Slavery Report, 1841*, pp. 450–1.

[5] Evidence of A. D. Campbell; *Select Committee Report, 1831–32*, Appendix K. The population of Tanjore in 1831 was 1,128,730.

[6] The number of Pallans, etc., was 129,520; the population of Tinnevelly in 1822–3 was 788,196.

[7] Collector, Trichinopoly to Board of Revenue, 1.7.1819; Trichinopoly Records, vol. 3677, p. 152.

[8] The caste break-down is very rough, there is a twofold division into 'Brahmins, Muslims, Soodras, etc.' and 'Pallars, Paraiyans, etc.'; P.B.R., 21.2.1831.

available for two other districts:[1] in Nellore the Paraiyans were 14·6 per cent of the population in 1827, and 16 per cent in 1830, and in Salem in 1830 they formed 12·2 per cent.[2]

These figures have been set out in Table 1, which also shows what each figure purports to represent: agricultural labour castes, 'slaves' in general, or 'agricultural slaves' (this distinction is important only in South Canara, since in the remaining areas the only quantitatively important form of servitude was agricultural). For purposes of comparison, the caste and occupation figures of the Censuses of 1871 onwards are also given.

According to these figures, during the first half of the nineteenth century the slaves in Malabar ranged between 13 per cent and 15 per cent of the total population, except in 1827 when the figure was just below 10 per cent. In South Canara the proportion of slaves to total population was at least 10–12 per cent. In the Tamil districts agricultural servitude was extensive in at least Trichinopoly and Tinnevelly; here the proportion of 'serfs' or of the agricultural labour castes was around 16 per cent, save for the exceptional figure of 20 per cent for Trichinopoly in 1830. It is known that serfdom was at least as extensive in Tanjore, a well-irrigated area, but no figures are available. In the other Tamil districts—both Arcots, Chinglepet, Salem, Madura and Coimbatore—the Collectors and Judges generally reported that there was very little 'slavery' or none at all.[3] The Collector of North Arcot reported, for instance, that the total number of 'slaves' in his district, all of whom were engaged in agriculture, was 688.[4] But it appears from some of their replies that not only were there some agricultural labourers, but that these labourers belonged to the agricultural labour castes: the absence of slavery pointed to social and political changes rather than to differences in the mode of production. Hence the Collector of Coimbatore could point out in 1819 that in many places where slaves did not exist the Pallans were in 'debt slavery' to their masters. In Madura, where the percentage of agricultural labour castes was high, the Collector wrote in 1819 that while slavery was not so common in his district as in the neighbouring districts, the system had been in full swing during the Nawab's time when the Paraiyans sold themselves or their relatives to the *raiyats*; this custom had probably been withering away in the British period because the Courts did not encourage it,[5] but

[1] Caste figures are also available for Guntur for 1830, but since the breakdown is into Brahmins, Muslims, Soodras, Paraiyans, etc., they cannot be used; P.B.R. 24.1.1831.

[2] P.B.R. 18.11.1830.

[3] See *Slavery Papers*, 1828, pp. 836–7 and *Report on Slavery, 1841*, p. 461.

[4] *Slavery Papers*, 1828, pp. 873–4.

[5] Collector, Madura to Board of Revenue, 26.10.1819; Madura Records, vol. 1166, pp. 91–3.

Table 1. *Serfs/Slaves or Agricultural Labour Castes as a Percentage of Total Population*

Year		Nellore	S. Arcot	Salem	Trichinopoly	Madura	Tinnevelly	Malabar	S. Canara
1800–1								13–15 (S)†	11·9 (S)
1807								13·7 (S)	
1819			3·7 (S)					15·2 (S)	9·6 (S)‡
1823							16·0 (C)		
1827		14·6 (C)						9·5 (S)	
1830		16·3 (C)		12·2 (C)	20·8 (C)				
1833								12·9 (S)	
1838								14·3 (S)§	
1841						16·0 (C)			
1857								11·7 (S)	
1871		20·5 (C)	25·3 (C)	13·8 (C)	13·0 (C)	9·5 (C)	9·8 (C)	13·2 (C)	15·0 (C)
1881		18·3 (C)	23·5 (C)	13·2 (C)	10·9 (C)	7·9 (C)	7·2 (C)	11·7 (C)	14·4 (C)
1891		14·9 (C)	24·4 (C)	11·2 (C)	18·2 (C)	13·2 (C)	21·0 (C)	11·9 (C)	13·2 (C)
1901	{	21·3 (C)	27·1 (C)	13·8 (C)	17·5 (C)	12·7 (C)	21·1 (C)	10·5 (C)	11·1 (C)
		21·3 (L)	23·0 (L)	15·7 (L)	16·4 (L)	14·1 (L)	17·3 (L)	29·5 (L)	21·0 (L)

S = Slaves/Serfs C = Agricultural Labour Castes L = Agricultural Labourers

Notes to Table 1

Sources. From 1871 onwards the figures have been derived from Census data. For earlier years the sources are mentioned in the text. From 1871 onwards only the main agricultural labour castes, i.e. Paraiyan, Pallan, Mala, Holeya, Cheruman and Pulaiyan, have been included. From 1871 onwards, Palli or Vannian are excluded from the caste figures, although some of the earlier figures may include them.

† Agricultural slaves alone.

‡ The proportion varies from 3·9 per cent in Tellicherry to 25·1 per cent in Tamaracheri and Walacheri, but for most other parts of Malabar, the proportion ranges from 10 to 17 per cent, and for the district as a whole the proportion would probably be nearer 13–15 per cent.

§ On the assumption that the slave population was a fraction more than one-seventh of the population.

in the Telugu districts it was reported that there were 'very many' slaves in Masulipatam and the adjoining districts; in the former they were so common that their upkeep was included in the ordinary cost of cultivation by the Collector in 1819,[1] but no figures are available.

Two important conclusions emerge. First, the contemporary evidence shows that 'slaves' and serfs were already a sizeable proportion of the total population in many areas at the beginning of the nineteenth century. In the second place, this evidence makes it highly probable that in Malabar, South Canara, and those Tamil districts where there was agricultural servitude, the vast majority of the agricultural labour castes were actually agricultural labourers.[2] This hypothesis is supported by the high proportion of the members of these castes who were agricultural labourers towards the end of the century, as the censuses show. The connection between caste and occupation justifies the attempt to attack the problem by extrapolating backwards from the Census figures of caste which are available for the later part of the century.

Census Data on Caste

Before using the Census data on caste, it is necessary to consider how reliable they are. The first problem is to define 'caste'; the point at which one distinguishes a caste from a sub-caste is almost a matter of individual preference.[3] But this would be no problem if all Census Reports followed

[1] *Report on Slavery, 1841*, p. 190.

[2] There are many references to show that agricultural 'slaves' or 'serfs' could be drawn only from the agricultural labour castes, e.g. replies of the Collector of Tanjore, 30.6.1819; *Slavery Papers, 1828*, p. 837; and the Magistrate of Madura, 21.1.1836; *Report on Slavery, 1841*, pp. 459–60.

[3] The following extract from the 1921 Census Report illustrates the difficulties of defining caste: 'In the India Census Report of 1911 caste was defined as an "endogamous group or collection of groups bearing a common name and having a common traditional occupation, who are so linked together by these and other ties, such as the tradition of a common origin, the possession of the same tutelary deity and the same social status, ceremonial observations and family priests, that they regard themselves and are regarded by others, as forming a single homogeneous community". As a rule a caste contains several endogamous groups or sub-castes, it is held by some authorities that each of these groups ought to be regarded as a caste, that the larger body commonly called a caste is merely a collection of true castes who follow the same profession. Be that as it may, the man in the street applies the term caste to the larger group, and this report adopts the same practice. The characteristics of a caste will then be endogamy, commensality, and a common name and common traditions, though intermarriage and commensality seldom extend to the whole caste and are generally restricted to sub-castes or endogamous groups within the caste. The common name is not always a safe guide nor is the common traditional occupation'; *Census Report, 1921*, pp. 153–4. Unless otherwise mentioned, references are to the Madras Census Reports, and if no volume reference is given, vol. I, containing the text of the report itself, is referred to.

the same principles of classification, and if all the sub-groups within a 'caste', as defined by the Census, followed the same traditional occupation. But neither of these two conditions holds. Under the term Palli and Paraiyan (Pariah) the 1871 and 1881 Censuses lump together a number of groups which are separately classified as castes in later reports.

Again, where the sub-division of castes is very broad there is the danger of including castes whose traditional occupation is not agricultural labour: the 1871 and 1881 group 'Palli' includes, for example, the two large castes of the Kallans and Marayans who were traditionally warriors or robbers. Even where the classification is more detailed the castes are too large for homogeneity. There were, for example, 4,439,253 Paraiyans in 1891, divided in the Tamil districts into 348 sub-divisions, including the Koliyans, who were weavers, and the Velluvans, who were medicinemen or priests.[1] Although the 1891 Census Report adds that the occupation of the vast majority of these sub-castes was agricultural or general labour,[2] it is still possible that some sub-castes whose traditional occupation was not agricultural labour were included, while others, who were traditionally agricultural labourers, were excluded.

Even when the definition of caste is roughly similar, as in 1891 and 1901, the lists of agricultural labour castes differ (see Table 2). This is not a serious problem, however, since there is general agreement about the main castes—the Cheruman, Holeya, Pallan, Palli and Paraiyan—in the various Census Reports, and in both 1891 and 1901 these form over 90 per cent of the total.

There are many other sources of error: certain titular terms could be used for members of many castes but were confused with caste names (e.g. Muppan); occupational terms were sometimes specific to one caste (Kusavan, potter), or applied to people of different castes performing similar functions (e.g. Pujari, the Tamil term for priest);[3] again, the same term would have varying meanings in different areas,[4] whereas the same

[1] *Census Report, 1901*, pp. 172–5.

[2] *Census Report, 1891*, p. 245.

[3] This type of error arose from the fact that each depressed caste would have its own functionaries—for caste reasons again. Thus 'each depressed caste [has] its own priests, medicinemen, bands, acrobats and orderlies. But in relation to the other castes the general body of a depressed caste and its accessory functionnaires form a unit having the same status and subject to the same social distance'; Reddy, 'Transition in Caste Structure in Andhra Desh with Particular Reference to Depressed Classes', pp. 16–17.

[4] Thus Pulaiyan is a synonym for Cheruman as well as the name of a Tamil caste of hill cultivators found in Madura and Coimbatore; *Census Report, 1901*, p. 175. Panchama is also a synonym for Mala or Paraiyan: in 1891 in the Tamil districts the Panchamas were included in Paraiyans but in the Telugu districts were registered as a separate caste; *Census Report, 1891*, p. 249.

Table 2. *Agricultural Labour Castes with more than 10,000 Population, as Classified in each Census**

1871†	1881	1891‡	1901	1911§
		Chandala		
		Cheruman (or Pulaiyan)‖	Cheruman	
		Holeya	Holeya	
		Kusa	Kusa	
		Mala	Mala	Mala
		Muppan		
		Paidi	Paidi	
		Pallan	Pallan	Pallan
Palli or Vanniyan	Palli	Palli or Vanniyan	Palli	Palli
		Paniyan	Paniyan	
Paraiyan	Paraiyan	Paraiyan	Paraiyan	Paraiyan
			Relli	
			Samantiya	
		Urali	Urali	
		Vettuvan		

* From 1921 onwards the Madras Censuses ceased to show traditional occupations. This was done in deference to feelings such as those of the Nadars. 'The traditional occupation of these Nadars has hitherto been shown as toddy-drawing, but they now claim that they are by tradition and inheritance lords of the soil and that toddy-drawing was the occupation only of comparatively few degenerate members of the caste'; *Census Report, 1921*, p. 154.

† 'The Pariahs or outcaste tribes . . . call themselves pariahs in Tamil, Malas in Telugu, Holia in Canarese, Poliyar in Malayalam and Dheda in Mahratti. . . . They are everywhere the menial servants of the country'; *Census Report, 1871*, p. 169. Vol. II (Supplementary Tables) of the *Census Report, 1871*, lists the names (pp. 108–30), of the 'sub-castes' grouped under each main head, from which it appears that Pallan included Palli.

‡ See caste glossary in *Census Report, 1891*. All those castes one of whose traditional occupations is listed as agricultural labour have been included. Thus the Paidis are agricultural labourers and weavers.

§ 'Field labour' castes; *Census Report, 1911*, p. 184.

‖ The term Cheruman was used in South Malabar, and Pulaiyan in North Malabar.

'caste' might have different names in different languages.[1] But on the whole these ambiguities were probably not very important: neither enumerators nor enumerated would be likely to make many mistakes, since caste was even more crucial then than it is today in Hindu society. Deli-

[1] *Census Report, 1901*, p. 127.

berate misrepresentation of caste would also be difficult, particularly in the rural areas.

It is true that new castes were constantly being created by changes in the occupation of a section of the old caste, by sections of several castes coming together in a common occupation, and so forth,[1] but these changes do not appear to have taken place on a significant scale in our period.[2]

The only major caste which is difficult to classify is the Tamil Palli or Vanniyan. Although the Pallis are included in all the Censuses in the agricultural labour castes they alone were not untouchables. Together with the fact that few of the early reports on serfdom in the Tamil districts mention them, this makes it unlikely that they were traditionally serfs. Indeed, the Collector of Tanjore wrote in 1819 that 'the slaves here are of two castes only, the Pallar and the Pariah'[3] whereas Ellis stated that the agricultural 'slave' castes were the Palli, Pallan and Paraiyans.[4] Again, Ellis states that the Pallis were the slaves of the Brahmins and that the other two castes served non-Brahmins, while according to the 1881 Census Report many of the Pallis 'probably were once the predial slaves, the *adscripti glebae* of the Vellala landlords'.[5] The Collector, South Arcot, wrote to the Board of Revenue in 1819 that 'the slaves in this collectorate are mostly of the *pulley* and *pariah* castes'—here 'pulley' may stand either for Palli or Pallan.[6]

In 1871 and 1901 again, less than 20 per cent of the Palli were actually agricultural labourers. On the other hand, the 1871 Census Report, stating that 70 per cent of them were 'cultivators' (as opposed to labourers and so on), remarked that 'a large proportion of the *Vunnies* (i.e. Vanniyans or Pallis) were abject slaves before the period of British administration, incapable of owning property, or of cultivating on their own account. Others were thieves and robbers by profession, and existed on plunder. A

[1] For examples of these and other types of caste formation see *ibid.*, p. 132.

[2] Also, entire castes or sub-castes could change their names, and it was naturally the lowest castes which actually did so. But the old despised caste names were forsaken on a large scale for new and (temporarily) more respectable ones only in the twentieth century, and this made a significant difference to the Census figures only in 1931. In fact 'the experience of seven censuses in this State confirms the view that the caste return is one of the most accurate of all the census tables, and is far more reliable than age-statistics for instance, or the return of infirmities or occupation'; *Census Report for Baroda, 1931*, p. 393.

[3] *Slavery Papers, 1828*, p. 837.

[4] Bayley & Hudleston, *Papers on Mirasi Right*, p. 335.

[5] *Census Report, 1881*, p. 110. See also *Census Report, 1891*, p. 249, and *Salem Gazetteer*, vol. I, Part I, p. 142.

[6] *Slavery Papers, 1828*, p. 871. On phonetic grounds, *pulley* should mean Palli, but from conditions in other districts Pallan is more likely.

wonderful change must have taken place in the last century to bring more than two-thirds of them into the class of small farmers, or peasant proprietors.'[1]

It would probably be safer to exclude the Pallis from the agricultural labour castes; here the proportion of such castes to total population has been calculated on two bases, first including and then excluding the Pallis. The five main castes which were definitely 'agricultural labour' castes—Pallan, Paraiyan, Cheruman, Mala and Holeya—together formed 12·0 per cent, 13·1 per cent, 12·9 per cent end 12·5 per cent of the total population in 1871, 1881, 1891 and 1901 respectively. If the Pallis are included, the proportion rises to aiound 20 per cent, and since they are largely a Tamil caste, the percentage of agricultural labour would be much higher in the Tamil districts than elsewhere.

Before discussing the significance of these figures, it will be useful to relate the data available for certain districts in the pre-Census years to the Census figures. This has been done in Table 1 above which shows, first, that there is remarkably little discrepancy between the early and later data: in fact it is only the 1819 figure for South Arcot which is incongruous with later data, and the figure is almost certainly far too low. Secondly, the agreement between the different sets of data is particularly significant in that the proportion of the agricultural labour castes to total population varies in the different districts. In the third place, the district figures do not throw much light on overall rates of growth: in Nellore, Salem and Tinnevelly, the proportion of agricultural labour castes to total population was higher in 1891 and 1901 than in 1827 or 1832, while in Malabar and South Canara the proportion was lower in 1901 than in 1801, but a little higher than in 1827 (Malabar) or 1819 (Canara).

A priori it is evident that the relative rates of growth of the different castes were affected by various factors which worked in different ways. The lower castes probably had a higher natural rate of increase than the upper castes, but they would undoubtedly have been more affected by famine. Again, emigrants from South India were largely drawn from the agricultural labour and other low castes. Finally, converts to Christianity and Islam came chiefly from the lower castes, but this became really significant only in the twentieth century.[2] Since these factors work in both directions, it can perhaps be assumed in view of the pre-Census data that

[1] *Census Report, 1871*, p. 158.

[2] Between 1871 and 1881 the Hindu population declined by 2·27 per cent, but the proportionate decline was greater for the Paraiyans. The decline was partly due to the effects of the 1876–8 famine, and partly due to conversion; *Census Report, 1881*, p. 115. For some districts, e.g. Malabar, conversions would be more significant; *idem*. In some years, the caste figures include converts, e.g. 1881.

the agricultural labour castes formed about 12 per cent of the population in the first half of the nineteenth century as well as in the second, if the Pallis are excluded, and about 20 per cent if the latter are included. So the crucial question then is: how strong was the connection between caste and occupation in the nineteenth century?

Although the 1881 and 1891 censuses do not contain actual figures on this point, they do make statements of relevance to it. For example, the 1891 Census Report stated that the bulk of the Pallis were still labourers,[1] and again that the vast majority of the Paraiyans were agricultural or general labourers.[2]

The 1901, 1911 and 1921 Censuses give figures of the actual occupations followed by members of each caste; while the 1901 figures relate only to selected castes in selected districts, the 1911 and 1921 figures relate to the total population of the castes selected. Two facts emerge from these figures: first, over 65 per cent of the workers in the agricultural labour castes followed their traditional occupations in 1901, and second, even though between 1901 and 1921 the proportion of each caste doing so had declined, it remained in most cases well above 50 per cent. The only exception to both these generalizations were the Pallis, of whom as few as 18·5 per cent were agricultural labourers in 1901. Since the proportion had risen to 56·5 per cent in 1921, it could be argued that the districts selected for 1901 may have been atypical, but for the fact that the 1871 figure, for what it is worth, is remarkably close to the 1901 figure of 18·5 per cent. Anyway, apart from the Pallis, the connection between caste and occupation was fairly close even in 1921, and was much closer in 1901 and 1911. And in the case of the Cherumans the connection was practically complete: over 90 per cent were still agricultural labourers even as late as 1921.

For certain districts details of the relation between caste and occupation are also given. Thus in 1871 in South Arcot, the Paraiyans and Vanniyans or Pallis formed the bulk of the labourers, while half the Paraiyans were cultivators;[3] and in Nellore, a Telugu district, the non-agricultural labour castes formed the bulk of the labourers.[4] Apart from the Census figures, there is a great deal of evidence in the literature on the continuing connection between caste and occupation. For instance, it was said of Ramnad that the Pallans, occupied exclusively in the cultivation of paddy lands, were predial labourers.[5] Indeed, unfree labourers were frequently con-

[1] *Census Report, 1891*, p. 246.
[2] *Ibid.*, p. 245.
[3] *Census Report, 1871*, p. 289. [4] *Idem.*
[5] *Ramnad Manual*, pp. 36–7. Ramnad is part of Madura district.

Table 3. *Percentage of Actual Workers following Traditional Occupation in Six Castes, 1871–1921*

	1871	1901 *	1911	1921
1. Cheruman		93·5	95·6	91·2
2. Holeya		65·7	79·7	44·2
3. Mala		75·5	79·0	60·9
4. Pallan		—	—	43·7
5. Palli	18·6†	18·5	—	59·4
6. Paraiyan	41·4†	64·2	—	56·5

Source: *Census Reports.*

* In selected districts only.

† *Census Report, 1871* (p. 170) states that 63·9 per cent of the male Pallis were occupied, of whom 11·9 per cent were labourers for hire; out of 63·5 per cent of the occupied Paraiyans, 24·4 per cent were 'labourers, agricultural or otherwise'.

centrated in the irrigated areas; thus in Trichinopoly the Pallans were bunched in the wet zones, while in Salem the few 'slaves' who existed under Muslim rule belonged to the wet lands near the river Kaveri.[1] In the Telugu districts as well the connection holds: as we have seen in Chapter III, it was reported as late as 1898 that most landless labourers in Anantapur were Malas, Madigas and Boyas.

Granted that the bulk of the so-called agricultural labour castes—say, 65–75 per cent—were in fact agricultural labourers towards the end of the nineteenth century, and that the proportion of these castes to total population remained constant at 12–20 per cent throughout the century, what inferences can be drawn about the numbers of agricultural labourers at the beginning of the century? Obviously the close connection between these castes and their traditional occupations around 1900 is not in itself proof that such a connection existed earlier.[2]

During the early nineteenth century, there can be little doubt that in those districts where agricultural servitude was rigorous, such as Malabar and some of the Tamil areas, most members of the agricultural labour castes were not only agricultural labourers but were also unfree. There is another consideration as well. Since only members of the agricultural labour castes could be deprived of their freedom,[3] the estimate of the

[1] *Slavery Papers, 1828*, p. 836.

[2] Indeed, those who hold that the class was created during the nineteenth century could find support in the fact that castes with other traditional occupations, such as the Madigas or leatherworkers of Andhra, as well as the Chakkiliyans or Tamil leatherworkers, were also for the most part agricultural labourers in 1901. It is in evaluating the significance of such data that the contemporary evidence about the existence of slavery is most useful.

[3] It is unnecessary to repeat the statements of every official who wrote on the

strength of these castes sets an upper limit to the extent of agricultural serfdom and slavery at the beginning of the nineteenth century.

It also seems likely that where these forms of servitude flourished, the bulk of labourers were unfree and hired; here free labourers of other castes were rare. This was almost certainly true of Malabar and South Canara. Thus in 1819 the Collector of Malabar reported that 90 per cent of the cultivation in South Malabar, particularly in the rice lands, was performed entirely by the Cherumans.[1] The Collector of South Canara remarked in 1801 that nearly all the cultivation was carried on by Holeyas 'or slaves of other sorts'. He added, 'an Estate indeed without a property in some of these people would be of little value because day labourers are not to be procured in this as in other countries'.[2] Again in 1843 the Collector replied, when asked to report on the condition of the working classes, that

> by the labouring classes, I conclude, the *dhers* or slaves are alluded to, by whom nearly the whole of the lands in Canara are cultivated, and indeed, with the exception of a certain number of free labourers, probably not more than four or five thousand, who annually contract to work in the Balaghaut Talooks, and an inconsiderable number of coolies who find employment at Mangalore, and several of the other principal seaports on the coast, there is no other class to whom the term can properly be applied.[3]

The caste figures are most revealing for those districts where 'slavery' or serfdom prevailed. Thus in Malabar it has been seen that during the early nineteenth century at least, nearly every member of the 'slave' castes, such as the Cherumans, was in fact an agricultural labourer; in other words at least 10–15 per cent of the total population were landless agricultural labourers. In addition, there were hired labourers. Buchanan stated that in Cannanore and Sheykal in North Malabar the greater part of the cultivation was done by hired labourers, who did not belong to these castes, such as the Nairs, Mappilas and Tiyans.[4] Again in 1819 the Collector of Malabar reported that in North Malabar hired

question that the 'slaves' could be drawn only from certain castes. The only contradictory statement was made by the Collector of North Arcot on 23.12.1819: 'The Slaves, though universally I believe pariahs [by which he meant untouchables] cannot be said to be of any particular caste,' which, he added, distinguished them from the slaves of Malabar; *Slavery Papers, 1828*, pp. 873–4. But all the weight of the evidence is against him, unless perhaps he was referring to debt slavery.

[1] Collector, Malabar to Board of Revenue, 20.7.1819; *Slavery Papers, 1828*, p. 846.

[2] P.B.R., 3.8.1801.

[3] P.B.R., 11.1.1844.

[4] Buchanan, *A Journey from Madras*, vol. II, p. 198.

labourers were mainly used.[1] Similarly in South Canara at least 10 to 12 per cent of the total population consisted of agricultural serfs or 'slaves'.

In those Tamil districts where serfdom was widespread, such as Tanjore, Tinnevelly and Trichinopoly, the caste figures are probably a fairly good guide to the strength of agricultural labour, particularly in the irrigated areas. It is in the remaining Tamil districts and in the Telugu districts (apart, possibly, from Kistna) that the caste figures are of less utility. But the agricultural labour castes were represented in these districts too; in fact even as late as 1830 the proportions were as high as 16 per cent in Nellore and 12 per cent in Salem.

It is likely that in these districts many members of the agricultural labour castes had also been 'slaves' or serfs at some earlier period, but that for various reasons they had already won their freedom by the beginning of the British period. The Malas of the Telugu districts, to take one instance, were traditionally weavers as well as agricultural workers, and at the beginning of the nineteenth century the weavers may not have been reduced to agricultural labour. Moreover, members of other castes may have been doing field work for wages. While the caste figures alone hardly allow us to estimate the numbers of agricultural labourers in these districts, the records do not suggest that the agrarian structure here was so widely different from elsewhere as to have made agricultural labour a negligible quantity.

Whatever their drawbacks, the data on the strength of the agricultural labour castes at the end of the nineteenth century, coupled with the scattered evidence on caste and serfdom at the opening of that century, suffice to show that at the earlier date there were a large number of persons belonging to the agricultural labour castes who were following their traditional occupation. It is highly unlikely therefore that agricultural labour was a quantitatively insignificant group at the time when British rule began.

[1] Collector, Malabar to Board of Revenue, 20.7.1819; *Slavery Papers, 1828*, p. 846.

V. OFFICIAL POLICY AND THE EMANCIPATION OF THE AGRICULTURAL LABOURER

Since the British officials of the time felt that many of the agricultural labourers of Madras Presidency, and in some other parts of India too, were 'slaves', India was bound to come within the scope of the anti-slavery movement in England, whatever the realities of the situation. But in fact their belief had sufficient basis not to make the connection with the abolitionist movement absurd; that many agricultural labourers were in some form of bondage or other was patent, and though the forms of servitude differed in many respects from the types of slavery familiar to European experience, certain features were similar. In Malabar, for instance, the labourers could be bought, sold and mortgaged. And in the early part of the century at least, in nearly all courts of law, following what were considered the traditional Indian practices 'slaves' were not allowed to testify in cases concerning themselves. Since the term 'slave' appears so frequently in the literature and since the measures we will discuss in this chapter were directed against those features of South Indian servitude which were more or less the attributes of full slavery, the term will be used more freely in this chapter than elsewhere.

But in spite of these attributes, slavery in India was very different from slavery in the West Indies or Brazil. The bonded labourer was an integral part of his society, belonging to the same race and culture as his master. He had certain rights as well as obligations, and in any case the traditional institutions of servitude had been modified over a long period of time and did permit a certain social mobility. At first at least, the new rulers were reluctant to take steps that might mean the destruction of the whole social and economic structure, and in any case their power to emancipate the labourer was limited precisely by the fact that he was so rooted in agrarian society.

Before British rule began, the labourer in most of the Telugu areas had already won his freedom, in a formal sense at least. Servitude persisted in both the West Coast and the Tamil areas, but it was in the latter that social mobility was the more likely. Here there was probably no formal prohibition against the ownership of land by the lower castes. Indeed, the Paraiyans, Pallans and the like performed such village offices as measuring the grain, marking the boundaries, watering the fields, burying the dead —and for these they were sometimes paid by being given rent-free lands.[1]

[1] Ellis in Bayley & Hudleston, *Papers on Mirasi Right*, p. 336.

Some of the Tamil districts sanctioned another liberating device: if the master's family were to die out, then his *pannaiyals* might offer themselves for hire. Again the *pannaiyal* was sometimes assigned land (dry land as a rule) by his master, which he would cultivate as a tenant, the master supplying him with the seed, the cattle and the implements; in return he would have to pay a higher rent than other tenants.[1] Indeed this practice might be pushed a stage further. In 1819 the Collector of Madura reported that there some of the Pallans owned lands.[2] In Tanjore again, 'when the master has no work for the slave, he allows him to work for another *mirasdar* who pays the man for his labour, by which means the slaves acquire personal property'.[3]

However unusual or however slow in developing it might be, emancipation was clearly possible under such a system. Whether as tenants or landowners or wage labourers, the *pannaiyals* were sometimes in a position to build up the funds needed for the commutation of their labour services.[4] Cases of this sort were reported from Tinnevelly in 1836, where some of the *pannaiyals* had purchased their liberty (although they had to pay double the market price for slaves to do so).[5]

Of course, this was not the general situation. Very often what might seem to be the road to commutation turned out to be a blind alley. Even in Coimbatore, where the labourer was rather liberally treated, the master had rights over his 'property'; for example, the cattle 'owned' by the bondsman were also at the disposal of the master.[6] Or again in Madura the *pannaiyal* had the right to own property, but after his death this reverted to the master, whether he had heirs or not.[7] But these local customs were powerless beside the basic economic and social forces working against emancipation. The general position in the Tamil areas was doubtless that the labourer could not collect enough funds to free himself or to buy land. Even when the *pannaiyals* were freed by the extinction of their master's family, they were so poor that they had frequently to sell themselves into bondage again in return for a small loan. They merely exchanged one servitude for another.

On the West Coast, where the caste system was more rigorous, the

[1] *Idem.*

[2] *Slavery Papers, 1828*, pp. 872–3.

[3] Minute of Acting Third Judge of the Provincial Courts, Southern Division; *Report on Slavery, 1841*, p. 13.

[4] For analogous developments in medieval Europe, see Marc Bloch, *Feudal Society* (English edition, London, 1961), pp. 278–9.

[5] Reply to Assistant Judge, Auxiliary Court, 15.5.1836; *Report on Slavery, 1841*, pp. 457–9.

[6] Collector, Coimbatore, 24.6.1819; *Slavery Papers, 1828*, pp. 836–7.

[7] *Report on Slavery, 1841*, pp. 455–7.

labourer's opportunities were correspondingly more contracted, and this was particularly true in Malabar. Admittedly, Buchanan mentions that a few of the 'slaves' (though not the Holeyas) of South Canara were permitted to rent lands,[1] and in 1822 Graeme noted that some of them were leased or were even given small plots of their own.[2] In Malabar any landowning by the Cherumans was so rare that officials specifically noted any cases of it. In 1819 Baber stated that he knew of two instances in Malabar of slaves owning property;[3] three years later Graeme remarked that it was very rare for slaves to hold land on any tenure.[4] As late as 1840 an official of the provincial court said that it was doubtful whether there were eight or ten cases in the whole district of bondsmen owning property. Even then, they might not dispose of it without the consent of their master; and if they died heirless, it reverted to these masters.[5] So it would seem that in Malabar the lower castes almost never held any lands,[6] and that their opportunities for emancipation through any of the commuting techniques were very small.

These differences in degrees of servility and in the possibilities of emancipation were partially reflected in official thinking. It was the administrators in Malabar (but not in Canara) who pressed hardest for reform, and those in the Tamil areas who were most reluctant to institute changes. Official British thinking passed through three phases before the coming of legal emancipation in 1843. In the first of these, the period when paramountcy was being won and was becoming consolidated, the new rulers of South India had no wish to tamper with so sensitive an institution as agrarian bondage. This was not surprising. Until the great European war ended in 1815 they had every reason not to court trouble in their colonial dependencies; in any case there was as yet no compelling movement in British opinion against the system of slavery itself. When the early administrators acted to check the sale of slaves this was usually for reasons which were quasi-mercantilist, out of a desire to deny foreigners a labour force. When the British discovered that slaves were being bought or kidnapped in Ganjam and other Telugu districts and were then shipped out of the

[1] Buchanan, *A Journey from Madras*, vol. II, p. 272.
[2] *Slavery Papers, 1828*, p. 921.
[3] *Select Committee Report, 1831–32*, Appendix K, p. 564.
[4] *Slavery Papers, 1828*, p. 921.
[5] *Report on Slavery, 1841*, p. 137.
[6] *Idem*. Admittedly, the Principal Collector reported at the same time that there were 377 slaves holding land on different tenures and paying revenue direct to government; the revenue paid ranged from Re. 1 to Rs. 92 per annum (Rs. 92 would be paid on a holding much larger than the average). But this seems improbable, and we prefer the testimony in the text.

Presidency, they issued a proclamation in 1790 which forbade such traffic.[1] Two years later, when they took over the administration of Malabar,[2] they found that children were being sold to the agents of vessels from the French settlement at Mahe[3] and the Dutch settlement at Cochin,[4] and at once issued a proclamation against dealings in slaves.[5] All this made it clear that they were not conquering South India merely to benefit the colonies of other European powers; but the social *status quo* in India itself was not disturbed.

In fact, the local servitudes were sometimes given official blessing. In 1801 the Collector of South Canara extolled the benefits of the system. It was not only necessary to industry and agriculture but 'productive of very important political as well as moral goods': in fact so admirable a practice was it that he urged that the Holeyas should be stopped from enlisting in the army, as they were in the habit of doing when they quarrelled with their masters.[6] Similarly, in the Tamil districts the tendency was for the British to look indulgently on the institution. When one of the Collectors of Tanjore heard in 1800 that Pallans and Paraiyans were absconding from his district, he ordered that they should all be returned to their masters from any landlord who had 'unjustly' harboured them. He went on to suggest that the police be empowered to force the slaves into working for the Government and for the landholders.[7] Again, it was common enough

[1] Proclamation of the Governor-General in Council, 8.3.1790; Godavari Records vol. 918, pp. 15–18.

[2] Unless other sources are stated, the account of reforms in Malabar follows Logan, *Malabar Manual*, vol. II, pp. 149–52.

[3] As the Magistrate of Malabar wrote on 9.10.1819: 'Mahe used to be a place notorious for kidnapping people of all ages and castes, who were sold as slaves and transported to Arabia and elsewhere.' Even in 1819 kidnapping of this sort had not been stamped out; Malabar Records, vol. 2293, pp. 25–7. There were several cases of the transportation of slaves to St Helena and other places as early as 1757; Letter of Court of Directors, 11.11.1757; the Rev. J. Long, *Selections from the Unpublished Records of Government for the Years 1748–1767*, vol. I, pp. 85–6.

[4] For cases of kidnapping at Cochin in 1799 and 1803, see Malabar Records, vol. 2034, pp. 111–12; P.B.R., 10.5.1803; P.B.R., 6.6.1803.

[5] The Regulations are contained in *Report of a Joint Commission from Bengal and Bombay Appointed to Inspect into the State and Condition of the Province of Malabar in the Years 1792 and 1793*, vol. III. The Government of Madras pointed out in a letter to Bombay of 22.3.1799 that the prohibition of slave traffic did not apply to the slaves of the Dutch who belonged to them prior to their surrender to the British; Malabar Records, vol. 2167, pp. 259–66. In 1830 the Advocate-General held that although the Act abolishing the slave trade did not apply to the internal traffic in slaves and those accused of this could not be committed under the Supreme Court, they could be tried before the Court of Circuit; Nellore Records, vol. 4174, pp. 375, 605.

[6] Collector, South Canara to Board of Revenue; P.B.R., 3.8.1801.

[7] Diary of the Proceedings of the Collector, Mayavaram Division, 6.7.1800; Tanjore Records, vol. 3254, pp. 40–1.

during this early period for the Collectors to co-operate with each other in the task of dragging runaway labourers back to their masters.[1] Thus the Collector of Trichinopoly wrote to the Collector of Coimbatore in 1828 that some Pallans who had absconded to the latter's territory were bound by a deed executed before the *tahsildar* of their village to return to their Brahmin master.[2] But the most telling evidence about the official attitude towards bondage is that the Government itself owned slaves in Malabar. Most of these were probably acquired when the Company took over the lands to which they were attached.[3] There were some two thousand of them, and they were either hired out or employed on the Government estates, such as the Randeterra plantation.[4] After the sale of the Randeterra plantation all the Government slaves were hired out; the hiring charges for most of them were included in the land revenue, so that the rent paid separately came to Rs. 168/9/2 per annum, though their total annual value would have been about Rs. 927/13/0. At prevailing prices in 1836 the slaves were worth Rs. 22,833/10/5.[5]

But this attitude of non-intervention became harder to sustain after the end of the war and the revival of the anti-slavery impulse. This feeling was still a long way from the high-water mark it was to reach during the eighteen-thirties; but even so, slavery was difficult to justify on the principles of Evangelical Christianity or of utilitarian economics, both of which were beginning to impinge on the Indian administration. Yet although Indian servitude might be hard to justify, it was no less hard to abolish. Unlike the plantations of the Caribbean, it was not a simple system of immigrant gangs driven by whip and cane into growing cash crops for white men. Far from that, it was deeply rooted in Indian society, and its sanctions were largely accepted by the serfs themselves. If these institutions were destroyed the roots of Indian society would be disturbed. While cushioning the slave from the worst abuses of the system,

1 E.g., Collector, Trichinopoly to Collector, Salem, 16.7.1810; Trichinopoly Records, vol. 3668, p. 213. Letter to Resident, Tanjore, 16.7.1815; Trichinopoly Records, vol. 3678, p. 188. The same problem arose about the flight of slaves from Malabar to Mysore; e.g., Malabar Records, vol. 1809, p. 87. The practice of collaboration to return runaways went on for several decades; letter from Collector, Salem; P.B.R., 8.11.1830.

2 Trichinopoly Records, vol. 4399, pp. 361 and 467.

3 Malabar Records, vol. 1695, p. 330–3.

4 See, for example, the correspondence between the Malabar Second Commissioner, and the manager (later, the owner) of the Randeterra plantation about the Cherumans and Pulaiyans employed there; Malabar Records, vol. 1695, pp. 330–7; vol. 1697, pp. 162–8. The Commissioner tried to help to recover Cherumans and their families who had escaped from the plantation; Malabar Records, vol. 1698, pp. 111–12.

5 *Report on Slavery, 1841*, Appendix X, p. 511.

the Government policy aimed to save South Indian society from sudden change and to spare the land revenue the risks of instantaneous emancipation. In 1819 the Board of Revenue in Madras felt it necessary to define its attitude. 'Slavery' ought to be abolished step by step, but

> it would be obviously unjust to interfere with the private property which there can be no doubt that the Raiyats at present possess in their slaves; it might be dangerous too suddenly to disturb the long established relations subsisting between these two orders. For the present, therefore, it would seem sufficient with the view to prevent oppression or abuse of authority, to define by legislative enactments the power which may be lawfully exercised by a Raiyat over his slaves.[1]

But what was this power? The Board did not know, and so it enquired of the Collectors. To these men, closer to the problem than the bureaucrats in Madras, the conflict between ethical and social considerations was clear, and it was well expressed in the reply from the Collector of Trichinopoly:

> There is something so revolting and abhorrent to an Englishman in the Idea of Slavery that the advocates of its continuance *in any shape* must ever labour under the disadvantage of prejudgement. Notwithstanding this, I shall endeavour to show that so far as it relates to the Revenue of the district (and I trust my opinion will not be supposed to extend further) any abolition of the Puller System would be attended with the most serious and ruinous consequences.

The Collector also pointed out that so long as there was caste and the Brahmins were debarred from cultivating it would be necessary to have Pallans. Further, emancipation would harm the Pallans themselves, for they would still be 'the lowest order of society', and they would still have to remain at the plough under less favourable circumstances, or else seek more arduous employment.[2] There was another powerful argument against emancipation. It was the serfs who maintained 'the river and Monument works . . . on which the very existence of the country depends'.[3] So far as Oriental slavery was concerned, the needs of humanitarian sentiment might point one way, but the needs of hydraulic society pointed another.

Such arguments as these confirmed the Board of Revenue in the belief that reform must be small in scale and long in coming. It recommended that the slaves' share of the harvest in the Tamil areas should be raised at the expense of the Government's share. It was calculated that this would not reduce the revenue by more than 2,000 pagodas, about Rs. 7,000.[4] To

[1] Minute of Board of Revenue, 25.3.1819; Bayley & Hudleston, *Papers on Mirasi Right*, p. 307.

[2] Trichinopoly Records, vol. 3677, pp. 155–9.

[3] *Ibid.*, pp. 366–76. [4] *Ibid.*, p. 159.

the President in Council this seemed too extreme, and the suggestion was turned down. But the Government consented to one measure of reform: it stopped the practice of selling the slaves to realize arrears of revenue.[1] By doing so the Government took a small step towards dissociating itself from the institution of slavery, but even this was more of a gesture than a policy, for the practice was probably not widespread even in Malabar and was definitely unusual elsewhere. It is true that one official wrote in 1818 that the sale of Cherumans for arrears of revenue was as common as the sale of land, but it is not at all clear how widespread the practice was in Malabar.[2] There are some references to actual sales; for example, the Judge on Circuit, Tellicherry, reported a complaint from a landholder that the local revenue officers had carried off four of his Cherumans and had sold them at public auction. The Collector had ordered them to restore these Cherumans, but this had not been done.[3] Consequently the Board of Revenue wrote to the Collector, Malabar, in 1820: It will be sufficient if the orders of the Board conveyed to you in my letter of 23rd December last prohibiting the sale of slaves for arrears of revenue be communicated to all your native servants and strictly enforced.'[4] Again, there is the petition to Government from the Rajah of Kollangode in 1808 asking for his Pallans, who were 'like slaves', to be restored to him by the Government.[5] In the other areas the Board went so far as to say in 1818 that it was not aware that slaves were ever sold to meet the demand for revenue payable directly to the Government; but it added that where the Government assigned the revenue, the assignee was at liberty to follow established practice in realizing his lawful demand.[6] But this is hardly consistent with the ruling of 1819. It was probably the case that the sales of slaves were not made by the Collectors, but by the minor revenue officials.

The canniness of the Government's attitude to radical reform was best expressed by Munro:

> ... a numerous class of slaves have not the free disposal of their own industry, but are in a peculiar state of servitude. Their condition may ... be regarded as capable of being improved by Government. But the consideration of the measures proper

[1] P.B.R., 25.3.1819; and Malabar Records, vol. 2269, pp. 3–5.

[2] He also felt that 'the partial measure of declaring them not liable to be sold for arrears of revenue will be a drop of water in the ocean; though why the Government should give up a right which every proprietor enjoys, is a question worthy of consideration'; *Select Committee Report, 1831–32*, Appendix K, p. 553.

[3] Coimbatore Records, vol. 589, pp. 143–63.

[4] Malabar Records, vol. 2269, pp. 3–5; cf. P.B.R., 25.2.1830.

[5] P.B.R., 4.3.1808.

[6] Minute of Board of Revenue, 5.1.1818; Bayley & Hudleston, *Papers on Mirasi Right*, p. 369.

to be taken . . . is a matter in which more good is to be expected from the gradual operation of justice and police administered in a spirit favourable to personal liberty than from direct interference on the part of Government.[1]

The Board of Revenue upheld this view in 1830 when they pointed out that while the Government should not sell slaves for arrears of revenue, all private sales where the slaves were separated from the land on which they had hitherto been employed could 'safely be left to the self-interest of those immediately concerned in the question, acting as of course they must under the restraint of law and the police'.[2]

But this spirit was not all-pervasive, and the courts generally upheld what they believed to be the local tradition. Most of the cases which came before them during this period were concerned with the question whether persons living in service and supposed to be slaves might in fact be sold by their masters.[3] In Malabar, for example, the Assistant Judge reported in 1819 that there had been 242 such cases: here the general practice of the court was to recognize the master's right to sell or to mortgage his slaves.[4] This was equally true of South Canara at this time, the court guaranteeing the right to sell slaves by decrees, and to sell them with the land or without it.[5] Moreover, there is no reason to suppose that such rigorousness was confined to the West Coast. There is evidence that the courts in the Tamil areas took the same attitude. So late as 1836 the Magistrate of Chinglepet was reporting the recognition of the master's right to sell or mortgage his *adimai*; cases were disposed of according to the 'laws of each class'.[6] In South Arcot, where the magistrate wanted to prevent practices of this sort, he could find no legal means of doing so.[7]

But various factors worked in the other direction, towards that emancipation on the instalment plan of which Munro had written. In the first place, the judgement of the courts was not always in favour of the master. Even when it might have been, the prospect of the legal charges involved sometimes stopped him from pressing a case; the cost of a civil suit for restoration of a runaway *pannaiyal* was estimated at more than the value of his labour for ten years.[8] In the second place, the mere presence of the

[1] Madras Presidency to Board of Control, 30.12.1825; Revenue Despatches preserved in the Madras Record Office (henceforth R.D.).

[2] P.B.R., 25.2.1830.

[3] W. H. Macnaghten, *Principles and Precedents of Hindu Law* (Calcutta, 1828–9), vol. II. p. 265.

[4] *Report on Slavery, 1841*, Appendix IX.

[5] Letter from Collector, South Canara to Board of Revenue, 10.7.1819; *Slavery Papers, 1828*, p. 843.

[6] *Report on Slavery, 1841*, pp. 449–50.

[7] Letter from Magistrate, South Arcot, 28.2.1836; *ibid.*, pp. 450–1.

[8] *Ibid.*, pp. 199–200.

British régime probably shook the stability of the system, since it was not a foregone conclusion that the courts would favour master against man. As early as 1819 the Collector of Trichinopoly remarked that he had received

> ...hundreds of complaints from landlords relative to the contempt and utter neglect with which their slaves treat all instructions given by them regarding the cultivation and the independence which they manifest since the institution of the courts. This evil, if not checked at the outset, will have the worst effect on the cultivation and ... the quiet of the country.[1]

Moreover, by the eighteen thirties the *dicta* of the magistrates, where they were in favour of the masters, were being nullified by the actions of the Collectors, who came more and more to share the ethical prejudices of the anti-slavery movement which had now grown strong in Britain itself. The Collector of Tanjore, for one, declined to assist the masters to recover runaways.[2] In Chinglepet, in fact, the Collector said as early as 1819 that the sale of the *adimais* was prohibited and that they could not be attached in liquidation of debt.[3] But these were probably local measures. In 1838 the Collector of Malabar remarked that the owners there still had the power of selling or mortgaging their slaves, but that in practice they seldom enforced it; if their Cherumans absconded they could count on no assistance from the authorities in getting them back.[4] Obviously, the bias of the administration was beginning to turn against the master, and this encouraged a measure of informal emancipation by weakening the practical sanctions for servitude. The attack on its legal sanctions was yet to come, except for one small measure. This was Regulation VII of 1829 which recognized that 'slaves' had the same rights of prosecuting and giving evidence as freeborn persons; till then cases had occurred in which slaves had not been allowed to give evidence when they were themselves involved, as in kidnapping charges.[5]

In Britain the vehement opposition to slavery reached its climax during the eighteen thirties and culminated in the famous Act of 1833, which converted the slaves in most British possessions into apprentices. But expropriating the wasting assets of Caribbean plantations and of obscure Afrikaner farmers was one thing; extending the attack as far as Indian slavery was another. The East India Company was not a wasting asset, and

[1] Collector, Trichinopoly, to Governor in Council; Trichinopoly Records, vol. 3677, pp. 366–76.

[2] *Report on Slavery, 1841*, pp. 119–20.

[3] Chinglepet Records, vol. 467, p. 113.

[4] Principal Collector, Malabar to Board of Revenue; P.B.R., 21.2.1839.

[5] D. R. Banaji, *Slavery in British India* (Bombay, 1933), pp. 307–11.

it was certainly not obscure. Its spokesmen expounded the arguments of the Old India Hands. Oriental slavery was quite different from the plantation system. It was part of the social order. It was essential for the land settlements. It was not slavery at all. Anyway, India was a special case. These considerations staved off the attacks of humanitarians. India was excepted from the operation of the Emancipation Act; and when the Company's charter was renewed in 1833, Parliament contented itself with directing the Governor-General to mitigate the position of slaves in India and to abolish the status of slavery as soon as might be practicable.

Having turned this difficult corner, the Indian Government saw no need for haste. Not until 1836 did the administration free its own slaves in Malabar, and even then it made a point of not proclaiming this too loudly, lest this enfranchisement should 'create any unnecessary alarm or aversion to it on the part of other proprietors, or premature hopes of emancipation on that of other slaves'.[1] Two years later, the Collector of Malabar could suggest no way of bettering the lot of the slaves other than remitting land revenue as a reward to benevolent masters.[2] All this was much too lukewarm for the humanitarians, who could still see a great deal of unfinished business in the fight against slavery. In 1837 they induced a House of Commons Committee to condemn all 'oppression' in British territories;[3] and the following year they forced the Government to scrap the whole apprenticeship system and to declare total and immediate emancipation of the former slaves.[4] Faced with pressures as strong as these, the Indian administration had to come into line. In 1841 a Law Commission reported on Indian slavery, recommending a restricted scale of punishments for Indian slaves.[5] But this was not sufficient for the humanitarians, and the Government of India was constrained to take visible action against the institution of slavery itself. Act V of 1843 attacked it in four ways: there were to be no more sales of slaves for arrears of revenue; no court should in future enforce rights arising out of the alleged possession of slaves; no man was to be deprived of his property on the ground that he was alleged to be a slave; and finally, any act which was a penal offence if

[1] *Report on Slavery, 1841*, Appendix X.

[2] Collector, Malabar to Board of Revenue; P.B.R., 21.2.1839.

[3] The Committee urged that Britain 'will no longer subject itself to the guilt of conniving at oppression, and that it will take upon itself the task of defending those who are too weak and too ignorant to defend themselves'; Report of House of Commons Committee on Aborigines in British Settlements, *P.P.* 1837, VII, partly printed in K. Bell and W. P. Morrell, *British Colonial Policy, 1830–1860* (Oxford, 1928), p. 546.

[4] W. L. Burn, *Emancipation and Apprenticeship in the British West Indies* (London, 1937), pp. 344–6, 352–9.

[5] *Report on Slavery, 1841*, p. 262.

committed against a free man was to be equally an offence if committed against a man on the ground that he was a slave. The salient feature of Act V is its hesitancy. Essentially the Government solved the problem of slavery by ignoring it: the Courts would not recognize the master's rights. The Indian institutions of servitude were too deeply rooted for a more direct attack.

And in actual fact these institutions survived for many decades, although the 1843 Act and even earlier legislation undoubtedly had some effect. For instance, the Collector of Canara (who seems to have been much less touched by the anti-slavery movement than most other officials) wrote to the Board in 1844 enclosing a petition from 27 *raiyats* who owned 'garden' lands entirely cultivated by Dheds. Formerly, when slaves fled to Mysore the Superintendent there fined any *raiyat* who employed them Rs. 30/-, but after a circular of 1841 saying that no one could detain the slaves against their will the Mysore Superintendent had not been able to help in returning them to Canara. The *raiyats* of Canara therefore wanted the Government to punish other landowners who employed their 'slaves'.[1] Thus the law was very slow to take effect. Although Act V of 1843 was published throughout Malabar, and the Collector proclaimed that the Courts would not investigate claims to 'slaves' as *janman* or *kanam* or force the 'slave' to work anywhere against his wishes, he also advised the Cherumans that their interest and their duty lay in staying with their master, if he was kind. And in Malabar in 1852 and again in 1855 the Government was informed that there was still a trade in slaves, but nothing was done about it,[2] perhaps because it was felt that the trade was very small.[3] In 1850 the Collector of South Arcot remarked that emigration was hard on the landholder since it 'draws away his agricultural serfts'.[4] Two years after Act V had been embodied in the Indian Penal Code of 1862 the true position was thus described:

> The relation of the agricultural labourer to his employer is for the most part hereditary; although when land changes he does not necessarily pass with it, still when there is a subdivision of the property among the owner's family, it will generally happen that the servants in it are allotted in the proportion of the shares. Thus the agricultural labourer is all save in name a serf.[5]

In some moods the Government was reluctant to recognize the strength of institutional servitude; in 1884 the Revenue Department laid it down

[1] P.B.R., 11.1.1864.
[2] *Malabar Manual*, vol. 1, p. 152.
[3] P.B.R., 5.2.1855; P.B.R., 29.3.1855; P.B.R., 16.4.1855.
[4] Collector, South Arcot to Board of Revenue, P.B.R., 13.5.1850.
[5] Collector, North Arcot to Board of Revenue; P.B.R., 29.1.1864.

that 'slavery having been abolished in British India, a reference to slaves in official correspondence is objectionable and likely to cause misapprehension'.[1] But they could not keep the objectionable word out of official reports and manuals, since the actual conditions of servitude had not everywhere been fundamentally altered. Towards the end of the century a few experiments were made by Collectors and missionary societies to go to the root of the problem by settling the Paraiyans on land of their own, but the Government did not permit these to be carried out in a really liberal manner or on a large scale; and since land was becoming scarce by then it may well have been difficult to do so. Thus the Government refused to permit the Collector of Kistna district to give land free to Paraiyan agricultural labourers; he was allowed to assign them a restricted quantity of land which they could cultivate as tenants, and could buy from the Government after an occupancy of at least ten years.[2] In any case these experiments were of minor significance, and conditions of bondage persisted even into the twentieth century. In 1906 it was thought that Malabar slaves were still 'with their full consent bought and sold and hired out'.[3] When land was sold in Tanjore the deed of sale often transferred to the new owner the debts owed by the *pannaiyal* to the old.[4] *Padaiyal* indentures were still being executed around 1916 in Salem and elsewhere.[5]

Why was it that serfdom proved so durable in practice? Part of the explanation must lie in the burden of indebtedness. Subsisting as he did on the narrowest of margins, it was impossible for the labourer to repay even small advances, and this inescapable bondage was reinforced by the tenacious traditions of serfdom. But such economic factors as indebtedness cannot alone account for the survival of the system of servitude. Indeed it is difficult to see what purely economic justification there was for the eighteenth- or nineteenth-century South Indian serfdom. This was not an economy of large-scale cash crops farming nor one where a labour force had to be raised by compulsion. Whatever the origin of the system, its

[1] P.B.R., 24.6.1884.

[2] Government Order (hereafter G.O.) No. 732. Proceedings of the Revenue Department, 17.10.1894. For the Secretary of State's approval of the Kistna experiment see G.O. No. 3831 (Misc. Series), Proceedings of the Revenue Department, 20.9.1895. Missionary Societies were also given lands on favourable rates of revenue on which they settled Paraiyans; e.g., for Trichinopoly, see P.B.R., 17.8.1901.

[3] *Malabar Manual*, vol. I, p. 153.

[4] R. F. Hemingway, *Tanjore District Gazetteer* (1906), vol. I, p. 111.

[5] See P. J. Thomas and K. C. Ramakrishnan, *Some South Indian Villages: A Resurvey* (Madras, 1940), pp. 174–6, for a description of the *padiyal* system in the twentieth century, and p. 181 for a translation of a '*padiyal* indenture' executed in 1916. A similar form presented for registration in the twentieth century is given in the *Salem Gazetteer*, vol. I, Part I, pp. 245–6.

durability must be explained in social rather than economic terms, in terms of the caste system rather than market needs. And these institutions were deeply rooted in South Indian society. British administration did not fundamentally alter this state of affairs. Moved sometimes by human kindness, sometimes by pressures from home, the administrators did try to change the relations between master and serf. But in reality these were minor adjustments—a far more fundamental attack on the social and economic position of the agricultural labourer was necessary if he was to be emancipated in fact.

VI. OFFICIAL POLICY: LAND TENURES AND LAND REVENUE

The chief administrative and legal levers for bringing about social changes lay not in the reform of 'slavery' but in land policy; and this was abundantly clear to the officials of the time. The point is obvious enough, since India was a largely agricultural society, and since it was from the taxation of land or its products that the Government derived the major portion of its revenue. Indeed revenue was the first concern of the British régime. So overstretched were the finances of the East India Company at the end of the eighteenth century that it was only the profits of the China trade which covered their Indian costs.[1] In the early nineteenth century these costs increased as the Company's territory spread, so that in this period the land revenue was often set at high, almost penal, rates. In South India the British had only to follow the example of their immediate predecessors: Tipu Sultan, for example, collected well over 50 per cent of the gross produce of the soil by way of land revenue and various other taxes.[2]

Apart from this helpful precedent, their predecessors bequeathed the British a host of problems. The political confusions of the eighteenth century had led to a breakdown of the revenue administration: the village registers were in chaos, with unauthorized 'renters' collecting a mass of illegal imposts, and having assumed various rights of ownership.[3] There were few written records of rights to guide the new administrators. And custom was an equally unreliable guide. There were several claimants to the land, ranging from feudal chieftains, through tax collectors, to actual cultivators, each invoking the authority of custom. To begin with, the

[1] H. Furber, *John Company at Work* (Cambridge, Mass., 1948), ch. IX.

[2] It is difficult to be more precise, since so many extra assessments were imposed, many of which could not be actually collected. It is also impossible to be more definite about the proportions actually collected by the ancient Hindu rulers. The traditional share of the ruler was one-sixth to one-fourth of the gross produce, but there is much controversy over whether these rates were ever operative. Sir Thomas Munro, for example, believed that the actual collections were generally much higher, though other administrators, such as Thackeray, took a different view; see Government of India, *Extracts from Records showing the Land Revenue Systems prevailing in India in pre-British Days & Contemporary Practice in Native States* (New Delhi, no date, probably 1913), *passim.*

[3] See, for example, Colonel Fullarton's description of Tinnevelly, written in 1783, quoted by R. Caldwell, *A Political and General History of the District of Tinnevelly in the Presidency of Madras, from the Earliest Period to its Cession to the British Government in A.D. 1801* (Madras, 1881), pp. 107–8.

policy of the new government tended to allow lands to become private property. But who should be proprietor? Four main types of superior tenure-holder confronted them: in the Telugu and some of the Tamil areas, the *zamindar*; in the Telugu and Tamil areas, the *inamdar*; in the Tamil areas, the *mirasdar*; and in Malabar and South Canara, the *janmi* and *mulwargadar*.[1] Recognizing such men as proprietors was only the first step; did they, or did they not, possess the rights which in English land law would accompany ownership in fee-simple?[2] What should be their relationship with the other occupants, if any, of their lands? And at what rates should they be assessed to tax?

In Bengal the Permanent Settlement of Cornwallis had boldly opted for private property in land by turning the *zamindars* into a form of gentry. But the experiment of casting these *zamindars* into the unlikely role of enlightened landlords had been a failure. Moreover, it hit the revenue, since the money which the new landlords had to hand over to the Government was fixed regardless of agricultural performances in the future.[3] Between 1802 and 1805 this system was introduced into the northern districts of Madras, greatly to the disgust of the military men, Read, Munro and Macleod, who had introduced a method of settlements with individual cultivators, and had applied it to Salem, Coimbatore, Madura, Malabar, Canara, Cuddapah, Bellary and Kurnool. *Zamindari* had its advantages in the nothern regions, but it proved difficult to carry farther south. Accordingly, the Government next experimented with a variant of it, in which lands were leased to villages, or in practice to the most well-to-do of the villagers; in effect, this was a sort of mitigated *zamindari* system, and in the nine districts in which it operated the results were not impressive. When Munro returned to Madras as Governor in 1820 he was quick to overthrow it, and to replace it with the system of individual settlements, or *raiyatwari*. This brought to an end the period of experimentation. As Munro left it, the lands in the Presidency were all held either on the tenure of *zamindari* or on *inamdari* or on *raiyatwari*. This last was to predominate, and to become characteristic of South Indian agriculture as a whole.

It is best to deal separately with these systems. The *zamindari* settlement introduced in Madras was generally on the lines of that adopted in Bengal; the 'ancient *zamindars*' were to be assessed at two-thirds of the revenue

[1] As we have seen in Chapter II, these categories were not always mutually exclusive; *mirasdars*, for example, might hold land under a *zamindar*.

[2] H. S. Maine, *Village Communities, East and West* (6th ed., London, 1890), p. 156.

[3] H. R. C. Wright, 'Some Aspects of the Permanent Settlement in Bengal', *Economic History Review*, 1954, vol. VII, No. 2, pp. 204–15.

they collected, while the *haveli* lands[1] in the Northern Circars, as well as *arjari* or Sarkar lands (belonging to the former rulers) in the Tamil areas, were parcelled out into estates and sold to the highest bidders. Under Regulation XXV of 1802, the land revenue (or *peshkash*) to be paid by the *zamindar* was to be fixed in perpetuity, and the *zamindaris* were made both heritable and transferable. The uncultivated arable lands and waste were given to the *zamindars* free of assessment.[2] Between 1801 and 1807 the permanent settlement had been introduced in Chinglepet (the 'Jagir'), the Northern Circars,[3] Salem, Chittoor, the Western and the Southern Poligar[4] estates, Ramnad, Krishnaguri, Dindigal and some other areas. The *peshkash* was generally calculated as two-thirds of half of the gross produce, this being assumed to be the *zamindar*'s collection. There was a great variety of modes in which the *zamindars* collected 'rent' from the cultivators—in cash or kind, as an absolute amount or a proportion of the crops, with or without a host of subsidiary levies—but in general, where it was fixed as a proportion of the crop, the traditional rate was half the gross produce, although there were certain cases where it went as high as two-thirds. Actual collections could rarely have been below the traditional rate and may frequently have been above it. For instance, Munro found in the Bobbili *zamindari* that the cultivator's share had been reduced nominally to one-third and actually to one-fifth of the gross produce on rice lands, and in other parts of Nellore too his share was from one-fourth to one-fifth.[5]

Regulation XXV of 1802 had vested in the *zamindar* 'the proprietory right of the soil', so that he was given powers of distraint and ejectment. The only restriction on him was that under Clause 14 of the Regulation he had to enter into engagements with his *raiyats* and give each *raiyat* a *patta* or *kaul*, defining the amount to be paid by him and explaining every condition of the contract between them. It was believed that these regulations would be sufficient protection against the evils of the *zamindari*

[1] The *haveli* lands belonged to the Muslim rulers; they were leased out to 'renters' who were later given the same rights of ownership as the *zamindars*; Sundararaja Iyengar, *Land Tenures in Madras Presidency*, p. 72.

[2] G.O., 15.10.1799; Vizagapatam Records, vol. 821, pp. 1–49.

[3] The Northern Circars included the districts of Ganjam, Vizagapatam, Godavari and Kistna. When these districts fell into the hands of the British, they consisted mainly of *zamindari* estates or *haveli* lands.

[4] The *poligars* were chieftains in the Tamil districts, particularly Madura and Tinnevelly; see C. S. Srinivasachari, 'The Poligar System in the Tamil Country: Its Origin and Growth', *Proceedings of the Indian Historical Commission*, vol. XI, 1928. See also the Report on Poligars submitted by the Collector of Madura to the Board of Revenue, 20.8.1799; Madura Records, vol. 1126, pp. 61–83.

[5] Arbuthnot, *Minutes of Sir Thomas Munro*, vol. I, pp. 204–5.

system, such as excessive rent collections.[1] But this belief was proved wrong. Accordingly, Regulation IV of 1822 declared that in passing Regulation XXV of 1802 the Government had had 'no intention of authorizing any infringement or limitation of any established rights of any class of its subjects whatever, such rights being properly determinable by judicial investigation only'.[2] The Collector was made the arbitrator between the *zamindar* and the occupant of the land, 'an arrangement which worked with some success until the courts began to admit claims to determine rents on a competitive basis, and to alter the customary methods of sharing the crops. Act VIII of 1865 (Rent Recovery Act), caused much greater confusion by declaring that all contracts for the rent, express or implied, must be enforced.'[3]

In 1883 the Government of India rejected the policy of 'a permanent settlement pure and simple',[4] This was hardly relevant in Madras, where the actual area under *zamindari* had been shrinking and not increasing. In fact, towards the end of the century the Government took steps to stop the breaking up of the estates: Act IV of 1899 authorized the Government, on request, to place estates embarrassed by debt under the Court of Wards, and Act II of 1904 (the Madras Impartible Estates Act) listed 121 such estates.

The *inamdari* system also involved a lighter rate of land revenue although by origin and social status the *inamdar* was far removed from the *zamindar*. When the first surveys and settlements were made, the Survey Officers had to deal with a vast number and variety of *inam* titles, many of which were false. Regulation XXXI of 1802 made it incumbent upon the Collectors to test the validity of these titles, but the rules were interpreted differently in each district,[5] and whether an *inam* was confirmed or not depended largely on the individual Collector or Judge. The arbitrary nature of the *inam* rules, together with the inevitable need to disfranchise some *inams*, led to dissatisfaction. This was brought to a head by the Poli-

[1] P.B.R., 14.4.1825, quoted in Masulipatam Records, vol. 4074, pp. 153–95.

[2] While the rights of *zamindars* were 'bound on the one hand by the obligation to respect whatever rights belonged to tenants, and to pay *peshkash* to Government', they had the same rights as other types of private property, which could be modified only by legislative enactment, and which ought not to be interfered with except on 'very sure grounds of policy'; P.B.R., 17.5.1825, quoted in Masulipatam Records, vol. 4074, pp. 247–58.

[3] *Cambridge History of India*, vol. VI, p. 45.

[4] Despatch No. 24, 28.3.1883; quoted in Baden-Powell, *The Land Systems of British India*, vol. I, p. 345.

[5] Letter from Taylor, Inam Commissioner, to the Revenue Department, 6.7.1859; Madras Government, *Collection of Papers Relating to the Inam Settlement in Madras Presidency* (reprinted 1948), p. 63.

gar rebellion of 1847, protesting against an order passed in 1845 to stay devolution by adoption and to limit private charitable grants to existing lives. A Special Commissioner was appointed in 1858 to validate titles and to enfranchise *inams*. The holder of a personal *inam* could now enfranchise it or convert it into his transferable heritable private property by paying or commuting an annual quit rent.

Raiyatwari, the third type of tenure, differs from *zamindari* and *inamdari* in that it was introduced by the British to take account of the specific conditions in Madras Presidency. As its leading advocate, Munro, remarked:

> It has been unfortunate for the territories under Madras that almost all the earlier discussions regarding Indian land and its owners or occupants were carried on in Bengal. . . . The opinions derived from Bengal regarding zamindars were extended to this Presidency, where in fact they are unknown, excepting in the Northern Circars.[1]

The champions of *raiyatwari* started from the premise that the most effective type of social change would be that which moved along the lines of local circumstances and tradition. As Munro put it:

> The land in most of the provinces under the Madras Presidency is occupied by a vast mass of small proprietors or ryots. . . . These properties are in general very small, but they are of that extent which necessarily results from the limited means of the owners, and the nature of the institutions of the country . . . [As for] the distribution of landed property . . . we ought to take it as we find it, and not attempt upon idle notions of improvement, to force a distribution of it into larger properties where every local circumstance is adverse to its continuance in that state.[2]

Taking things as they found them meant that the British ought to work through local custom, wherever this was practicable, and above all, to work slowly: 'We proceed, in a country of which we know little or nothing, as if we knew everything. . . .'[3]

Nevertheless, there was to be change. Munro meant to widen the market in land, and he wanted to encourage the *raiyats* to improve it, and to look on it as permanent hereditary property. This made it necessary to assess the rents at rates moderate enough to encourage enterprise and fixed enough to shelter them from accident or caprice. Taxation in kind, he thought, would fluctuate too much; taxation in cash based on tradi-

[1] Gleig, *The Life of Sir Thomas Munro*, vol. II, pp. 267–8.

[2] Munro, 'On the State of the Country and the Condition of the People,' 31.12.1824; Arbuthnot, *Minutes of Sir Thomas Munro*, vol. I, pp. 253–4.

[3] *Ibid.*, vol. I, p. 237.

tional rates would be too arbitrary. The best course would be a moderate money assessment, fixed specifically on every field and then formally registered. The assessment itself was calculated as a given percentage of the gross value of the crop; each *raiyat*'s liabilities would be settled from year to year, not because the rate itself varied, but because the *raiyat's* holding might have varied. He should be free to sublet or transfer his property, and to have the additional options of adding to it from the waste, or of abandoning it altogether. While not liable to extra assessment for any improvements on his land, unless these had come through the agency of the Government, nevertheless he should be entitled to ask for remission of liability because of a bad year or other due cause. To all intents and purposes, he should be the proprietor, with all the incentives and less of the risks than the proprietor elsewhere:

> The Government rent should be that which is produced by the ordinary degree of cultivation in ordinary seasons—what the Ryot may easily pay without any labour or expense beyond what is usually employed. Whatever increase of produce may be derived from extra labour or expense should be his own.[1]

Obviously, such a system of assessment was laborious; but in the eyes of its champions, *raiyatwari* had great advantages. Sanctioning a host of small proprietors would recognize the social realities of South India. Linking the assessment with the area cultivated would create an elastic revenue which would grow when the increase of prosperity put more land under the plough. Leaving to the *raiyat* all the surplus which his own efforts had produced would stimulate him to produce further surpluses. Yet although there were such strong arguments in favour of small ownership, more than half a century elapsed before the main features of this ideal were realized.[2]

The history of the *raiyatwari* system is traditionally broken up into three periods: early *raiyatwari* up to 1822, middle *raiyatwari* up to 1855 and late *raiyatwari* from 1855 till the present day. The first settlement of this sort was made by Read in Salem in 1792 and was later extended by Munro and others in the Ceded Districts and the Carnatic districts. The main feature of the settlement was that it was made with the individual cultivator, who, once he accepted (or sometimes, had been forced to accept) a plot of land was not always free to give it up. The land revenue on the plot had to be paid whether he cultivated it or not, although remis-

[1] Madras Presidency to Board of Control; R.D., 21.6.1822, p. 13.
[2] Baden-Powell, *Land Systems of British India*, vol. III, pp. 32–50.

sions were made for bad seasons. The rate of assessment was extremely high; the cultivator often got only a fifth of the crop or even less.[1] Generally, however, the rate was assumed to be 50 per cent of the gross produce, though there were frequent fluctuations in the assessment in these early experimental years. It is impossible to be more precise than this without going into the details for each district; indeed the rates varied within each district. Further, the rates were not always fixed on a general principle, such as that land revenue should amount to 50 per cent of the gross produce. And even when such a principle was adopted modifications were made; for example, 'administrative charges' were deducted before the calculation of the gross produce, or they were deducted from the Government's share of the produce. Actual collections frequently exceeded the recorded collections in the early years of the century, since corrupt officials collected on their own account also. One of the most significant features of the system was that from the beginning the revenue was almost always collected in cash and not in kind.[2]

After the abortive experiments in the *zamindari* settlements and village leases between 1813 and 1822, *raiyatwari* settlements were reintroduced. Now began the so-called middle *raiyatwari* period which lasted up to 1855. During this period the rates of assessment were theoretically 50 per cent of the gross value of the crop on wet (i.e. irrigated) lands, and 33 per cent on dry lands, but here again practice swerved widely from theory. Usually, the traditional rates recorded in the village registers, most of which were well above the theoretical rates, were adopted; the real burden of these rates[3] was increased by the fall in prices over most of this period, as Table 4 shows.

From 1826–7 to 1852–3, the prices of food grains were substantially below those prevailing in 1816–26, except for the famine years 1832–3, 1833–4 and 1838–9. For most of this period when prices were low, the *raiyat* was not allowed to surrender lands, and consequently he had to pay the full revenue on all the lands registered in his name. Free surrender was

[1] P.B.R., 5.1.1818; *East India Papers*, vol. I, p. 940.

[2] In the pre-British period the revenue was frequently collected in kind, particularly in the Tamil districts. For example, in Trichinopoly the ruler took half the gross produce in kind; *East India Papers*, vol. III, p. 529.

[3] The actual assessment for a period would be an absolute amount, determined by the application of a certain rate to estimates of the crop, the resulting figure being qualified by various factors. The methods of estimation and the various factors taken into account—which sometimes included the *raiyat's* caste, his means, and even his health—were determined largely by local custom, so that they differed even within each district. To make generalizations about rates of assessment in middle *raiyatwari* is therefore peculiarly difficult.

Table 4. *Index Numbers of Food Prices, 1825–55* (with 1816–25 prices as base)

1825–6	110	1840–1	74
1826–7	79	1841–2	56
1827–8	68	1842–3	51
1828–9	79	1843–4	50
1829–30	85	1844–5	60
1830–1	71	1845–6	96
1831–2	65	1846–7	91
1832–3	120	1847–8	76
1833–4	150	1848–9	61
1834–5	98	1849–50	61
1835–6	66	1850–1	63
1836–7	83	1851–2	60
1837–8	84	1852–3	60
1838–9	111	1853–4	106
1839–40	82	1854–5	107

Decennial average 1846–55 81·3
Decennial average 1856–65 121·5

Note: The foodgrains covered include rice, *cholum*, *ragi*, *varagu* and *cumbu*.

Source: P. J. Thomas and B. Natarajan, 'Economic Depression in Madras Presidency, 1825–1854', *Economic History Review*, vol. III (1936), pp. 67–75.

later permitted,[1] but the assessments remained high throughout, as well as unsystematic and unequal.

Middle *raiyatwari* was brought to an end in 1855, when systematic surveys and assessments were started, but it was not until 1864 that the principle which in theory is valid even today was laid down: the land revenue should be half of the value of the crop, net of cultivation expenses; and the period of settlement, that is the period during which the assessment should remain unchanged, was fixed at 30 years.[2] The other features which marked the modern system of *raiyatwari* were that the

[1] The rules appear to have varied from district to district. For example, the Board of Revenue, reviewing the report of the Collector of Coimbatore on 21.12.1818, said that the cultivator should have the liberty to give up his lands; *Guide to the Records of the Coimbatore District*, p. 102. Sometimes the *raiyat* was only allowed to relinquish his lands if he gave up some good lands with the bad; *ibid.*, p. 2. Again in Salem the Board ruled that the *raiyat* had no right to pick out the best fields and leave the remainder waste, and this policy held until the 1850's; J. W. B. Dykes, *Salem, an Indian Collectorate* (London, 1853), p. 307.

[2] This period was later left to the discretion of Government. Before 1855 no period of settlement was fixed, and the general belief was that the *raiyatwari* rates were fixed in perpetuity; *Cambridge History of India*, vol. VI, p. 49.

raiyat or registered occupant of the land, could mortgage, sell or gift his land as he pleased, and as long as the transaction was registered, it would be recognized by the Government; he could not be ejected from the land so long as he paid the land revenue; and he could relinquish any portion of his holding to the Government (subject to minor qualifications); these rights were not invariably granted before 1859.

In theory the *raiyat* was the actual cultivator, and he was usually referred to as the tenant of the State; thus there were *zamindari* and *inamdari raiyats*, under the *zamindar* or *inamdar*, as well as the 'Government *raiyats*', that is those paying land revenue direct to the Government. Yet when a market in land developed, and land was used as security for debt, the *raiyat*, as the registered occupant, was often in effect a landlord who hired his land out. But the fiction that the *raiyat* as registered in the Government records was the actual cultivator was so pervasive that during the nineteenth century no laws were passed protecting *raiyatwari* tenants.[1] The theory is particularly odd, in view of the fact that in several districts the settlement had to be made with landholders who were clearly not mere cultivators, and who enjoyed far more of the rights of ownership than the term 'tenant of the State' would imply.

In the *raiyatwari* areas there were, as we have seen in Chapter II, three main types of these superior landholders, the *mirasdar* of the Tamil districts, the *janmi* of Malabar, and the *mulawargadar* of South Canara, but their status, and still more their claims to various rights, differed very widely.

It is almost universally agreed that the *mirasdar* had the right to sell and to mortgage his land, although in joint villages this right may have been qualified. In many instances, however, this nominally saleable land had hardly any value, unless the Government kept the village tank in good repair.[2] *Mirasdars* were supposed to pay for communal services and charities, such as feeding Brahmins, shoring up the village walls and keep-

[1] 'The sub-tenants [i.e., tenants of the *raiyats*, who were themselves "tenants" of the State] in the ryotwari areas of Madras are not protected by any legislative enactment. It is understood that custom or contract can be utilized as proof of occupancy right and powers of transfer, but the cases covered thereby would be exceedingly few'; Government of India, *Note on Land Transfer and Agricultural Indebtedness in India* (not dated, but probably published in 1895), para. 414.

[2] 'From these causes it happens that in Arcot, and still more in districts where the soil is richer, the more substantial ryots are found engaged, not in the cultivation of the wet lands, where Government supplies the water, but in that of dry, where they can improve without the help of Government, and derive the exclusive benefit of every improvement', Sir Thomas Munro: 'Minute on the State of the Country and the Condition of the People', 31.12.1824; Arbuthnot, *Minutes of Sir Thomas Munro*, vol. I, p. 241. For a discussion of why *mirasi* rights were less valuable than those of the *janmi* of Malabar, see Bayley & Hudlestoe, *Papers on Mirasi Right*, pp. 381–2.

ing the temples in good repair.[1] They enjoyed certain allowances (*merais*) in return, and these the British began by recognizing. Thus they agreed to deduct the value of these allowances from the gross output of all cultivated lands paying the Government tax,[2] and they conceded the *mirasdars* the right to favourable rates of land revenue.[3] Perquisites of this sort did not survive long however, and after the first decade or so of the century they were withdrawn. Most of the hereditary rights of ownership claimed by the *mirasdars* went the same way. But in the early part of the century these rights were still important, for at that time the Collectors had still to decide with whom to make the settlements, and this involved deciding whom to recognize as the occupants of the soil.[4] Once conditions had grown stable, and British law had given rights of sale and occupancy to all registered tenants, the line between *mirasdars* and other types of *raiyats* became a distinction without a difference.[5]

This left them with only one important claim—their right to the waste lands of the village. In addition to the barren areas, these claims ranged over fallow land and land which was cultivable, although classed as 'immemorial waste'. In fact the nature of traditional rights was determined by the nature of the waste. The *mirasdars* could cultivate or let fallow lands (*sheykal*), but they could not do so with 'immemorial waste', where, however, they had exclusive rights of quarrying, and the like. The classification of the waste lands was laid down in the village accounts, and it could not be changed without Government permission.[6] But the real point at issue was whether the Government had the right to let the waste lands for cultivation without reference to them. The significance of this was that when waste lands were taken up for cultivation, a lower rate of revenue was charged to compensate for the expense of breaking up the land.[7] No clear policy was followed, though the tendency was of course to arrogate rights to the Government. In 1823 the Board of Revenue held that the division of rights between the Government and the *mirasdars* was

[1] *Standing Information on the Administration of the Madras Presidency* (Madras, 1877), p. 85.

[2] Bayley & Hudleston, *Papers on Mirasi Right*, pp. 375–6.

[3] See, for example, the Settlement Report on Tanjore for 1805.

[4] See, for example, Trichinopoly Records, vol. 3651, pp. 184–97, for a case involving *mirasdars* and renters, in which land had to be sold for revenue arrear in 1811. In 1820 the Board of Revenue decided that where a *mirasdar* claimed a traditional right which he had long relinquished and which he could not satisfactorily establish, the actual occupant should not be displaced; Bayley & Hudleston, *Papers on Mirasi Right*, pp. 415–18, 422.

[5] *Ibid.*, p. 373.

[6] *Ibid.*, p. 184.

[7] P.B.R., 2.5.1831.

uncertain.[1] In 1841 the Court of Directors resolved that the *mirasdars* should be given the first choice of cultivating waste lands: 'We consider that the Government has a clear right to the revenue to be derived from the conversion of waste land into arable, but we at the same time think it preferable that this object should be attained, whenever practicable, without causing the intrusion of strangers into the village community.'[2]

In the West Coast areas of Malabar and South Canara, the revenue system deviated in some respects from that in the other *raiyatwari* districts. These differences reflected differences of social structure. Villages in Malabar and South Canara were not of the standard Indian pattern, for here there was no sharply demarcated area composed of all the village houses. Instead, there was an almost continous stretch of plots, with a family residence in the centre of each. For administrative convenience, groups of plots were aggregated into an administrative unit,[3] but these did not have the corporate life of other Indian villages. Furthermore, these units were not subject to the elaborate survey and settlement, field by field, which marked *raiyatwari* elsewhere.[4] Here, on the contrary, assessments were made on the basis not of the field but of the holding, and they tended to be lighter.

In Malabar the British had to deal with the *janmi*, whose status was even more complex than that of the *mirasdar*. There was a great variety of relations between the *janmi* and the inferior right-holders, including the *kanamdars*. But one thing is clear. In certain types of *kanam* at least, the *kanamdar* had permanent rights of occupancy.[5] In fact it was with the *kanamdars* that the rulers of Mysore had made their revenue settlements, since the *janmis* had all fled. But the *janmis* returned when the British took over the district in 1792, and the British not only made settlements with them but issued a proclamation[6] recognizing them as 'landlords' with the

[1] The Board resolved to ask the Collectors about the rights formerly granted to *mirasdars*, but this was never done; Bayley & Hudleston, *Papers on Mirasi Right*, p. 429.

[2] *Ibid.*, p. 456. In 1856, the Government stilled the Board's fears that to admit the *mirasdars'* rights to waste land would increase the cost of land for railways, etc.; these rights only applied when the land was used for cultivation; *ibid.*, pp. 534–5, 556.

[3] In Malabar these were termed *amishams*, in South Canara *tarfs* or *maganes*.

[4] Even in 1890, 'we have no land register, we have no regular register of gardens, and we have no register of dry lands. In fact, we have nothing whatever reliable about the land revenues, and we know next to nothing about them, ...' Collector of Malabar, 1880; quoted by C. A. Innes, *Gazetteer for Malabar and Anjengo* (Madras, 1908), p. 341.

[5] For a fuller discussion, see Chapter II, *supra*.

[6] When Malabar was annexed it formed part of Bombay Presidency, and a joint commission of officials from Bengal and Bombay was appointed to examine its affairs; it was this Commission which issued the proclamation about the rights of the *janmis* in October 1793. The Commission was wound up and a Principal Collector appointed in 1801.

right to expel the *kanamdars* when their leases expired. Rebellions and unrest followed. These were not assuaged by the revision of the assessment made by the first Collector of Malabar in 1803; indeed, he made matters worse by levying a high assessment and compounded this by raising the rate of exchange between the various coins then in circulation against the revenue payer. In 1805 a new settlement was put into effect under which 33⅓ per cent of the gross produce on wet lands was allowed to the cultivator for expenses and his 'profits'; of the balance 60 per cent was paid to the Government and 40 per cent to the *janmi*. On garden lands the cultivator, Government and the *janmi* got 33⅓ per cent each. Thus no provision was made for the *kanamdar* on the ground that his rights were secured by the terms of the mortgage.

At that time this did not matter very much to him because the settlement was not stringently put into effect (partly because prices were low), and because the *janmis* were very heavily in debt to the *kanamdars*. But in 1817 the assessment was reduced,[1] and in 1832 prices rose sharply, so that the *janmis* were enabled to wipe out their debts. They were also beginning to realize that under the new system they were given full rights of ownership. The *kanamdars* were then brought face to face with the fact that under the new legal and administrative system they had lost their customary rights. Not only did the usual litigation follow; many of the *kanamdars* were Mappillahs or Muslim converts who had obtained their rights at the time of Hyder Ali's conquest,[2] and there was a series of riots, in which one cannot disentangle the religious from the economic motive. But apart from the Malabar Tenants' Compensation Act of 1900 which provided for compensation for improvements made by the tenant, no action was taken to protect the rights of the *kanamdars*.

Such was the hierarchy of groups which in 1800 were concerned with winning a living from the soil. In fashioning a revenue policy to match this structure, the British made two important decisions. The first was to extend and to codify rights of ownership. They did so in order to regulate claims intolerably vague and in flagrant contradiction with the principle of *nulle terre sans seigneur*. Admittedly, the bias of their policy was to whittle down the rights of the *mirasdars*, but that was because *mirasi* claims and Government claims to the waste could hardly co-exist. But in the *zamindari* areas they confirmed the *zamindar*'s claims to the right to own and the right to evict. In fact throughout the nineteenth century the

[1] Not only were the *raiyatwari* rates in Malabar lower than in the other districts, but not all the produce was assessed; J. Sullivan, *Report on the Provinces of Malabar and Canara, 1841* (Calicut, 1916), pp. 1–2.

[2] *Malabar Manual*, vol. 1, p. 616.

courts held that the onus of proving the right to occupancy was on the tenant.[1] In Malabar and South Canara too, the effect of their decisions was to settle on the 'landlords' firmer rights than they had previously enjoyed.

What was chiefly entailed by their settlements was a reshuffling of the upper levels of the tenurial hierarchy. Both *zamindari* and *raiyatwari* re-aligned the position of rent-collectors, superior landholders and sub-proprietors. While it is true that the simple cultivator occasionally lost certain traditional rights, he probably also gained others that previously he had not held at all, or had not held securely, such as the right to buy and sell land. But none of the changes made during the first half of the century impinged on the landless labourer at the bottom of the social scale.

Towards the end of middle *raiyatwari*, the stiff rates of land revenue brought a good deal of hardship to the *raiyats*. The bleak tone of the Collectors' reports in the early eighteen fifties finally stirred the Government into a change of outlook. In 1853–4 there was a general enquiry into the rates of assessment, and the hardships it revealed had the effect of bringing Madras to the clear attention of London. New settlements were introduced in every district after 1855, though in some districts they did not come into operation until the 1880's. The dates of these new settlements and the principles on which they were made are set out in Table 5.

In nearly every district the basis for the new settlement was that the collection would be 50 per cent of the net produce, though even here the rule was not uniform—in some *taluks* of South Arcot, even after the new assessment of 1861–2, revenue rates were approximately two-thirds of the net produce. Again in Masulipatam in Kistna district the new assessment of 1866–7 approximated to one-third of the gross rather than half the net produce, and amounted to considerably more than half the net produce on poorer soil. In such cases there was no material change in the incidence per acre compared to early *raiyatwari*, but as a general rule there was a reduction in the incidence per acre, particularly in the Telugu districts. The real relief was afforded by the fall in prices. The settlements were generally made on the basis of prices prevailing from 1845 to 1861, or in some cases (as in Trichinopoly) on the basis of average prices over the last 60 years, but prices throughout the second half of the century were very much higher than in the first half. Thus, the average price of rice from 1819 to 1823, when prices reached their peak in the first half of the century, was Rs. 1·54 per *seer*,[2] whereas from 1864 to 1900 prices fell below Rs. 3 per

[1] Government of India, *Note on Land Transfer and Agricultural Indebtedness in India* (n.d., probably 1895).

[2] 1 *seer* equals about 2·057 lb.

Table 5. *Settlements in the Late* Raiyatwari *Period*

District	Date of old settlement	Rate	Date of new settlement	Rate	Increase/ decrease in total demand
North Arcot			1881	½ N.P.	plus 12·6%
South Arcot	1801	45–70% G.P. on wet land	1861–2	⅔ N.P.	plus 4%
Chinglepet	1803	Half average out-turn of last ten years, less 20 per cent for expenses	1875–9	½ N.P.	plus 12·3%
Coimbatore	1801–2	½ G.P. on wet, ⅖ G.P. on dry	1881–2		plus 5%
Cuddapah			1878		plus 7·1%
Ganjam*		⅘ G.P. on wet, ½ G.P. on dry under the original *zamindari* settlement; but these reduced by the *raiyatwari* settlement	1878 and 1883		plus 14·2% *in two taluks*
Godavari			1862–5	½ N.P.	plus 26·6%
Masulipatam			1866–7	⅓ G.P. on wet, much more than ½ N.P. on dry	plus 20·3%
Guntur			1873–4	½ N.P.	
Kurnool			1864–79	½ N.P.	minus 9·9%
Nellore	1801	55% G.P.	1873–5	½ N.P.	plus 9·6%
Salem			1871–4	½ N.P. minus 10%	minus 9·3%
Tinnevelly	1801	½ G.P., but this was reduced	1873–8	½ N.P. minus 10% for poor areas	plus 6·4%
Trichinopoly			1864–5	½ N.P. minus 20%	minus 7·7%

Source: compiled from *Manual of the Administration of the Madras Presidency* (Madras, 1885), vol. II, pp. 406–19.

Abbreviations: G.P. Gross Produce
N.P. Net Produce

Notes to Table 5:

1. It is sometimes impossible to summarize the old settlement rates, since they varied so widely from one part of a district to another.

2. It is sometimes impossible to summarize in one figure the new settlement rates for the same reason and at other times because the work of resettlement was still incomplete.

3. 'Old settlement' figures relate generally to the original *raiyatwari* settlements by the British. These rates were often reduced, and the last column compares the new settlement not to the old settlement but to the total revenue demand just before the new settlement.

* At the time this calculation was made full settlement rates had not been imposed.

seer only in seven years, and from 1883 onwards were generally well above that level. Price movements are set out in Table 6.

On the other hand, the new settlements did not immediately benefit the cultivator, since with more systematic surveys a larger area was brought within the revenue net and the immediate result of the settlement was almost always to increase the total demand, except in Salem, where the demand was reduced by 9·3 per cent by the new settlements of 1870–1 and 1873–4, and in Trichinopoly and Kurnool.

Table 6. *Average Annual Prices of Common Rice, 1809–1901*
(Rs. per *maund*)*

Year	Price	Year	Price
1809–13	1·47	1880	2·803
1819–23	1·53	1881	2·594
1828–32	1·33	1882	2·780
1841–53	1·13	1883	3·329
1861	2·666	1884	3·396
1862	2·866	1885	3·902
1863	2·943	1886	3·779
1864	3·055	1887	3·303
1865	3·536	1888	3·282
1866	3·770	1889	3·708
1867	4·305	1890	4·012
1868	2·900	1891	4·659
1869	3·187	1892	5·064
1870	2·003	1893	4·723
1871	3·347	1894	4·380
1872	2·892	1895	4·226
1873	2·399	1896	4·284
1874	2·797	1897	5·005
1875	2·501	1898	4·948
1876	3·014	1899	3·898
1877	4·884	1900	4·779
1878	4·751	1901	4·593
1879	3·613		

* *maund* = 82·28 lb.

These are prices for the 'second sort of rice'; famine years have been included.

Prices before 1861 have been calculated from S. Srinivasa Raghavaiyangar, *Memorandum on the Progress of the Madras Presidency during the Last Forty Years of British Administration* (Madras, 1893) p. 4.

Prices from 1861 onwards are from the series *Prices and Wages in India*, published by the Director General of Commercial Intelligence and Statistics.

These increases brought critical despatches from London. At first this was no more than a retrospective scolding: 'It is greatly to be regretted that a system originally designed . . . in a humane and liberal spirit . . . should have been permitted by the controlling local authorities so long to be subverted in practice. . . .'[1]

Two years later London permitted itself some self-congratulation on the working of the new system:

> In nearly every instance the reduction of the land tax has resulted in a considerable increase in the cultivation, and a consequent addition to the revenue, while over-assessed Ryots have been relieved from taxation to the amount of Rs. 25,95,423. The success of the liberal system of taxation which has thus been commenced is most encouraging. . . .[2]

In the decade following 1855, when the period of late *raiyatwari* was being ushered in by an elaborate process of resurveying and reassessing, London and Madras did not see eye to eye on a number of points. Should there be any temporary remissions? Should there be remissions on fallow land? The Presidency thought not, the India Office disagreed.[3] Should the new settlements give the Government a share of the gross produce or of the net? Madras wanted the former, London the latter.[4] But the economic upturn of the eighteen sixties brought them into a satisfying unanimity on the main issues of policy. It was reported that 1864 had seen the revenue increase by Rs. 20 lakhs, and the cultivation extend by 621,720 acres. From these figures, both London and Madras drew the same conclusion: '. . . On the whole there is sufficient evidence to show that the condition of the agricultural labourers particularly, and of the lower classes of the people generally, is improving.'[5]

But this complacency was not to last. The new settlement policy had tightened up the procedure for collection of revenue. Until 1858 attachment for property for arrears had been regarded as a sign of inefficient administration, but Act XXXIX of that year had encouraged this by simplifying the procedure. Act II of 1864 lowered the interest on arrears, but it also greatly increased the Government's powers to sell land once it had been attached. These new powers of coercion were quickly put to use, and this proved disastrous for some of the poorer *raiyats* (see Table 7).

[1] President of the Board of Control to Madras, Revenue, No. 38, 22.10.1857; Revenue Despatches from India Office, preserved in the Public Record Office, Madras (hereafter I.O.), 31.

[2] Secretary of State to Madras, Revenue, No. 12, 26.3.1859; I.O., 33.

[3] Secretary of State to Madras, Revenue, No. 22, 29.3.1860; I.O., 34.

[4] Secretary of State to Madras, Revenue, No. 7, 24.2.1864; I.O., 38.

[5] Secretary of State to Madras, Revenue, No. 4, 25.1.1865; I.O., 39.

Table 7. *Revenue Demand and Arrears, 1855–6 to 1872–3*

Year	Arrears for which coercive processes issued (Rs.)	Amount realized by sales for arrears (Rs.)	Total revenue demand in Presidency (Rs.)	Col. 2: Col. 4 (%)	Col. 3: Col. 4 (%)
1	2	3	4	5	6
1855–6	2,73,191	14,776	370,39,916	·13	·04
1856–7	4,01,625	25,791	386,03,010	1·04	·06
1857–8	2,11,223	8,327	373,02,516	·56	·02
1858–9	3,37,068	13,901	411,80,881	·81	·03
1859–60	2,51,989	31,172	404,25,406	·62	·07
1860–1	2,35,325	34,040	381,11,261	·61	·08
1861–2	2,09,518	21,337	395,41,020	·52	·07
1862–3	2,38,820	44,237	408,12,217	·58	·1
1863–4	3,56,376	48,510	408,61,096	·86	·11
1864–5	2,78,447	31,880	398,57,442	·7	·08
1865–6	3,87,225	65,709	406,22,384	·95	·16
1866–7	5,00,190	81,219	423,05,876	1·18	·19
1867–8	6,71,827	1,33,631	404,75,405	1·66	·33
1868–9	6,70,981	1,05,490	427,54,042	1·57	·25
1869–70	8,56,255	1,49,966	446,81,927	1·92	·37
1870–1	18,87,286	3,04,179	457,76,283	4·12	·66
1871–2	24,21,206	3,97,345	448,78,526	5·39	·83
1872–3	25,08,606	4,52,789	453,38,597	5·58	·99

Source: P.B.R., 1.4.1874.

Madras saw nothing ominous about these figures. The increase in forced sales simply reflected a necessary change from the old 'persuasive methods'. Fortunately, 'what with roads and railways and high prices and spreading education, the people are getting richer every day, the agricultural stock is improving, and the population is increasing rapidly and living less abstemiously'.[1]

Indebtedness seemed to be on the increase, to be sure; but 'we look to the improvement in village institutions as the best means of preventing the accumulation of arrears'.[2] But, unaffected by this hopefulness, the India Office began to scrutinize the new settlements more sharply. The settlement in Cuddapah they felt 'reluctant' to sanction,[3] the new system in Kistna made them feel 'anxiety'.[4] By 1875 the two governments came

[1] P.B.R., 1.4.1874.
[2] Governor, Madras to Secretary of State, 16.3.1875; R.D., 61.
[3] Secretary of State to Madras, Revenue, No. 19, 26.8.1873; I.O., 48.
[4] Secretary of State to Madras, Revenue, No. 5, 31.3.1874; *ibid.*

to a sharp clash. The Secretary of State had enjoined the Governor to use 'great caution' in distraining;[1] and this exhortation so irritated the Council at Madras that they overrode Lord Hobart, the Governor, and refused to publish the dispatch, since it seemed to suggest that such caution had been lacking hitherto, and since 'to suspend the rigour of the law . . . is likely to lead to evasions and corrupt dealings'.[2]

The great famine of 1876 took the edge off this controversy, since it forced the Government into a headlong policy of remissions to stave off disaster. But by 1880 London was uneasily noting that attachments were on the increase again, and that whereas in 1874–5, 336,000 persons had been coerced, by the end of the decade the number had increased more than sixfold.[3] The criticisms continued. In 1881 London pointed out that less land was now occupied than before the famine, but that the revenue demand was higher.[4] The statistics were becoming ominous once more. In 1878–9 the sum collected in revenue and arrears was Rs. 43 lakhs greater than the current demand; the following year it was still Rs. 13 lakhs greater, and in 1880–1 Rs. 8·66 lakhs greater.[5] In the two years 1879–81 the property of nearly 278,000 persons was sold to pay off arrears,[6] and in 1881–2 the property of 126,704 persons more.[7] In the seven districts of the Presidency which had suffered most from the famine, the acreage under cultivation had gone down by 11·7 per cent.[8] All this stirred the Earl of Kimberley into a vehemence unusual in the correspondence of the India Office:

'The facts disclosed . . . cause me grave uneasiness, and it does not seem to me that their full significance is apparent to Your Excellency's Government . . . the condition of the agricultural classes throughout a large part of your Presidency calls for the most serious attention . . . and [I must] express the hope that you will be able to take such measures as may result in a great and speedy improvement.'[9]

The improvement took place, at least at the level of policy-making. By the eighteen nineties, it was the accepted doctrine that the Government was prepared to sanction a greater elasticity in revenue collection and a general reduction of assessments in cases of local difficulty.[10]

[1] Secretary of State to Madras, Revenue, no No., 3.12.1874; I.O., 49.
[2] Governor, Madras to Secretary of State, 16.3.1875; R.D., 61.
[3] Secretary of State to Madras, Revenue, No. 13, 26.2.1880; I.O., 54.
[4] Secretary of State to Madras, Revenue, No. 9, 10.3.1881; I.O., 55.
[5] Proceedings of the Revenue Department, No. 7988, 22.11.1883.
[6] Proceedings of the Revenue Department, No. 1092, 25.1.1883.
[7] Proceedings of the Revenue Department, No. 7988, 22.11.1883.
[8] Proceedings of the Revenue Department, No. 2586, 29.3.1883.
[9] Quoted in the Proceedings of the Revenue Department, No. 1092, 25.1.1883.
[10] Government of India, *Papers Regarding the Land Revenue System of British India*, pp. 16–17.

What were the effects of *raiyatwari* on the agrarian structure of the Presidency? The soils of South India were poor, and so were its farming practices. This was pre-eminently the region which stood most in need of a moderate system of assessment, yet the financial strains of the Madras government had kept the rates high. Munro had deplored this, and so had many of the Collectors after him, and the assessment policy of late *raiyatwari* had nominally been meant to scale it down. But, as we have seen, actual collections were often raised.

Apart from the effects of high assessments, the *raiyatwari* system had other consequences. In Madras the *raiyat* was allowed to pick and choose amongst his fields those he would keep and those he would abandon. A good season would induce all sorts and conditions of *raiyats* to take up land, often more land than they could properly cultivate. The Government made no enquiries about their resources, took no security, exacted no penalty for early abandonment. Moreover, its procedural rules encouraged inefficiency, because in the allotting of lands preference was given to relatives of the last tenant, to neighbours, to fellow-villagers, any of whom would take up the option rather than allow strangers to enter. Between them, the rules of the Government and the xenophobia of the *raiyats* made it as difficult as possible for vigorous farming entrepreneurs (not that there was a plentiful supply of these) to get a footing.[1]

Since the resources of these *raiyatwari* farmers were so meagre and their situation so precarious, the result was a high turnover in occupancies. As the Madras Government admitted:

> 'Whilst prices are rising every ryot who has land is eager to invest all his savings in more land, and to forestall other applicants for the fields surrounding his farm if they are unoccupied. . . . If regulations were devised for preventing men without means from taking up small pieces of land, the extent to which coercive processes are used might be reduced. . . .'[2]

But the Board of Revenue was unwilling to do this, for it would discriminate against the small man. From this point of view, the same statistics of eviction which alarmed London so much seemed to Madras a healthy sign. Every eviction put more land on the market, and it gave another small *raiyat* a chance. One man's loss might be another man's luck. Table 8 shows how the increase of coercion could lead to an increase of turnover, during a time of high prices.

[1] H. A. D. Phillips, *A Blacker Pamphlet; or an Attempt to Explain the Severity of the late Famine and the Causes of the Poverty of the Madras Ryot* (Madras, 1878), pp. 4–5, 15.
[2] P.B.R., 1.4.1874.

Table 8. *Attachments and Sales of Property for Arrears, 1855–6 to 1872–3*

Year	Estimated value of property attached for arrears (Rs.)	Estimated value of property sold for arrears (Rs.)	Col. 3: Col. 2 (%)
1	2	3	4
1855–6	1,25,064	12,761	10·2
1856–7	1,37,382	16,313	11·8
1857–8	1,38,917	6,994	5·0
1858–9	2,86,730	11,634	4·1
1859–60	2,00,188	24,594	12·2
1860–1	1,93,116	24,097	12·4
1861–2	1,59,856	19,533	12·2
1862–3	1,81,692	38,667	21·3
1863–4	2,80,467	41,322	14·7
1864–5	2,82,838	29,124	10·2
1865–6	3,00,997	63,346	21·0
1866–7	3,23,953	71,394	22·0
1867–8	4,30,342	1,15,688	26·8
1868–9	4,58,997	98,853	21·5
1869–70	5,89,192	1,50,185	25·4
1870–1	13,77,678	2,91,440	21·1
1871–2	16,63,998	4,22,294	25·3
1872–3	15,08,715	4,52,789	30·0

Source: P.B.R., 1.4.1874.

Nevertheless, the Madras Government saw the need to check this high turnover of tenancies. Not only did they tighten the screw on revenue defaulters, but they also gradually increased the charges on the waste. By 1874–5 the *raiyats* were being assessed at Rs. 25,38,251 on 2,211,777 acres of waste and allowed only Rs. 2,66,552 of remission for them. In the following year—the eve of the famine—Rs. 23,55,748 were demanded as revenue for a waste of 2,229,719 acres.[1] The administrators saw this as a policy of fiscal prudence. 'This,' they observed, '. . . has, to some extent, checked rash speculation.'[2] But once the famine broke out, what seemed prudent to the men in Fort St George seemed punitive to the *raiyats* in the districts, where dispossession and death marked the last years of the eighteen seventies.

The high eviction rate of the years immediately before and after the

[1] Phillips, *A Blacker Pamphlet*, p. 3.
[2] P.B.R., 1.4.1874.

great famine leads to a second question. To what extent can the changes in the *raiyatwari* system be held responsible for the growth of landless labour in South India? When they scrutinized the reports from five of the famine districts, the India Office suspected that many persons were being transformed from landholders into labourers, and that this was 'clearly much aggravated by the way in which the revenue was collected'.[1] No doubt there were cases in which this was so. But the connection was much more indirect and uncertain than it appeared. In the first place, not all the tenants on the eve of the famine were established landholders. In 1874 the Board of Revenue had noted that:

'Even day-labourers have indulged in the hope of becoming farmers, and the . . . rules codified in fasli 1273 [1863–64] have allowed them to get land as a matter of right in cases where their applications would formerly have been often rejected on the ground that the applicants were without means.'[2]

In the second place, suits for eviction were sometimes only moves in a game whose end had little or nothing to do with driving tenants off the soil. A suit for eviction might arise solely out of a dispute between rival claimants for land; filing the suit might be no more than a manœuvre for establishing the validity of one's title. Thirdly, eviction orders applied to leases, not to persons, and it was not unusual for one tenant to hold more than one lease. Fourthly, many eviction decrees were not executed. Lastly, eviction did not necessarily drag a tenant down to the status of a landless labourer, for a man evicted from one piece of land might simply shift to another. The statistics of evictions conceal many cases which involved no more than a reshuffling of tenancies.[3] For all these reasons, the growth of landlessness cannot be simply correlated with the growth in evictions. In any case, the coercive policy, for all its harshness, was short-lived. In Malabar, for example, the eviction suits filed, which had been some 1,800 per annum at the end of the eighteen seventies, had dropped to a total of 1,700 for the quinquennium 1900–4.[4]

Towards the end of the century the incidence of land revenue in real terms may have been reduced by the rise in prices. But it remains true that the burdens of British revenue administration were inordinately heavy,

[1] Secretary of State to Madras, Revenue, No. 10, 23.2.1882; I.O., 56.

[2] P.B.R., 1.4.1874

[3] For an application of this reasoning to one district of the Presidency see T. W. Shea, 'The Land Tenure Structure of Malabar and its Influence upon Capital Formation in Agriculture' (unpublished thesis presented for the degree of Ph.D., University of Pennsylvania, 1959), p. 158.

[4] This is also related to the passing of the First Malabar Compensation Act for Tenants in 1887 and its revision in 1899; *Gazetteer for Malabar and Anjengo*, vol. 1, p. 237.

and had serious social consequences. In Malabar, Logan found a correlation between rates of eviction and heavy rates of crime.[1] And there is no doubt that the revenue system accentuated the drift towards greater fragmentation of holdings.[2] Madras was by far the most heavily taxed Presidency in India; it was computed in 1854 that for every 100,000 of the population, the land revenue was Rs. 10,05,455 in Bengal, Rs.16,71,965 in Bombay and Rs. 23,12,465 in Madras, and this difference almost certainly continued throughout the century.[3]

Nor were these tendencies confined to the *raiyatwari* areas: in the latter half of the nineteenth century, the *raiyatwari* cultivator may well have had to pay less than the *zamindari raiyat*,[4] particularly since the latter's occupancy rights were not guaranteed by law.[5]

[1] Government of Madras, *Report of the Malabar Special Commission, 1881–82* (Madras, 1882), vol. 1, para. 311.

[2] This was already apparent before the famine. In 1862 1,864,026 tenures were held on single titles, and 262,009 on joint titles. By 1872 1,946,929 tenures were held on single titles, and 445,135 on joint titles; P.B.R., 1.4.1874.

[3] Raju, *Economic Conditions in Madras Presidency, 1800–1850*, p. 50.

[4] The gap between the *zamindari* and the *raiyatwari* rates appears to have widened sharply in the twentieth century; in 1938 the Andhra Pradesh Congress Committee found that *zamindari* rates were four to five times higher than the *raiyatwari* rates; A. V. Raman Rao, *Economic Development of Andhra Pradesh, 1766–1957* (Bombay, 1958), p. 271.

[5] It was only towards the end of the century that the Madras High Court started to recognize the permanent occupancy rights of *zamindari* tenants.

PART II

VII. LAND AND POPULATION

One of the crucial factors in the growth of landless labour is obviously the pressure of population on land as measured by changes in the land-labour ratio, this basic ratio being qualified by changes in technique and in crop patterns. But there are, of course, several other very important factors to be considered. As we have seen, the land revenue was particularly important in Madras; when the rate was very heavy, it may well have induced some cultivators to throw up their lands and to work as agricultural labourers. Another important factor may have been the decline of village industries or other avenues of employment. No quantitative information is available on this up to 1870 but thereafter the Censuses do contain some data on the change in the proportion of the agricultural population to total population; this will be discussed in Chapter X. Again changes in the terms of trade between agricultural and other commodities and changes in exports of agricultural commodities outside Madras were obviously relevant—particularly after the opening of the Suez Canal in 1869.[1] But foreign trade in agricultural commodities is not of much significance here since the quantities exported were a small proportion of the total output of the Presidency.

The first estimate of population for Madras (in the British period at least) was made in 1687[2] but we need go back only as far as 1802 when the population was estimated at 9·57 millions.[3] Estimates of population, including figures for each district, are also available for 1823, 1827, 1830 and 1839. These were compiled from the figures sent in by the Collectors and are likely to be far more reliable than the estimate for 1802, which included 'in some cases calculations of population based on comparative revenues'.[4] More and better census data are available for Madras than for any other part of India in this period,[5] but even these censuses suffered from a number of grave defects, particularly the first two returns. Instead of taking an actual count of the inhabitants, the population was some-

[1] For example, the exports of foodgrains from India went up from less than 0·65 million tons in 1867–8 to 1·25 million tons in 1879–80. See B. M. Bhatia, *Famines in India—1850–1945* (Bombay, 1963), p. 38.

[2] In 1687 the Court of Directors estimated the population of Madras, i.e. of Fort St George and the surrounding villages, at 300,000; *Census Report, 1931*, vol. 1, p. 1.

[3] General Reports of the Board of Revenue, vol. 7, p. 77.

[4] *Census Report, 1931*, vol. 1, p. 1.

[5] For the various estimates of all-India population before 1871, see Kingsley Davis, *The Population of India and Pakistan* (Princeton, 1951), p. 25.

times estimated by applying a certain ratio of persons per house to the number of houses. This method naturally led to grave mistakes. The Collector of Salem felt that the fall in population between 1827 and 1830 could be explained only by the fact that the 1827 estimate used a ratio of $4\frac{1}{2}$ persons per house, while the 1830 Census, based on a count of heads, showed the ratio to be $3\frac{1}{8}$.[1] Where such a ratio is applied, it is of course difficult to decide in which direction the figures would be biased. But when an actual count of heads was taken the estimates probably erred on the low side, since it would have been difficult for the enumerators to obtain accurate figures of the female population. Other errors in classification, such as the omission of the figures for soldiers from the population figures, must also be noted.

Figures for certain districts were particularly subject to error. These included the districts where there were extensive *zamindari* areas, and Malabar and Canara, where the revenue administration was less detailed than in the other *raiyatwari* districts; and finally the areas where there was great unrest. For example, 'it is doubtful whether any figure for Ganjam before 1840 would be anything but a guess so far as the interior parts are concerned, so constant was the preoccupation with internal commotion, rebellion and zamindari truculence'. Again, for Canara the Collector himself stated in 1830, while forwarding the census figures, 'it is evident however that little confidence can be placed in such an account as this'.[2]

From 1851–2 onwards, four quinquennial censuses were taken on a more systematic basis. Not only were better administrative arrangements made, although the figures continued to be collected by the revenue officials, but more details were asked for, so that for the first time separate figures for agricultural population were given.[3] In 1856 nearly all the Collectors reported that the previous Censuses were fairly accurate—apart from Ganjam, where the returns were still 'very approximate', and Madura, where the returns for Madura city and one other town were serious underestimates, since 'respectable Hindus' would not disclose the size of their families; and on the other hand, the census return for Vellore appeared to be an overestimate.[4]

The figures for the rural districts were generally much more accurate than those for the cities before 1881; the figures for the *zamindari* tracts were also bad. The returns for Madras city were particularly inaccurate, as

[1] P.B.R., 18.11.1830.

[2] Collector, Canara to Board of Revenue; P.B.R., 16.9.1830.

[3] Details of the forms, instructions to enumerators, etc., are given in *Census Report, 1871*.

[4] Proceedings of the Revenue Department, 12.12.1856, No. 66, and 1.7.1856, Nos. 40 and 41.

the figures in Table 9 will show.[1] It is hardly likely that the population of Madras city fell steadily from 600,000 in 1801 to 379,552 in 1871. The figures given in the table are for those years for which figures of the total population of the Presidency are also available, but estimates made for other years show a much lower population for the city. Thus the Collector of Madras estimated the population in 1808 at 275,000, and in 1818 the population within the jurisdiction of the Supreme Court was stated to be 339,000.[2] The 1823 figure was apparently based on actual enumeration, but even so it was too high. The Census Commissioner for 1871 felt that the enumerators in 1823 had probably been paid by the number of persons they were supposed to enumerate; he calculated that on the basis of 8 people per house (which was the 1871 ratio) the population would have been around 237,000,[3] which he felt was a likely figure, but which appears, if the former estimates of population are taken into account, too low. After 1823 the next actual enumeration made for Madras city was in 1871; an estimate made in 1850 had been adopted in 1852 as well as in the later three quinquennial censuses.

From 1871 onwards decennial censuses were taken on an all-India scale and with increasing elaboration. It is clear that from 1802 onwards the accuracy of the censuses improved more or less steadily but it is not so obvious that inaccuracy generally implied underestimation, as has been suggested.[4] It is true that the early censuses probably tended to underestimate the female population. Even in the 1851–2 Census the Government felt that the number of women was understated.[5] This is perhaps borne out by the fact that the male population was 51 per cent of the total in 1823 and 1851–2; just over 50 per cent in 1871, and 49 per cent in 1881, 1891 and 1901. On the other hand, a source of error in the opposite direction is the gross overestimation of the population of Madras city in the pre-1871 Censuses, but this error is of too small a magnitude to counteract the errors making for underestimation, except for the period 1801–23. The overestimation of the population of Madras city in 1801 is particularly large. Assuming that the population of the city was 200,000 in 1801 and 350,000 in 1823, the annual increase in the population of the Presidency over the period would have been 1·2 per cent instead of 1·6 per cent. (The

[1] See Statistical Appendix to this chapter.

[2] H. Dodwell, *Report on the Madras Records* (Madras, n.d.), p. 60.

[3] *Census Report on the Town of Madras, 1871*, p. 13.

[4] 'Continuing improvement is observable from 1802 onwards in closeness of enumeration and . . . unusual accretions in populations were rather to be expected at each census'; *Census Report, 1931*, vol. I, p. 2.

[5] Chief Secretary, the Government of Madras, to Board of Revenue, 19.7.1852; P.B.R., 18.10.1852.

population in 1801 was also inflated by the inclusion of Seringapatam and North Canara.)

The likelihood of inaccuracy, or its broad magnitude, cannot be deduced even from a scrutiny of the figures for each district, since as a result of wars, epidemics, famines and mass emigration to neighbouring states, sudden changes in population were possible. For example in 1810 and 1811 an unspecified epidemic fever is estimated to have killed over 5 per cent of the population of Madura, Coimbatore and Tinnevelly.[1] Another factor making for changes in the district, but not in the overall figures, was the changes in district boundaries. The major change was the reformation of the districts of Rajahmundry, Masulipatam and Guntur into the two districts of Godavari and Kistna in 1859.

The most serious fluctuations were, of course, due to the famines; in fact many of the epidemics followed and were caused by them. Except in the 1880's, there was no decade of the nineteenth century which was untouched by famines or scarcity, and there was no district unaffected. Even Malabar suffered from the scarcity of 1865, and Tanjore from the great famine of 1804–7 which covered all the southern districts and even Nellore.[2] South Canara, although less immune to famines than Malabar, was also one of the better-off districts in this respect. The worst affected were the dry Telugu districts, and in particular Bellary and Anantapur. From 1799 to 1834 there were several famines, the most severe occurring in 1799, 1804–7, 1811–13 and 1824. Typical of these is the report from the Collector of Chinglepet in 1824: 'a crowd still covers the face of the country seeking food and numbers die daily along the public roads'.[3] But although they were widespread, these outbreaks caused less destruction, and probably less mortality, than the famine of 1833–4 which ravaged Guntur. In this one area alone the loss of life was estimated at one-third to one-half of the total population, and the loss of cattle at nearly two-thirds.[4] Although the famine was severest in this area, it was not confined to it; all the northern districts were affected. Between 1834 and 1865 there was no severe or widespread famine, although there were instances of severe scarcity in 1837 in six districts, in 1839 in Bellary, in 1847 in Coimbatore and Madura, in 1854 in Bellary again. In 1865–6 there was another

[1] Revenue letter to Fort St George, 6.6.1814; *East India Papers*, vol. 1, p. 546. For the cholera epidemic in Coimbatore of 1827 which killed 2·4 per cent of the population, see P.B.R., 4.11.1830; for the smallpox epidemic in Canara of 1833, see P.B.R., 23.9.1833.

[2] The Collector reported on 25.12.1804 that there was a great scarcity of grain in some districts and he proposed to ban exports to Ceylon; Tanjore Records, vol. 3214, p. 218.

[3] Chinglepet Records, vol. 3845, pp. 121 and 134.

[4] Settlement Report for 1833–4; P.B.R., 11.6.1835.

famine which covered a very widespread area, in particular the East Coast north of Madras, but this was only the prelude to the worst famine of the nineteenth century, that of 1876–8, which covered the whole of the Presidency, apart from the districts of Ganjam, Vizagapatam, Godavari, Tanjore, Malabar and South Canara. An area of 74,000 square miles with a population of 36 millions was affected; on an average, three-fourths of a million were on daily famine relief for a period of 22 months, and the loss of population was estimated at nearly 4 millions.[1] There were again severe famines in 1896–7 and from 1898 to 1900 in the Telugu districts.[2]

These catastrophes were not always reflected in changes in the rate of growth of population; in fact it was remarked after 1876–8 that the recovery of the population had been exceptionally rapid. But in general the very severe famines did slow down the rate of growth of population, as the following table will show. The figures as they stand (see Table 9) show increases in population in every inter-censal period, apart from the periods 1830–9 and 1871–81, in both of which there were several severe famines.

Table 9. *Rate of Growth of Population, 1801–1901**

Year	Rate of Growth per annum (%)†
1801 to 1823	1·6
1823 to 1827	2·4
1827 to 1830	1·8
1830 to 1839	−1·2
1839 to 1851–2	3·6
1851–2 to 1856–7	0·7
1856–7 to 1861–2	1·5
1861–2 to 1866–7	1·5
1866–7 to 1871	3·3
1871 to 1881	−0·1
1881 to 1891	1·5
1891 to 1901	0·9

* Calculated from the population figures in Table 11 (pp. 120–3).

† Compound rates of growth have been calculated, but no account has been taken of the fact that the censuses were not taken at the same time of year, i.e. the 1871–81 inter-censal period was not 10 years but 9½ years. This omission is unlikely to make any material change to the rate of growth.

[1] See Raghavaiyangar, *op. cit.*, pp. 42–3, and William Digby, *The Famine Campaign in South India, 1876–78*, 2 vols. (London, 1878).

[2] Government of Madras, *Report on the Famine in Madras Presidency during 1896 and 1897*, 2 vols.; Government of India, *Report of the Indian Famine Commission, 1898*; Government of India, *Report of the Indian Famine Commission, 1901*. Famines, as well as periods of drought, are listed in Table 12 in the Appendix to this chapter.

The variations in rates of growth are clearly to some extent a matter of chance: if a census had been taken not in 1823, but in 1825 just after the famine, there would have been a much smaller rate of increase in the preceding inter-censal period. And, in some periods the rate of change may merely have reflected the underestimation of the earlier census. The Census Commissioner of 1881 calculated that probably half a million females had been omitted from the 1871 count, as well as a floating population of 359,779; taking these omissions into account, and allowing for the population of 35,000 in the new areas annexed to Godavari in 1874, the actual decline in population between 1871 and 1881 was 1,310,000 instead of the decline of 454,064 shown by the census figures.[1] Changes in the area of the Presidency would also affect the rate of growth, though it is difficult to see in which direction, since the totals for each year relate to the actual Presidency at the time. The important changes are the acquisition of Kurnool in 1839 and the cession of North Canara to Bombay in 1861. The population of North Canara in 1871 was 398,498; the population of Kurnool was given as 273,190 in 1851–2, and 959,640 in 1871.

An interesting feature of the figures is that the rate of increase jumps up sharply whenever there is a change in the method of enumeration: that is, between 1839 and 1851–2, when the system of quinquennial censuses was introduced, and between 1866–7 and 1871, when the decennial census was introduced. This supports the presumption that each improvement in the system of taking the census reduced the degree of underestimation. If this presumption is correct, then the actual rate of growth of population over the century would have been lower than the figures show.

Between 1801 and 1851–2 the population increased, according to the figures, by about 130 per cent. This rate of increase is probably too high; the presumption that this rate of growth is an overestimate is supported,

[1] The Census Commissioner calculated that the effect of the famine should be measured by the increase in population between 1871 and 1881 that would have taken place (as estimated from previous rates of growth) if the famine had not occurred. This he put at 3,551,414, calculated as follows:

Population censused in 1871	31,597,872	(corrected figures)
Add females uncounted	488,800	
Floating population	359,779	
Corrected population in 1871	32,446,451	
Estimated increase at 0·795% for 9¼ years	2,466,181	
Estimated population in 1881	34,912,632	
Difference	3,551,414	

(These population figures differ from those in Table 11 (pp. 120–3), since they include the population of Puddukottah, a native state.)

Census Report, 1881, pp. 23–4.

to a slight extent, by the facts that the estimated rate of growth of population for Asia as a whole for 1800–50 was only 10–24 per cent, and for India for 1800–55, 46 per cent. On the other hand, for the latter half of the century, when the figures are far more accurate, the rate for Madras is 75 per cent as against 23–30 per cent for Asia and 62 per cent (between 1855 and 1900) for India.[1] But even if the actual rate in the first half of the century was only half the 130 per cent which the figures imply, it would still raise the question: was this substantial rise in population accompanied by any increase in area under cultivation?

There are no systematic data on cultivation for the first half of the century, but at least it is clear that extensive lands were available for cultivation at the beginning—either virgin soil, or lands which had gone out of cultivation because of political unrest or for other reasons. Buchanan supplies much evidence on this point for the beginning of the century: referring to Pollachi, in South Coimbatore, he mentions 'the immense extent of uncultivated land that is everywhere to be seen'.[2] In Malabar about 6 per cent of the rice lands that had formerly been cultivated were lying waste, and about 15 per cent of the garden lands.[3] In South Canara, about 5 per cent of the rice lands were waste, 'owing to want of tenants', and in addition there were 127,808 acres of lands cultivable for pasture, rice or garden crops.[4] In North Tulava in Canara where the land-tax was low,[5] there were no waste lands, although there were many near Sadasivghar in the same district.[6] According to Munro 'it is reckoned that the population of the country has been diminished one-third within the last forty years; and there can be no doubt that its property has suffered a much greater reduction'.[7] Again, in Baramahal in the Salem district, less than a third of the arable area was cultivated.[8]

Similar conditions prevailed in the Telugu districts, which Buchanan does not cover. Munro estimated that in the Ceded Districts there were

[1] Estimates for Asia are from United Nations, *The Determinants and Consequences of Population Trends* (New York, 1953), pp. 10–11; the figures for India are from Davis, *The Population of India and Pakistan*, pp. 25–7.

[2] Buchanan, *A Journey from Madras*, vol. II, p. 32.

[3] *Ibid.*, p. 62.

[4] Information supplied by the Collector, South Canara; *ibid.*, p. 202.

[5] The State did not claim ownership of land here. Buchanan disagreed with the landowners about the burden of the land tax: 'most . . . [of the landowners] who were as fat as pigs, gravely told me that they were reduced to live upon *kanji*, or rice-soup'; *ibid.*, p. 226.

[6] *Ibid.*, p. 334.

[7] Minute of 31.5.1800; Arbuthnot, *Minutes of Sir Thomas Munro*, vol. I, p. 67.

[8] 'The Chief Officer . . . says that at present he has 2,700 ploughs and that it would require 6,000 more to cultivate the whole arable land in his district'; Buchanan, *op. cit.*, vol. II, p. 504.

over 3 million acres of 'good land unoccupied, which may be ploughed at once, without the labour and expense of clearing away forests'.[1] In 1815 out of the 9·2 million acres of *raiyatwari* lands in Bellary and Cuddapah (not all of which were cultivable), only 3·2 million acres were being cultivated.[2] The fact that in the beginning of the century at least lands which formerly had been cultivated were lying waste reflected to some extent the political instability of the late eighteenth century. But it is clear that the high land revenue was another and perhaps the chief reason for the restriction of cultivation, and not just at the outset of the century but throughout its first five decades.

It is difficult to generalize about the rates of land revenue in any period, because of the complexity of the *raiyatwari* system of assessment. This is particularly true of early and middle *raiyatwari* when the method of assessment was not only complex, but varied in each district. But, as we have seen in Chapter VI, it is established that actual collections of land revenue were often more than one-half the gross produce, the cultivator sometimes being left with only one-fifth of the crop.

Conditions were no better in the *zamindari* areas. In theory, the cultivator on *zamindari* lands got the same proportion of the crop as the cultivator on *raiyatwari* lands, since it was only the Government's share of the crop that was split up between the Government and the *zamindar*. But the actual collections varied enormously, since the revenue administration in the *zamindari* areas was even less uniform than in the *raiyatwari* areas. Munro found, for example, in the Northern Circars and Nellore that some *zamindars* collected their revenue in kind, either because they were traders or because the cultivators were poor; some fixed the total amount in money; in others the collections varied with prices and production; and some *zamindars* made settlements not with the cultivator but with a village renter.[3] Payments in kind were more common in the Tamil than in the Telugu areas; where there were payments in kind in the Telugu areas they were usually on irrigated lands.[4] Perhaps in some long established *zamindaris* the cultivators were better off—at the beginning of the century at least—than in the *raiyatwari* areas, since rents were probably

[1] Letter from Board of Revenue to the Governor-in-Council, 25.4.1808; *East India Papers*, vol. I, p. 486.

[2] *Ibid.*, p. 634.

[3] Minute of 7.1.1823; Arbuthnot, *Minutes of Sir Thomas Munro*, vol. I, p. 206. In Chinglepet the majority of the *zamindars* were paid a part of the crop, but money rents fixed every year or for a period of years were also paid; Settlement Report on Chinglepet, 12.11.1827; Chinglepet Records, vol. 3849, p. 30.

[4] E.g., Letter of Collector, Masulipatam to Board of Revenue, 20.10.1829; Masulipatam Records, vol. 4063, pp. 239–43.

not increased to the same extent as the *raiyatwari* land revenue. But there is no evidence that this was generally the case. Again, even when *zamindari* assessments were high, remissions were perhaps more frequently made by the *zamindars* than by the Government.[1] However, in certain *zamindari* areas also the high collections led to land lying to waste; hence the Assistant Collector of Masulipatam reported in 1802 that several acres of land in each village were lying waste because of the exorbitant rents charged by the *zamindars* and their ill-treatment of the cultivators.[2] But the high rents charged by *zamindars* would probably be given more publicity in the official records than the effects of the high land revenue taken by the Government.

In fact, there might have been an even greater decline in cultivation if the *raiyats* had not been forced to cultivate their lands. In 1805 Munro estimated that in the Ceded Districts the *raiyats* were forced to plough not less than 12 per cent of the total cultivated area,[3] and that if they were completely free they would probably give up about 25 per cent of their land. 'The same causes which make land unsaleable and several others, concur to render it impracticable to establish a lease for a term of years, and far less a permanent settlement, *with the Ryots individually*. Many of them are so poor, that it is always doubtful whether they will next year be in the rank of cultivators or labourers, and few of them are so rich as not to be liable to be forced, by one or two bad seasons, to throw up a considerable part of their farms.'[4]

Physical force had to be used to compel some of the *raiyats* to cultivate their lands. The early records are full of letters from one Collector to another asking for help in bringing back *raiyats* who had run away from their villages because they could not pay the land revenue, or were unwilling to cultivate their lands at the prevailing rate of assessment.[5] The Collectors generally wrote to each other asking for the return of revenue defaulters and occasionally even for other fugitives, although in 1803 the Board of Revenue ruled that public servants or revenue defaulters alone could be compelled to return.[6] The shortage of cultivators led to arrange-

[1] Settlement Report on Karvetnagar Zamindaris for 1841–2.

[2] Letter from Assistant Collector to Collector, Masulipatam, 10.2.1802; Masulipatam Records, vol. 3071, p. 92.

[3] Raju, *Economic Conditions in the Madras Presidency, 1800–1850*, p. 49.

[4] Minute of Board of Revenue, 5.8.1813; *East India Papers*, vol. 1, p. 589.

[5] E.g., letter from Collector, Trichinopoly to Collector, Dindigul, 21.10.1802, asking for the return of *raiyats* who were revenue defaulters; Trichinopoly Records, vol. 3661, pp. 262–4.

[6] The Board of Revenue wrote to the Collector, Trichinopoly on 16.9.1803 that he could not compel the return to his district of the *raiyats* or any one else who was not a public servant, unless the Government had claims of arrears of revenue; Trichinopoly Records, vol. 3644, p. 167.

ments to exchange runaway *raiyats* (the Collectors taking care to do so after the harvest)[1] and even to occasional disputes between Collectors.[2] Most of this type of emigration appears to have been from Trichinopoly,[3] though there were also cases recorded for other districts, including Nellore, Vizagapatam and Godavari.[4]

Probably it was the flight of the cultivators which compelled the Government to moderate its demands. In 1810 the Board of Revenue rebuked the Collector of the Ceded Districts who had complained that many villagers were fleeing to Mysore: 'The object of the Government and of the Board is to collect the greatest possible revenue that is consistent with the permanent prosperity of the country, which must necessarily imply such a degree of ease and comfort to the inhabitants as shall prevent their quitting their houses. . . .'[5] But this did not mean that the Board would sanction any great reduction in the revenue, and the burden of assessment continued to be heavy throughout the first half of the century; even as late as 1855 the Government was using force to extract the land revenue.[6]

In some districts the Collectors suggested special terms for waste lands in order to induce emigrants to return,[7] but the general policy of theBoard was laid down in 1827: it was averse to encouraging cultivation, especially where there was a deficiency of population, by offering unusually favourable terms, since this would only attract cultivators from elsewhere.[8]

[1] E.g., the correspondence in 1800 between the Collectors of Coconada and Godavari; Godavari Records, vol. 932, pp. 329–30, 373, 405–6.

[2] E.g., the Head Assistant Collector, Madura protested in 1801 against the return of fugitives to Trichinopoly, since most of them were cultivating lands in Madura; Trichinopoly Records, vol. 3642, pp. 18–19.

[3] Trichinopoly Records, vol. 3644, pp. 12, 45, 53, 167; vol. 3656, pp. 769–71; vol. 3661, pp. 187–8, 262–4; vol. 3663, pp. 8, 111, 122, 129, 197; vol. 3665, pp. 23–9, 38–43; vol. 3668, p. 261; vol. 3669, pp. 44, 170, 264–5, 286, 307; vol. 3670, pp. 1–2, 38, 94, 122, 141–2, 147, 165, 272, 280–2, 300.

[4] Nellore Records, vol. 3126, pp. 157–9, 283–4; vol. 3145, pp. 73, 185; vol. 3146, pp. 191, 251–3, 298; vol. 4108, pp. 227, 248, 250, 259; vol. 4137, pp. 33, 133, 149, 270; vol. 4157, pp. 284, 691–3. Vizagapatam Records, vol. 3776, pp. 45–7. Godavari Records, vol. 847, p. 27. See also Revenue Letter to Fort St George, 6.6.1814; *East India Papers*, vol. 1, p. 544. In 1816 the Board of Revenue objected to an order passed by the Collector of Vizagapatam preventing *raiyats* from absconding to neighbouring *zamindari* estates; Vizagapatam Records, vol. 3754, pp. 335–41.

[5] P.B.R., 6.1.1810. See also P.B.R., 4.1.1810; Revenue letter from Fort St George, 12.8.1814; *East India Papers*, vol. 1, p. 656.

[6] Report of the Madras Torture Commission, 1854–5, in J. B. Smollett, *Madras, its Civil Administration* (London, 1858).

[7] Board of Revenue to Collector, Coimbatore, 9.10.1820; Malabar Records, vol. 2272, pp. 118–19; Board of Revenue to Collector, Trichinopoly; Trichinopoly Records, vol. 3642, pp. 58–9, vol. 3643, pp. 66.

[8] Board of Revenue to Collector, Trichinopoly, 3.5.1827; Trichinopoly Records, vol. 4378, pp. 213–15.

Another factor, obviously connected with the incidence of the land revenue, was the scarcity of the capital required to take up inferior or previously uncultivated lands.[1] This sometimes resulted in the abandoning of the better lands too, where a higher initial outlay of seed, labour and so on, would be required; thus the Collector of North Arcot found that the best lands were kept out of cultivation by the exorbitant revenue on them.[2]

In the *mirasi* areas, the uncertainty of the Government's right to dispose of the waste lands[3] frequently prevented their cultivation. When the original settlements were being made the *mirasdars* tried to prevent cultivation, in order to depress the value of the lands.[4] In the first half of the century, when the whole nature of the *mirasdar's* rights to his land was being debated, valuable areas were frequently not cultivated since the wet lands were generally held by the *mirasdars*.[5] In Malabar the waste lands were acknowledged to be the property of the *janmis*, and here there were special types of leases to encourage new cultivation. For instance, in the *kuzhikanam* lease, the sum to be spent by the tenant on improvements was considered to be an advance to the landlord, and the tenant paid at most a nominal rent for twelve years, at the end of which he obtained an ordinary lease from the landlord, or surrendered the land after receiving the value of his improvements. There were many variations on this type of lease.[6] The special leases at low rates given to tenants in Malabar who improved lands were apparently successful, since a great deal of jungle was converted into garden lands in the first decade of British rule.[7]

[1] Which factor one chose as an explanation of agrarian backwardness often depended on the political bias of the writer. Thus Buchanan is reluctant to connect waste lands with land revenue. For instance, he disagrees with the Assistant Collector of Dharapuram in South Coimbatore that the poverty of the peasants is due to the high land revenue; he ascribes it to the fact that the peasants lease from the Government more land than they have the stock to cultivate properly: 'One great cause indeed of the poverty of the farmers and consequent poverty of crops, in many parts of India, is the custom of forcing land upon people who have no means of cultivating it. Thus all the lands are apparently occupied; but it is in a manner that is worse than if one half of them were entirely waste'; Buchanan, *A Journey from Madras*, vol. II, p. 24.

[2] Collector, North Arcot to Board of Revenue, 28.8.1853, Raju, *op. cit.*, p. 51.

[3] The correspondence, minutes, etc., dealing with this issue are fairly fully covered in Bayley & Hudleston, *Papers on Mirasi Right*.

[4] Report of the Collector of Tanjore; *ibid.*, p. 85.

[5] Board of Revenue to the Collector, Trichinopoly, 3.5.1827; Trichinopoly Records, vol. 4378, pp. 217–21.

[6] See e.g. *Malabar Manual*, Chapter IX.

[7] No figures are available, but this has been deduced from the number of court decisions regarding *kuzhikanam* leases (for improvements); T. W. Shea, 'The Land Tenure Structure of Malabar', pp. 160–1.

The depressing effects of the high rates of land revenue are also revealed by the fact that cultivation increased most in areas such as Malabar and South Canara, where the rates were the lowest, and increased least in Andhra, where the rates were generally the most severe. In 1800 Malabar did not grow enough rice for its own consumption; by 1837 the value of exports of rice (including exports to other districts) was equal to nearly half the collections of land revenue, although population had increased by 150 per cent.[1] In both Malabar and Canara the land revenue system appeared to encourage cash crops such as pepper and coffee. Sullivan reported that in Canara there had been a very considerable extension of cultivation of all types of land, including coconut plantations, and that no land was left waste. The only exception to this growing prosperity was the decline in betelnut plantations in one part of the district. Sullivan estimated that in 1838–9 the value of the gross produce from the land was Rs. 67,11,280, of which the land revenue took Rs. 18,20,123 or 27 per cent; and that crops worth Rs. 24,52,186, or 36 per cent, were exported.[2] In Tanjore also there was a steady increase in the gross produce of the wet lands from 1801 to 1841, though the rate of increase slackened after 1830. But these districts were, as usual, atypical: in most of the other districts wide fluctuations in cultivation were recorded. In general, an improvement in cultivation took place around 1830, especially in the southern and some Telugu districts; indeed rice cultivation had been improving even earlier in many of the southern districts. In Chinglepet, for example, the cultivation rose from 117,056 acres in 1828–9 to 214,933 acres in 1850–1[3] in response to the increased demand for food and commercial crops. On the other hand, in Trichinopoly there was a fall in land under cultivation between 1840–1 and 1844–5 as compared to the preceding five years, the increase in the irrigated and garden lands being more than offset by the fall in the dry cultivation; there was a fall in total cultivated area as well as in revenue collections.[4] There was also a fall in the land revenue collections of the whole Presidency in the ten years up to 1840.[5] This was at least in part a result of the high rates of land revenue.

In many Telugu districts cultivation either continued to decline or failed to increase up to 1851. The famines which occurred from 1833 on-

[1] Sullivan, *Report on the Provinces of Malabar and Canara, 1841*, pp. 4–5.

[2] *Ibid.*, pp. 16–17.

[3] Raju, *Economic Conditions in the Madras Presidency, 1800–1850*, p. 64. *Cawnies* have been converted into acres at the rate of 1·32 acres per *cawnie*.

[4] P.B.R., 13.5.1850.

[5] The average annual collections of land revenue (and a few minor taxes) was Rs. 34·1 lakhs in 1831–40, as compared to Rs. 37·3 lakhs in the previous decade; Raghavaiyangar, *Progress of the Madras Presidency*, p. cxxviii.

wards are proof of this. Thus there was a complete failure of cultivation during the famine of 1833, which affected Guntur the worst. In 1839 again there was a failure of crops in most of the Telugu districts, and there was another in the Ceded Districts in 1853.[1] Some of these failures were caused by weather conditions, but the high rates of land revenue were partly to blame for the low level of cultivation. In 1846 the Collector of Bellary wrote that 'were it not for the aid of the Collector through his revenue subordinates half or at least one-third of the highly assessed lands would ere now have been thrown up'.[2] But in Nellore, the cropped area rose from 244,139 acres in 1801 to 389,802 acres in 1850; in Godavari also the cultivated area went up after the extension of irrigation in 1844.[3]

There was some improvement in the cultivation of cash crops in the first half of the nineteenth century, though it fell far short of expectations. The Company had at one time very high hopes of the possibilities of introducing improved varieties of cotton, indigo, cinnamon from Ceylon, cloves from Amboyna, and spices from the Straits. The statement by a member of the Board of Revenue that the Presidency possessed 'so many natural advantages of situation and climate and so rapid a progress of vegetation that innumerable sources of industry and wealth might be introduced by way of manufacture'[4] was optimistic but not atypical. The heavy rate of assessment and the numerous duties on particular crops, such as betelnut, may also have prevented the introduction of commercial crops. Munro pointed out that if the taxation were reduced, the cultivation of betel, coconut, sugar and cotton would be encouraged, rather than that of the food crops.[5]

From 1877 onwards the Company made many attempts to introduce various commercial crops, including the establishment of experimental farms, the grant of advances for cultivation and of rewards for excellence, and the distribution of seeds. These measures were taken for nearly all the cash crops, but more particularly for cotton; the only exception was indigo, where the Company felt that there was a danger of over-production, and where the interests of Madras had to yield to those of Bengal. The Madras Government wrote to the Court of Directors in 1809 as follows: 'The capacity of these provinces to produce indigo is such that there is always ground to apprehend that the manufacture will be extended far beyond

[1] See Dalyell's Memorandum on Madras Famines in Government of India, *Report of the Indian Famine Commission, 1880*.

[2] Report from the Collector, Bellary to the Board of Revenue; P.B.R., 25.7.1846.

[3] Raghavaiyangar, *op. cit.*, p. 31.

[4] Minute by C. N. White, 25.3.1793; *Fifth Report from the Select Committee of the House of Commons* (ed. W. K. Firminger), 3 vols., Calcutta, 1917, vol. III, pp. 135–6.

[5] Arbuthnot, *Minutes of Sir Thomas Munro*, vol. I, p. 29.

the ordinary consumption and demand, and we shall therefore feel it incumbent upon us to act with extreme caution in making our purchases of indigo.'[1]

These measures succeeded in increasing the cultivation of cotton to nearly 1 million acres by 1852. There is little information on the cultivation in earlier years in the Presidency as a whole, but the growth can be gauged from the fact that while at the beginning of the century exports of Indian cotton were negligible, in 1854 they were valued at Rs. 11,63,422. The increase in certain districts was particularly marked. In Tinnevelly the area under cotton rose from 45,000 acres in 1812 to 190,000 acres in 1852, and in Bellary it grew by nearly 130,000 acres over the half century. In Coimbatore it was estimated that around 256,000 acres were under cotton in 1848, but that this could easily be trebled.[2] The cultivation of indigo grew rapidly in particular districts such as Trichinopoly,[3] Nellore and Cuddapah. In the Presidency as a whole the total area under indigo was somewhat under 200,000 acres in 1852. Again, the land under sugar-cane was only 38,400 acres in 1852, and the Presidency continued to import sugar on a large scale. Oil seeds, which are now amongst the most important cash crops in South India, were of no importance in this period.

It is difficult to generalize about the progress of cultivation in the Presidency as a whole during the first half of the century. One indicator is the actual collections of land revenue; from these it would appear that over the period as a whole there was no significant extension of cultivation. Thus the average collections of land revenue in the first 10 years of the century were Rs. 38·4 lakhs per annum, while the average collections during the decade ending 1849–50 were Rs. 39·5 lakhs per annum, an increase of less than 3 per cent.[4] The collections in the decades ending 1829–30 and 1839–40 fell by 3 per cent and 11 per cent respectively. There were of course changes in the rates of land revenue per acre, in the efficiency of collection and the leniency with which remissions were granted, all of

[1] Quoted in Raju, *Economic Conditions in the Madras Presidency, 1800–1850*, p. 79. This book contains a fairly full description of the measures taken to stimulate the growth of cash crops, and if no other source is mentioned the data for this paragraph are from it. For the attempt at cotton cultivation and the setting up of the experimental farms, see also P.B.R., 14.3.1842 and 23.12.1848.

[2] Letters from the Superintendent, Government Cotton Farm, to the Govt. of Madras; P.B.R., 23.12.1848.

[3] In Trichinopoly the acreage under indigo in 1840–1 to 1844–5 was three times that in the preceding five years; P.B.R., 13.5.1850.

[4] Raghavaiyangar, *Progress of the Madras Presidency*, p. cxxviii. These figures include the collections of taxes on trades and houses, the excise, and the proceeds of the tobacco monopoly in Malabar and South Canara, but these form a small proportion of the total.

which would qualify any inference from the land revenue figures regarding the extension of cultivation. But these are not insuperable limitations. There was on the whole no substantial fall in the rates of land revenue during this period, although there was some decline in comparison with the first *raiyatwari* settlements, and it would therefore appear that the cultivation of land did not in fact increase rapidly. Since it seems fairly certain that the population did increase rapidly, though probably at less than the recorded rate of 130 per cent, it is strange that a more substantial increase in cultivation was not recorded. While no firm statement can be made concerning the overall figures of the increase in cultivation, it seems beyond doubt that one of the main factors restraining the increase was the high rate of land revenue, a presumption which is supported by the fact that cultivation appears to have increased more rapidly in the second half of the century, when there was a reduction in the burden of the land revenue.

More data are available for the second half of the nineteenth century. During this period too population grew, although the rate of growth was not on average as rapid as in the first half of the century. There is no doubt that there was a significant extension of cultivation after 1850, but the question is whether, taking into account the type of new land brought under cultivation, and the changes in the crop patterns, the increase in production was at the same pace as the growth of population, which went up by 75 per cent between 1851–2 and 1901.

There would certainly appear to have been ample scope for the extension of cultivation in the 1850's: the Board of Revenue found that the total amount of cultivable waste land at the disposal of the Government amounted to 13·5 million acres, of which 2 million acres were irrigated. These figures, which exclude Malabar and Canara, were calculated by deducting from the total recorded cultivable area in each district the *peramboke* or waste land which could not be cultivated, as well as the *inam* lands and the lands actually under occupation in the year 1857–8. Most of these were scattered over the country, and a large portion of them was covered with thick jungle and could not be brought under cultivation without the expenditure on a large scale of capital and labour.[1] But even so, it is clear that there was room for significant expansion of cultivation; indeed even in 1890 the Madras Government felt that the reserve of cultivable waste would not be exhausted for some years.[2]

Between 1856 and 1874 the acreage of occupied land under *raiyatwari*

[1] Government of Madras, Memorandum Regarding the Cultivable Waste Lands at the Disposal of Government; P.B.R., 27.2.1890.

[2] *Ibid.*

increased from 12,205,313 to 19,691,408, a rise of 61 per cent;[1] in contrast, between 1856–7 and 1871 the population had increased from 22·8 million to 31·3 million, or by less than 40 per cent. Admittedly the famine of 1876–8 checked this trend; in 1878–9 the cultivated acreage was less than it had been four years earlier.[2] But by 1880–1 there was an increase of 5·4 per cent from this low point,[3] and thereafter the figures continued to rise (see Table 10).

Table 10. *Area Under Raiyatwari, 1881–8*

Year	Acres
1881–2	18,772,370
1882–3	19,095,867
1883–4	19,326,097
1884–5	19,438,274
1885–6	19,875,750
1886–7	20,324,503
1887–8	20,499,137

Source: P.B.R., 27.2.1890.
N.B. This excludes South Canara.

Although these figures give valuable evidence about the rising trend of cultivation, they refer to the *raiyatwari* districts alone. But the series, *Agricultural Statistics of British India*, which begins from 1884–5, provides cultivation figures for all three systems—*raiyatwari*, *zamindari* and *inamdari*—and includes South Canara. Furthermore, it contains details about the crops grown and the areas irrigated; figures for all these are set out in the Statistical Appendix to this chapter, Tables 13, 14 and 15. Since the starting date of this series is inside the period of accurate censusing, it is possible to establish some reasonably accurate correlations between the growth of population and that of the area under cultivation during the last two decades of the century. On this basis, the total area cultivated went up from an annual average of 23,377,000 acres in 1884–6 to 26,823,000 acres in 1899–1901, or by 14·7 per cent; if one compares only the years 1885–6 and 1900–1, the cultivated area went up from 24,082,628 acres to 27,849,683 acres, or by 15·6 per cent. If the 1886 population is assumed to be the arithmetic mean of the population in 1881 and in 1891, the population increased from 33·1 million in 1886 to 38·6 million in

[1] P.B.R., 1.4.1874. Part of the increase may have been due to more accurate measurement.
[2] Secretary of State to Madras, Revenue, No. 9, 10.3.1881; I.O., 55.
[3] Proceedings of Revenue Department, 25.1.1883, No. 1092.

1901, or by 16·6 per cent. Thus in the last fifteen years of the nineteenth century the increase in cultivation barely kept pace with the increase in population.

But this conclusion must be qualified by taking account of changes in crop patterns, the quality of new lands, and irrigation. And the figures require further adjustment since there was a sizeable area sown to crops more than once in the year, and to arrive at the total area cropped it is necessary to count twice this double-cropped area; this has been done in Table 14.

The question of yield is particularly important; it appears that inferior lands were being taken up under cultivation, especially towards the end of the century. It was found, for example, that in 1888 the average yield of cotton was probably less than in 1850, and the staple no finer. Forty years previously the yield of clean cotton in Bellary, Cuddapah, Coimbatore and Tinnevelly had been 90, 50, 50 and 80 lb. per acre, respectively; the average was 62½ lb. per acre, which was not lower than the averages prevailing in 1880. In 1848 it was reported that the average produce per acre in Coimbatore was nearly 111·0 lb.[1] The great external demand for cotton had been met by the extension of cultivation rather than the improvement of yields or of the quality of the cotton. The Agricultural Committee of 1880 also attributed the extremely low yield of cereals, which was little more than one-third of the yield in England (11 bushels per acre as against 30 in England), partly to the extensive taking up of bad soils which had never been tilled before and for which the *raiyats* had no experience: 'it was the failure over vast areas of poor and poorly tilled soil probably at a minimum degree of productiveness that intensified the recent famine'.[2] Again the ploughing up of forest land may well have led to a decline in rainfall.[3] This evidence on declining yields is of course far from conclusive,[4] but it seems to fit in with the fact that wages declined towards the end of the century (see Chapter IX). The agricultural practices of the time, particularly as regards dry cultivation, led to the rapid exhaustion of the soil, since the land was not left fallow frequently enough nor was it sufficiently fertilized.

[1] Government of Madras, *Report of the Agricultural Committee*, 1880, Appendix C, pp. 64, 158–9.

[2] Collector to the Board of Revenue; P.B.R., 23.12.1848. According to the Superintendent of the Cotton Farm at Coimbatore the yield on red sandy soil was 150–200 lb. per acre; *ibid.*

[3] W. R. Robertson, *Reports on the Agricultural Conditions . . . of the Neilgherry and Coimbatore Districts* (Madras, 1881), pp. 99–100.

[4] Raghavaiyangar denies that yields were declining (*Progress of the Madras Presidency*, pp. 53–7), but the evidence he adduces is inconclusive.

When relating changes in the land–labour ratio to movements in wages, however, the specific effects of changes in irrigation and in crop patterns on the demand for agricultural labour must also be taken into account. A study of farms in Salem and Coimbatore in 1954–5 gives some information on yields and labour inputs which can serve as a rough indication of the weight to be given to these factors.[1] Since even in 1954–5 the method of cultivation was purely extensive, and only one cultivator in all the thirty-two villages studied had a tractor, while only a few farmers in seven of the villages had even iron ploughs, the figures will be about as correct for 1884 or 1900 as for 1954–5, particularly since we are interested in the differences between inputs for different crops rather than the absolute amounts.

The study showed a very wide variation between labour inputs per acre for the different crops,[2] and between irrigated and unirrigated areas under the same crop. The greatest variation was between paddy and the other crops: the labour input per acre for paddy was 129·7 to 156·3 man-days per acre, which was about double the input on the second most labour-intensive irrigated crop, *ragi* (68·2 to 86·6). Again, the labour input on irrigated lands was also at least double that on unirrigated lands for the same crop.[3] Now, as Table 14 shows, the increase between 1884–5 and

[1] Two methods were used, the cost accounting and the survey method, and twenty villages were studied under each (eight were common so that there were 32 villages studied out of a total of 2,851). Under the cost accounting method 10 holdings in each village (making 200 holdings in all) were studied; under the survey method 20 (400 holdings in all). Differences in figures of inputs, yields, etc., may therefore arise on account of differences either of method or coverage; Ministry of Agriculture, Government of India, *Studies in the Economics of Farm Management in Madras, Report for 1954–55* (New Delhi, 1957).

[2] Labour was assessed in terms of days of eight hours; female and child labour was converted into adult male labour on the basis of the ratio of prevalent wage rates for men, women and children. Family labour and exchange of gift labour is included and valued at the rate paid to permanent farm servants; *ibid.*, Appendix 6.

[3] The labour inputs, in man-days per acre, for various crops were as follows:

		Cost Accounting Method	Survey Method
Irrigated	Paddy	129·7	156·3
	Ragi	68·2	86·6
	Cotton	63·2	68·6
	Cholum	54·4	57·8
	Cumbu	31·5	62·1
Unirrigated	Groundnut	43·7	44·6
	Ragi	31·0	43·6
	Cotton	25·2	22·1
	Cholum	16·8	15·9
	Cumbu	15·4	15·8

Figures for unirrigated *cholum*, cotton and *cumbu* seem too low, even if allowance

1900–1 was more in the cultivation of food crops than in commercial crops. The area under rice went up by 20 per cent, under *cholum* by 17 per cent, under *ragi* by 14 per cent, under *cumbu* by 34 per cent, while the area under cotton went up by only 3 per cent, under coffee by 5 per cent, and the area under indigo declined by 12 per cent. The exceptions were oil seeds, with an increase of 55 per cent, and tobacco, with an increase of 40 per cent, but the acreage under the latter was relatively small. But the overall figures of area under each crop are an insufficient measure of the demand for labour since irrigation made such a difference to labour inputs, and from 1892–3 onwards figures of irrigated area under each crop were not collected. The total area irrigated increased by 8·3 per cent over the period, but the effect on output and on the demand for labour would have been much larger since there would have been more double and triple cropping on irrigated than on dry lands.

To sum up, from 1885 onwards the cultivated area, taking into account the double and triple cropped area, was growing at a slightly lower rate than the population. In addition, it seems likely that the marginal lands brought under cultivation were of inferior quality. To some extent the effects of increased irrigation have already been taken into account, since the double and triple cropping made possible by it has been allowed for in calculating total acreage. The evidence regarding changes in crop pattern is admittedly inconclusive. When all factors are taken into account the balance of probability is that towards the end of the century the extension of cultivation was beginning to fail to keep pace with the growth of population. This conclusion is supported by movements in emigration and wages.

is made for the fact that many of these are second or third crops. The simplest explanation is that crops failed the year the study was made, since average yields were particularly poor.

STATISTICAL APPENDIX

Table 11. *Population of Madras Presidency, 1801–1901*

	1800–2	1823	1827	1830	1839
1. Ganjam	—	332,015	468,047	438,174	438,174
2. Vizagapatam	—	772,570	1,008,544	1,104,744	1,047,414
3. Godavari/ Rajahmundry	—	738,308	660,906	695,016	695,016
4. Masulipatam	—	529,849	519,125	544,672	544,672
5. Guntur	135,877	454,754	476,787	518,318	267,426
6. Nellore	—	439,467	730,608	846,572	328,726
7. Bellary	—	927,857	941,612	1,128,839	1,129,907
8. Kurnool	—	—	—	—	—
9. Anantapur	—	—	—	—	—
10. Cuddapah	—	1,094,460	1,000,957	1,063,164	1,081,261
11. Chinglepet	271,372	363,129	289,828	331,821	331,821
12. N. Arcot	—	892,292	730,410	772,068	523,248
13. S. Arcot	—	455,020	549,795	553,388	484,800
14. Salem	612,871	1,075,905	955,480	822,107	898,233
15. Trichinopoly	459,055	481,292	476,720	536,697	485,242
16. Tanjore	—	901,353	1,165,560	1,128,730	1,128,730
17. Madura	—	564,957	1,122,979	1,135,411	552,477
18. Tinnevelly	571,000	788,196	766,746	850,891	850,891
19. Coimbatore	—	638,199	854,050	854,834	783,392
20. Malabar	465,594	907,575	1,003,466	1,113,497	1,165,791
21. Nilgiris	—	—	—	—	—
22. S. Canara*	396,672	657,594	665,652	709,571	768,123
23. Madras City	600,000	462,051	462,051	462,051	462,051
TOTAL	9,574,458	13,476,843	14,726,690	15,552,135	13,967,395

* Except for 1801, all figures for South Canara till 1866, include North Canara.

	1851–2	1856–7	1861–2	1866–7
1. Ganjam	926,930	949,947	1,136,926	1,235,790
2. Vizagapatam	1,204,272	1,284,243	1,415,652	1,934,558
3. Godavari/ Rajahmundry	1,012,036	1,081,703	1,366,831	1,427,472
4. Masulipatam	520,866	623,808	1,194,421	1,296,652
5. Guntur	570,083	593,213		
6. Nellore	935,690	952,032	999,254	1,168,664
7. Bellary	1,229,599	1,181,087	1,234,674	1,304,998
8. Kurnool	273,190	287,726	775,768	770,857
9. Anantapur	—	—	—	—

Table 11—*continued*

10. Cuddapah	1,451,921	1,351,151	1,050,104	1,144,759
11. Chinglepet	583,462	605,221	675,390	804,283
12. N. Arcot	1,485,873	1,588,104	1,654,557	1,787,134
13. S. Arcot	1,006,005	1,135,961	1,128,430	1,261,846
14. Salem	1,195,377	1,268,200	1,493,221	1,619,233
15. Trichinopoly	709,196	809,580	939,400	1,006,826
16. Tanjore	1,676,086	1,657,285	1,652,170	1,731,619
17. Madura	1,756,791	1,792,737	1,856,406	1,946,380
18. Tinnevelly	1,269,216	1,339,374	1,370,221	1,521,168
19. Coimbatore	1,153,862	1,176,831	1,215,920	1,430,738
20. Malabar	1,514,909	1,602,914	1,493,221	1,856,378
21. Nilgiris	—	—	—	—
22. S. Canara	1,056,333	1,126,938	788,042	839,688
23. Madras City	450,000	450,000	450,000	450,000
TOTAL	22,031,697	22,857,855	24,656,509	26,539,052

	1871	1881	1891	1901
1. Ganjam	1,520,088	1,749,604	1,896,803	2,010,256
2. Vizagapatam	2,159,199	2,351,680	2,802,992	2,933,650
3. Godavari	1,592,939	1,641,002	2,078,782	2,301,759
4. Masulipatam } Kistna 5. Guntur }	1,452,374	1,548,480	1,855,582	2,154,803
6. Nellore	1,376,811	1,220,236	1,463,736	1,496,987
7. Bellary	1,668,006	1,336,696	900,126	947,214
8. Kurnool	959,640	709,305	817,811	872,055
9. Anantapur	—	—	708,549	788,254
10. Cuddapah	1,351,194	1,121,038	1,272,072	1,291,267
11. Chinglepet	938,184	981,381	1,136,928	1,312,122
12. N. Arcot	2,015,278	1,817,814	2,180,487	2,207,712
13. S. Arcot	1,755,817	1,814,738	2,162,851	2,349,894
14. Salem	1,966,995	1,599,595	1,962,591	2,204,974
15. Trichinopoly	1,200,408	1,215,033	1,372,717	1,447,770
16. Tanjore	1,973,731	2,130,383	2,228,114	2,245,029
17. Madura	2,266,615	2,168,680	2,608,404	2,831,280
18. Tinnevelly	1,693,959	1,699,747	1,916,095	2,059,607
19. Coimbatore	1,763,274	1,657,690	2,004,839	2,201,752
20. Malabar	2,261,250	2,365,035	2,652,565	2,790,281
21. Nilgiris	49,501	91,034	99,797	111,437
22. S. Canara	918,362	959,514	1,056,081	1,134,713
23. Madras City	387,552	405,848	452,518	509,346
TOTAL	31,597,872	31,170,631	35,630,440	38,199,162

Notes to Table 11

1801

(*a*) Guntur figures are ambiguous. In his letter to the Board of Revenue of 2.5.1802, the Collector states that these estimates were arrived at from the accounts sent by village headmen four years previously and seem to include only the male population of each village. If the number were doubled to include the female population, this would raise the total population to 271,754 or 9 persons per house, which, he states, would be an overestimate; Masulipatam Records, vol. 3071, p. 211.

(*b*) The Chinglepet figures relate to 1798–9; Place, Report on the Jaghire, p. 238.

(*c*) Salem: Includes S. Salem and Coimbatore; *Salem Gazetteer*, 1916, vol. I, Part I, p. 90.

According to the Collector, writing in 1806, the population in 1801 was 386,442, and fell the following year to 377,004 as a result of the bad harvest, but these figures are much too low; Collector to Board of Revenue, 24.5.1806; Salem Records, vol. 3159, pp. 50–7. On the other hand the population of 1,075,905 in 1823 seems too high,

(*d*) According to the Collector, Trichinopoly had a population of 507,552 in 1802, excluding 'military men, camp followers and their families, which must be a considerable number', Letter from Collector to Board of Revenue, 15.5.1802; Trichinopoly Records, vol. 3661, pp. 188–91. Apparently, later corrections were made, since in 1822 the records have a figure of 459,055, excluding Manargudi *taluk*; P.B.R., 10.6.1822.

(*e*) Tinnevelly figures from letter from the Collector to board of Revenue, 22.10.1823. The Collector states that this figure includes the population of the *zamindaris*. The population in 1817 (the year is not covered in the table) was 629,000; Tinnevelly Records, vol. 4364, pp. 169–71.

(*f*) South Canara: Buchanan, *A Journey from Madras*, vol. II, p. 208.

(*g*) Figures from Sullivan, *Report on Malabar and Canara, 1841*. According to the Collector the population of Malabar in 1806–7 was 700,000; *Select Committee Report, 1831–32*, Appendix K.

(*h*) Madras City: *Census Report, 1931*, vol. I, p. 1.

(*i*) Total: This figure includes 'calculations of population based on comparative revenues'. North Canara and Srirangapatam are included; General Reports of the Board of Revenue, vol. 7, p. 77.

1823

(*a*) All figures except those for Ganjam and Madras from P.B.R., 3.11.1823

(*b*) Ganjam: Excludes the hill *zamindaris*; P.B.R., 24.11.1823.

(*c*) South Canara: Includes North Canara.

(*d*) Madras City; P.B.R., 8.5.1823.

1827

(*a*) All figures from P.B.R., 11.5.1829, except for amended figures for Ganjam, and the total, which are from P.B.R., 4.3.1833.

(*b*) Ganjam: Excluding hill *zamindaris.*
(*c*) South Canara: Includes North Canara.
(*d*) A breakdown of the population according to sex and age (adults and children) for Tinnevelly is contained in the letter from the Collector, 27.12.1827; Tinnevelly Records, vol. 4365, p. 104.

1830–1
(*a*) All figures for 1830–31 from P.B.R., 4.3.1833.
(*b*) Trichinopoly: The increase of 59,977 since 1827 was apparently too high, because the inhabitants of certain villages held on special tenures, as well as of two temples, were left out from the earlier figures. The real increase was only 38,937, P.B.R., 21.2.1831. The figures in the table have however not been changed since the Board did not alter them. In any case the difference made to the totals would be minute.

1839
(*a*) All figures from P.B.R., 19.7.1852.

1851–2 to 1866–7
(*a*) Figures from *Census Report, 1881*; the figure for Madras City was 720,000 in the original figures (P.B.R., 19.7.1852); this was obviously revised later. Some of the other district figures were also revised, i.e. Vizagapatam, Tinnevelly and Kurnool. In addition, the total figure for 1861–2 contains 600,041 which has not been attributed to any district; *Census Report, 1881*, vol. III, Appendix A ('Native Life Tables for Madras Presidency'), pp. 1–2.

1871 to 1901
(*a*) The figures for each year are taken from the *Census Report* of that year, instead of the corrected figures available in later Censuses, since detailed figures relating to caste and occupation for any year are available only in the Census of that year.

Table 12. *Famines in Madras Presidency, 1800–1900*

Year	Area of drought	Area of famine or scarcity
1804		High districts of Tanjore*
1805–6	Southern districts*	
1806	Central districts, from Trichinopoly to Nellore	
1807		Central districts; southern districts*
1812	Madras Presidency	
1813		Madras Presidency
1819	Nellore*	

Table 12—*continued*

1823	Madras Presidency	
1824		Madras Presidency, chiefly in the north
1832	Northern districts, except Ganjam; also Madura*	
1833		Northern districts
1837	Coimbatore, Ganjam, Vizagapatam, Guntur, Madura, Tinnevelly*	
1839	Bellary	
1847	Coimbatore and Madura*	
1853	Bellary, Cuddapah	
1854		Famine in Bellary and scarcity in adjoining areas
1865	Northern districts	Malabar, Madura, Trichinopoly*
1866		Ganjam and Bellary
1876	Madras Presidency	
1877		Madras Presidency
1896–7		Bellary, Cuddapah, Anantapur, Kurnool, Ganjam, Vizagapatam, and parts of Godavari*
1898		Madras Presidency, mainly northern districts

Droughts or famines marked with an asterisk are mentioned in P.B.R. All others are from the *Manual of Administration for Madras Presidency*, 1885, vol. II, pp. 470–1.

Table 13. *Area Cultivated and Uncultivated in Madras Presidency, 1884–5 to 1900–1*

(*acres*)

Year	Forest	Not available for cultivation	Cultivable waste other than fallows	Current fallows	Net Area cropped	Total area
1884–5	8,980,725	11,101,192	10,600,707	5,662,995	21,331,674	57,677,293
1885–6	7,611,480	12,339,878	8,052,375	5,017,653	22,463,253	58,106,157
1886–7	8,549,000	11,238,960	7,777,298	4,966,086	23,004,643	58,049,643
1887–8	9,366,866	12,482,149	8,376,156	4,940,990	23,326,272	58,492,433
1888–9	9,459,492	12,184,424	8,461,340	5,096,589	23,157,408	58,359,253
1889–90	11,424,269	11,850,938	8,021,292	4,972,995	23,797,936	60,066,539
1890–1	11,541,881	11,960,222	7,869,272	5,176,218	23,702,280	60,249,873
1891–2	11,038,448	11,880,742	7,972,561	6,637,481	22,094,985	59,624,217
1892–3	10,367,042	12,475,634	7,720,959	5,617,169	23,761,300	59,942,104

Table 13—*continued*

1893–4	8,064,256	12,210,896	6,992,817	5,185,972	24,411,300	56,865,241
1894–5	11,953,815	12,870,101	6,746,546	5,467,893	24,420,321	61,458,676
1895–6	12,096,723	13,150,287	6,401,604	5,261,035	24,844,140	61,753,793
1896–7	11,937,101	13,368,833	6,423,855	6,362,161	23,602,319	61,694,269
1897–8	12,082,354	13,336,707	6,269,680	5,896,998	24,250,708	61,836,447
1898–9	12,157,824	13,164,080	6,299,569	5,658,341	25,511,162	61,790,976
1899–1900	12,262,902	12,985,856	6,388,186	6,930,963	23,122,191	61,690,098
1900–1	12,386,285	12,638,197	6,259,615	5,762,668	24,509,613	61,556,378

Sources: Agricultural Statistics of British India, 1884–85 to 1886–87; 1887–88 to 1891–92; 1892–93 to 1896–97, vol. 1; *1897–98 to 1901–02*, vol. 1.

Table 14. *Crops Cultivated in Madras Presidency, 1884–5 to 1900–1*

(*acres*)

Year	Rice	Cholum	Ragi	Cumbu	Total food-grains and pulses	Oilseeds
1884–5	5,630,106	4,070,206	1,459,938	2,202,835	18,539,030	1,169,079
1885–6	5,795,644	4,077,607	1,565,533	2,210,650	19,688,058	1,364,093
1886–7	6,165,132	3,845,595	1,487,951	2,542,039	19,819,569	1,548,194
1887–8	6,293,242	N.A.	N.A.	N.A.	20,283,363	1,509,347
1888–9	6,285,806	N.A.	N.A.	N.A.	20,233,435	1,566,935
1889–90	6,458,668	N.A.	N.A.	N.A.	20,579,835	1,908,022
1890–1	6,159,628	4,429,084	1,639,109	2,746,812	20,534,915	1,918,705
1891–2	5,771,182	4,667,666	1,675,805	2,496,078	19,703,047	1,501,638
1892–3	6,408,236	4,698,448	1,557,196	2,894,724	21,387,594	1,687,929
1893–4	6,710,212	4,570,378	1,622,563	2,857,900	21,558,912	1,881,071
1894–5	6,557,590	4,271,274	1,701,966	2,787,913	21,474,377	1,700,261
1895–6	6,881,043	4,494,060	1,649,905	2,709,412	21,874,421	1,993,406
1896–7	6,612,567	4,730,741	1,724,057	2,463,243	21,225,899	1,688,020
1897–8	6,935,159	4,510,973	1,683,717	2,700,936	21,864,667	1,646,628
1898–9	7,166,072	4,827,997	1,713,333	2,806,084	22,667,013	1,515,601
1899–1900	6,429,045	4,375,168	1,699,071	2,456,354	20,694,678	1,516,826
1900–1	6,591,611	4,777,215	1,672,537	2,966,266	22,310,235	1,819,026

Table 14—continued

Year	Cotton	Tobacco	Indigo	Coffee	*(acres)* Double cropping	Total area
1884–5	1,326,718	82,673	321,339	60,933	1,340,307	22,671,981
1885–6	1,358,260	80,561	292,757	57,509	1,619,375	24,082,628
1886–7	1,487,204	74,717	424,534	54,924	1,654,149	24,658,656
1887–8	1,463,669	83,727	501,721	56,333	1,859,197	25,185,469
1888–9	1,507,556	87,860	509,290	56,094	2,176,723	25,334,131
1889–90	1,640,843	102,637	447,343	55,618	2,322,016	26,119,052
1890–1	1,737,722	89,989	255,511	70,219	2,393,238	26,095,508
1891–2	1,318,042	72,747	212,255	63,371	2,163,752	24,308,292
1892–3	1,326,242	104,662	301,201	62,927	2,673,381	26,434,687
1893–4	1,723,985	125,062	442,439	59,156	3,014,703	27,410,038
1894–5	1,519,120	108,516	527,081	62,069	2,608,463	27,028,784
1895–6	1,623,913	112,055	486,938	60,125	3,012,036	27,856,176*
1896–7	1,394,134	86,650	454,748	60,773	3,014,091	26,616,410†
1897–8	1,509,135	103,357	323,931	64,402	2,961,377	27,212,085
1898–9	1,321,698	118,488	210,610	65,191	3,274,634	27,785,796
1899–1900	1,382,716	82,276	276,210	59,581	2,674,229	25,796,420
1900–1	1,373,345	117,428	252,054	64,181	3,340,070	27,849,683

* Includes 3,037 acres in Vizagapatam for which details of crops not available.
† Includes 3,052 acres in Vizagapatam for which details of crops not available.

Sources: As in Table 13.

Table 15. *Irrigated Area in Madras Presidency 1884–5 to 1900–1*

(*acres*)

Year	Government canals	Private canals	Tanks	Wells	Other sources	Total area irrigated
1884–5	2,282,223	14,766	2,134,795	788,621	325,786	5,546,191
1885–6	2,447,282	25,360	2,290,453	803,479	248,804	5,815,378
1886–7	2,517,389	23,261	2,374,815	816,648	267,809	5,999,922
1887–8	2,659,449	27,852	2,289,300	1,055,912	201,919	6,234,432
1888–9	2,642,153	24,712	2,286,992	1,100,083	177,418	6,231,358
1889–90	2,700,698	28,289	2,314,932	1,169,141	185,225	6,398,285
1890–1	2,634,708	27,129	2,187,521	1,248,581	173,268	6,321,207
1891–2	2,471,623	24,494	1,697,620	1,034,020	135,019	5,362,776
1892–3	2,518,998	27,831	2,034,268	994,193	128,908	5,704,198
1893–4	2,601,774	27,659	2,099,773	1,059,888	123,155	5,912,249
1894–5	2,621,086	28,549	1,942,536	1,084,060	127,706	5,803,937
1895–6	2,540,165	30,182	2,103,539	1,053,458	131,413	5,858,758
1896–7	2,591,740	25,977	1,882,246	1,084,619	156,754	5,741,336
1897–8	2,644,650	30,966	1,969,678	1,083,014	147,066	5,875,374
1898–9	2,704,772	31,308	2,079,626	1,138,326	162,315	6,116,347
1899–1900	2,648,160	26,289	1,832,527	1,129,804	146,986	5,783,766
1900–1	2,802,284	25,392	1,881,160	1,106,502	155,675	5,971,013

Sources: As in Table 13.

VIII. EMIGRATION

'It is doubtful if economic conditions in India have had any effect at all [on emigration]; we may assume, indeed, that the pressure to emigrate, in an economic sense, has always been great enough to provide a stream of emigrants much larger than the actual stream, given opportunity.'[1] If it were true that, as Dr Kingsley Davis holds, the two factors controlling emigration were economic conditions abroad and legislative enactments in India, then trends in emigration could throw little light on economic conditions in India. Emigration would reflect solely the pull of demand from abroad, after allowing for changes in the law in India. But such a view contains some elements of exaggeration. During the first half of the nineteenth century at least, employment opportunities were not always scarce since land in particular was not in short supply. Also the pressure of home supply of labour varied considerably: there was sometimes a sharp increase in emigration following famines in India, one instance being the spurt in emigration from Madras following the great famine of 1876–8. Thus supply did affect movements in migration, although there can be no doubt that movements in the demand for labour abroad were far more important.

The earliest emigration from South India in the British period was the Tamil exodus to the Straits Settlements which had apparently started before the beginning of the nineteenth century; these emigrants were employed abroad as domestic servants and agricultural labourers.[2] The attempts made by the Government early in the nineteenth century to encourage emigration to Ceylon were at first unsuccessful. In 1815 the Collector of Tanjore, when asked by the Government of Madras to employ all the means in his power to send coolies and cattle to Ceylon, said that the Government of Ceylon would have to send agents and offer special inducements, since the people of his district were 'averse to any exodus from their native land of cheap living'.[3] Apparently the Government of Ceylon found private enterprise more efficient than official agencies; in 1818 the Assistant Commissioner-General, Ceylon, wrote to the Collector that the Government had entered directly into a contract with *maistries*

[1] Kingsley Davis, *The Population of India and Pakistan*, p. 99.

[2] T. Geogeghan, *Note on Emigration from India* (Calcutta, 1873), p. 1.

[3] Collector, Tanjore, to Chief Secretary to Government, 31.1.1815, Tanjore Records, vol. 3276, pp. 12–13.

(labour contractors) who had agreed to find 600 labourers for them.[1] The first batch of 150 indentured labourers from South India was brought into Ceylon in 1828 by the Governor to work on his plantation, but all the labourers deserted, and presumably returned to India, within a year.[2] The development of the coffee plantations in Ceylon after 1830 gave rise to a sustained demand for labour.[3] Systematic recruitment to Ceylon started in 1839 when 2,432 indentured labourers were brought in,[4] and two years later an ordinance was passed enabling planters to take criminal action against the labourer who broke his contract and deserted. But desertion was difficult to check when the homeland was so near, so that the indenture system had to be abandoned for the *kangany* system of labour contractors. Even in 1847 the emigration to Ceylon from Madras was not considerable, but in later years it increased very substantially; between 1843 and 1867 there were 1,446,407 emigrants from Madras to Ceylon, of whom 839,897 returned.[5]

The published figures of emigration from Madras to Ceylon are incomplete (the figures available are set out in Tables 16 and 17). The Ceylon records give figures of emigration from and to Ceylon from 1871 onwards; separate figures are not available for India, but nearly all the migration was Indian: the Ceylon Census figures for 1871, 1881 and 1891 show that 98 to 99 per cent of the foreign-born in Ceylon were of Indian origin.[6] It has been estimated that about 90 per cent of the emigration from India was from Madras; an estimate which is supported by a comparison of the Madras figures with the Ceylon figures, as in Table 16. These figures relate only to estate labour; Dr Sarkar estimates that movements of non-estate labour would be as large again.

Emigration to Ceylon reached a peak of 150,000 (recorded figures only) in 1877–8, following the great famine (see Table 17, p. 134). Emigration declined sharply with the collapse of the coffee plantations from 1880 to 1890 but was revived again by the growth of tea and rubber production in Ceylon.

After the conquest of southern Tenasserim in 1826 emigrants from India (probably at first from Bengal alone) went to Burma as domestic servants or miscellaneous labour. In 1840 both the Collector of Godavari

[1] Assistant Commissioner-General, Ceylon to Collector, Tanjore, 25.3.1818; Tanjore Records, vol. 3316, pp. 352–3.

[2] G. C. Mendis, *Ceylon Under the British* (second revised edition, Colombo, 1952), p. 50.

[3] N. K. Sarkar, *The Demography of Ceylon* (Colombo, 1957), p. 27.

[4] C. Kondapi, *Indians Overseas, 1838–1949* (New Delhi, 1951), p. 30.

[5] *Moral and Material Progress Report, 1872–73*, p. 133.

[6] Sarkar, *op. cit.*, p. 170.

Table 16. *Average Annual Migration between Ceylon and India, 1871–99 (in 000's)*

Year	Migration to Ceylon (Ceylon figures)	Madras to Ceylon (Indian figures)	Migration from Ceylon (Ceylon figures)	Net (Ceylon figures)
1871–4	95		75	20
1875–9	119	99·8	90	29
1880–4	43	42·4	58	—12
1885–9	61		52	9
1890–4	96	} 119	63	33
1895–9	122		94	28

Sources: Ceylon figures are from Sarkar, *The Demography of Ceylon*, pp. 168–9; the figures for Madras are from the *Moral and Material Progress Reports*.

and the Commissioner, Tenasserim, reported a large movement of labour from the North Coromandel Coast. After the annexation of Pegu in 1862 the Government of India took steps to encourage emigration to Burma; these became increasingly active after the opening of the Suez Canal had increased the demand for Burmese rice; in 1876 provision was made for the appointment of a recruiting agent for labour from Madras.[1]

Ceylon and Burma account for the bulk of emigration from South India, of course, but there was also emigration to other British colonies and to Dutch and French possessions. The Commissioner of Police in Calcutta stated that emigration to Mauritius and Bourbon had started as early as 1819, but Geogeghan was unable to find records of it before 1830.[2] In any case, it was the abolition of slavery in the British Colonies in 1834 which gave the first great impetus to emigration from India[3] to countries other than Burma and Ceylon.

In 1834 the Collector of Godavari, wrote to the Board of Revenue that men from his district, usually washermen and weavers thrown out of employment by the abolition of the Company's factories, were going to Bourbon in large numbers[4] and to Mauritius,[5] and in 1843 the emigration

[1] Kondapi, *Indians Overseas, 1838–1949*, pp. 46 *et seq.*

[2] See also I. M. Cumpston, *Indians Overseas in British Territories, 1834–1854* (Oxford, 1953), p. 11.

[3] Geogeghan, *Note on Emigration from India*, p. 2. The Act of Emancipation was passed in 1833 but went into force on 1 August 1834.

[4] Collector, Godavari to Board of Revenue, 14.4.1834, Godavari Records, vol. 4647, pp. 72–3.

[5] The total emigration from India to Mauritius alone was 25,000 in 1838, of which

to Mauritius was estimated at 11,000.[1] Emigration to British Guiana started in 1838 but was on an insignificant scale as far as Madras was concerned since the large majority of the migrants sailed from Calcutta: it was estimated that from 1838 to 1890 there were only 14,026 immigrants from Madras into British Guiana as compared to 156,995 from Calcutta.[2]

Systematic emigration to Malaya and the Straits Settlements for work on the plantations started about 1833, and a depot for recruiting indentured labour was set up by the Government of the Straits Settlements at Negapatam.[3] Following a petition from the planters of Natal in 1859, emigratior from India to South Africa began in 1860.[4] After the abolition of slavery in the French Colonies in 1849 and in the Dutch Colonies in 1863, the Government of India entered into Conventions with France and Holland in 1861 and 1868 respectively, permitting emigration to their colonies.[5] But it was always very small compared with that to the British possessions. The emigration from Madras and the French ports in South India to Mauritius, Réunion, Natal and the West Indies between 1842 and 1870 was put at 533,595, of whom around 112,178 returned.[6]

This period was marked by a number of laws controlling both the flow of emigration as well as the terms offered to the migrants.[7] Act XIV of 1839 prohibited contracts with a native of India for labour to be performed outside the territories of the East India Company, or the abetting of emigration for this purpose; the Act was repealed piecemeal over the following years. In 1842 emigration to Mauritius from Madras, Calcutta and Bombay under certain conditions was again permitted; in 1845 emigration to the West Indies and in 1847 to Ceylon was permitted, although the prohibition itself had probably never been applied in practice.[8] The

15,000 was from Bombay and Calcutta, and the remaining 10,000 from the rest of India, probably chiefly Madras. Geogeghan, *op. cit.*, p. 3.

[1] *Ibid.*, p. 13. Scattered data for earlier years, are given in *P.P.* 1841, III (66), *Correspondence Regarding Introduction of Indian Labourers in Mauritius.*

[2] D. W. D. Comins, *Notes on Emigration from India to British Guiana* (Georgetown, 1894), p. 20.

[3] Kondapi, *Indians Overseas, 1834–1949*, pp. 41, *et seq.*

[4] *Ibid.*, p. 21.

[5] *Ibid.*, pp. 5–6. Slavery was formally abolished in France in 1848, though the Act went into force in 1849. The Dutch abolished slavery in the Netherlands West Indies in 1863; the abolition of slavery in Indonesia in 1860 is not relevant here.

[6] These figures are said to be very poor; Geogeghan, *Note on Emigration from India*, p. 66.

[7] On the pressure exerted by the Anti-Slavery Committee on the Government of India to prevent the emigration of labourers from India, on the grounds that it obstructed the emancipation of the slaves, see Cumpston, *Indians Overseas in British Territories, 1834–54*, pp. 175–6.

[8] When the Ceylon Government proposed an ordinance for the protection of

ban on emigration to Natal was lifted in 1860, and to the Seychelles in 1862. These Acts were consolidated in Act XII of 1864. This specified that every migrant had to be taken before a district magistrate who was to register the district of his residence, his occupation and the place to which he was emigrating. This was superseded by Act VII of 1871 which consolidated all previous Acts and provided for a Protector of Emigrants in each Presidency who would, in addition to his other functions, collect emigration figures.

Emigration to Natal was again prohibited between 1866 and 1874, and to the Straits Settlements in 1867, following their separation from British India. But people moved none the less; in 1870 the Sub-Collector of Tanjore stationed at the port of Negapatam publicly pointed out that the recruiting was not only illegal, but also 'a regularly organized system of kidnapping'.[1] After the Government of the Straits Settlements urged upon the Colonial Office that Indian labour was necessary to the agriculture of the colony and promised to safeguard these labourers' interests, emigration was permitted in 1872 under certain conditions; but emigration from Madras alone to the Straits Settlements was further controlled in 1876 and 1877.[2] One reason for this was that the Colony wrote to the Government of Madras, asking them to prevent the emigration of coolies who were physically unfit for agricultural labour;[3] this may have meant either that agricultural labourers were not emigrating or, which is equally likely, that they were in a miserable condition. The Straits Settlements, together with Ceylon, were expressly exempted from the provisions of the Indian Emigration Act, 1883, which regulated the terms and conditions of Indian emigrant labour.[4]

When considering the effect of emigration on the supply of labour in Madras, movements to other parts of India must also be taken into account. Such movements took place throughout the nineteenth century: for example, labourers from Malabar went to work in the coffee plantations in Coorg and Wynaad, and from the beginning of the century there was emigration to Mysore from the neighbouring districts of Madras. Tamils and Telugus moved to Hyderabad, and Telugus to the Central

Indian coolies in 1847, the Government of India pointed out that emigration to Ceylon was illegal, but agreed to permit it by law if the Ceylon Government took steps to prevent Ceylon from becoming an entrepot for emigration to the other colonies; Kondapi, *Indians Overseas, 1838–1949*, p. 30.

[1] Geogeghan, *Note on Emigration from India*, p. 63.

[2] See *Moral and Material Progress Report for India, 1887–88*, p. 154.

[3] P.B.R., 31.3.1877.

[4] For further details of legislation on emigration see Geogeghan, *op. cit.*, and Kondapi, *Indians Overseas, 1838–1949*.

Provinces and Orissa.[1] After the cultivation of tea was introduced in Assam around 1840, workers from the Telugu districts moved up to the plantations there. The abuses of the system of labour recruitment for the Assam tea gardens led to Act V of 1866, which provided for the licensing of all contracts and recruiters of labour from other parts of India, and the examination and registration of labourers by the Protector of Labourers. In 1867 recruitment for Assam was prohibited absolutely, but it was discovered in 1899 that emigration from Ganjam 'in considerable numbers' had been taking place nevertheless, and that most of the emigrants from Ganjam were landless labourers. It was decided to permit recruitment from Ganjam and Vizagapatam, but no emigration from the other districts was permitted. In 1897, following the severe famine of 1896–7, there were 1,044 registered emigrants to Assam, in 1898 269, in 1899 197, and in 1900 none.[2] Another measure of the volume of emigration is the Census figures of people born in Madras but living in Assam: 753 in 1881, 9,901 in 1801, 21,571 in 1901.

Following the famines there were movements to other parts of India; after the great famine of 1876–8, 39,229 people went from Bombay and Madras to Berar.[3] In 1888 the Collector of Bellary reported that labourers had left to work on the Southern Mahratta Railway because of the failure of the rains.[4] But on the whole these movements to other parts of India were much smaller in volume than emigration outside the country, and insignificant in relation to population as a whole.

It is only in the last forty years of the century that emigration grew to significant quantities. Table 17 shows the annual averages of migration in the inter-censal periods from 1861 to 1901, and Table 18 gives more details for the nine years 1875–6 to 1883–4.[5] These figures show that between 1861 and 1871 recorded emigration to Ceylon alone was over 70,000 per annum and the actual emigration must have been considerably larger. The growth of population in this period in Madras was nearly nine times as high as the recorded figures of gross emigration to Ceylon, Mauritius and the West Indies. Between 1871 and 1881, the annual net emigration amounted to 22,624; for the nine years 1875–6 to 1883–4

[1] Davis, *Population of India and Pakistan*, p. 109.

[2] *Report of the Assam Labour Enquiry Committee, 1906–7*, pp. 54–5 and p. 181.

[3] *Moral and Material Progress Report, 1877–78*.

[4] Proceedings, Revenue Settlement, Land Records & Agriculture Department, 31.8.1888.

[5] More figures may be available in the records of the Protectors of Emigrants and the Collectors of the maritime districts which have not been consulted. Geogeghan has used the former source in compiling his statistics from 1843 onwards; these have already been discussed. The latter have been used in the Censuses.

Table 17.

Annual Averages of Migration from Madras Presidency for Inter-Censal Periods, 1871–1901

Year	Ceylon	Burma	Straits Settlements	Natal	Mauritius, Bourbon and West Indies	Total to foreign countries	Rest of India	Grand Total
1861–71	70,667	—	—	—	5,557 −888	—	—	—
1871–81	—	—	—	—	—	22,624 (net)	—	—
1881–91	—	—	—	—	—	98,011	—	—
1891–1901	119,238	61,904	21,917	2,140	354	−75,248 205,554	49,158	254,712 −210,226

Note: Negative figures refer to returning migrants.

Source: Census Report, 1871, p. 76; *Census Report, 1881*, p. 42; *Census Report, 1901*, p. 33.

Table 18.

Emigration from Madras Presidency, 1873–4 to 1888

Year	Ceylon	Burma	Straits settle-ments	Natal	Mauritius and Réunion	British West Indies	Total to outside India
73–4							99,282
							−82,114
74–5				0	1,186		132,692
				−172	−1,231		−85,444
75–6	87,509	3,118		0	294	908	98,258
				−373	−1,247		−82,053
76–7	99,146						197,979
							−91,145
77–8	150,000	4,018		23,901	2,572		169,089
							−92,317
78–9	99,146	7,337			3,697	105	117,148
							−88,864
79–80	63,344	10,377			6,548	3,147	88,386
							−89,572
80–1	43,292	6,682	1,074		3,192	2,733	61,183
							−74,665
81–2	46,594	8,020	1,759	1,763	996	640	59,945
							−64,603
82–3	45,045	22,188		1,358	2,598	796	75,250
							−62,776
83–4	35,292	12,659					54,347
							−57,537
84–5	41,751	5,993					55,427
							−57,548
86			20,625	496	747		84,815
			−17,432				−54,335
87							129,650
							−89,844
88							143,045
							−97,318

Note: Negative figures relate to returning migrants.
Sources: Moral and Material Progress Reports. Wherever possible, figures have been taken m Reports later than the years to which they relate, to allow for corrections.

gross emigration amounted to an annual average of 92,335, and net emigration to 21,873, which was not a significant increase over 1861 to 1871; on the other hand population declined by 0·1 per cent per year between

1871 and 1881. Total recorded gross emigration between 1881 to 1891 amounted to less than one-fifth of the increase in population. Thus emigration became a larger proportion of the growth in population. In the last ten years of the century there was a very considerable spurt in emigration to 200,000 per year (250,000 per year if emigration to other parts of India is included). Net emigration amounted to a little over 0·1 per cent of the mean population, and gross emigration to over 0·6 per cent; during this period population grew at the rate of 0·9 per cent per year.

But emigration is underestimated in these statistics. These are drawn from two sources. First, where emigration was protected under the Indian Emigration Act XXI of 1883, the detailed lists of emigrants were filed in the offices of the Protectors of Emigrants and were more or less complete. This applied to emigration to Natal and Mauritius, and by land to Assam. But to the really important countries, such as Ceylon, the Straits Settlements and Burma, migration was free, and statistics were collected under executive orders based on the Sea Customs Act VIII of 1878 and others.[1] The method of registration was such that immigrants were recorded more completely than emigrants. The Censuses in general include only emigration by sea but even the figures in the *Moral and Material Progress Reports*, which ostensibly include migration by land, do not always include all the travellers to Arakan.[2] Similarly, in the case of emigration to other parts o India, statistics of emigration to the Indian states were frequently incomplete. The definition of an emigrant also varied. For Ceylon, as we have seen, the unrecorded emigration may well have been as much again as the recorded figures. And even in the case of other countries, since a number of regulations were imposed as regards wages, conditions of passage and so on, emigration outside the law and the records must have taken place. It is not therefore improbable that actual emigration was at least 50 per cent higher than the recorded figures; in the last ten years of the century gross emigration from the Presidency may have equalled the increase in population.

For measuring changes in domestic labour supply, gross emigration may be more revealing than net emigration. A distinction must be drawn between three types of movement: permanent emigration, emigration for periods of over a year, and seasonal migrations where the migrant would return within the year. The purely seasonal movements, such as the flow of labour to Burma for the rice harvesting season, took place particularly during the slack season in Madras, April to June.

[1] For more details, see *Census Report, 1901*, p. 26.
[2] See, e.g., *Moral and Material Progress Report, 1878–79.*

In the case of long-term emigration, it is net emigration which ought to be taken into account in measuring labour supply, for it would reduce the labour supply permanently (or rather, over the lifetime of the worker) and raise the wage level throughout the year. But with seasonal emigration, it is the gross figures which are significant. Even if net emigration were nil, the migration of workers during the slack season in India would raise wage rates during that season, while the busy season rates would remain constant. From the statistics it is not possible to distinguish seasonal from other movements, but it can be assumed that during the nineteenth century a large part of the emigration to Ceylon and a smaller proportion of the emigration to Burma was seasonal; since Ceylon took around 46 per cent of the total emigrants and Burma 30 per cent (in 1892–1901), a fairly large proportion of the emigration from Madras must have been seasonal. This is supported, but not proved, by the fact that immigration was around 80 per cent of emigration on an average.

As regards the non-seasonal movements of labour, the length of stay abroad depended partly on the distances involved. Emigrants to Africa, the West Indies and other distant places tended to settle abroad permanently, in contrast to those going to Burma, Ceylon and Malaya. However, even in Fiji as late as 1931 it was found that 'family repatriation is commonest with the Madrasi, who is reported to retain longest his connection with his home country and ancestral lands'.[1] In the nineteenth century at least, emigrants to Burma, Ceylon and Malaya tended to return to India;[2] from a study made of Indian migration to Burma from 1900 to 1940, it was found that the average length of stay in Burma before World War I was five to seven years,[3] and this was probably roughly true of the latter part of the nineteenth century also. (It was reported, on the basis of observation presumably, that emigrants to Burma during the nineteenth century went for periods of one to five years, or for the season.)[4]

Another relevant distinction is that between the single emigrant and the migrant family; the presumption is that if the emigration for any period consisted solely of single labour it would have more effect on the labour supply than if it included women and children. But this must be qualified, since both women and children worked as agricultural labourers in India.

[1] *Census Report, 1931*, pp. 80–90.

[2] Kondapi, *Indians Overseas, 1838–1949*, p. 6.

[3] H. Bernadelli, 'New Zealand and Asiatic Migration', *Population Studies*, July 1952, pp. 39–54. This average has been calculated from moving averages of the total number of Indians in Burma and/or their rate of departure.

[4] Geogeghan, *Note on Emigration from India.*

Another presumption is that family migration would be more permanent but for Ceylon at least this was not true.[1] That whole families moved for relatively short periods was probably a peculiarity of emigration to Ceylon, since it was there that work could be found on the plantations for women as well as children, and that emigration was assisted.[2] During the nineteenth century emigrants to Burma were generally single men.

The full impact of emigration cannot be judged in relation to the population of the whole Presidency, since emigration was always confined to a few districts. But district figures for emigration are only rarely available. Moreover, the centres of emigration, so to speak, themselves changed in response to such factors as famines. In 1857, Tanjore, Trichinopoly, South Arcot, Vizagapatam, Rajahmundry and Ganjam were said to be the main areas of emigration, whereas in 1860–1 and 1861–2 the main centres of emigration to Ceylon were Madura and Tinnevelly.[3] In 1872 the Protector of Emigrants said that emigration from districts other than Godavari, Vizagapatam, Ganjam, Madras and Chinglepet was rare,[4] but it seems very unlikely that there was no emigration from the other Tamil districts—all the more so, because according to the 1881 Census, the emigration to Ceylon was entirely from Madura, Tanjore and Tinnevelly. From 1870 to 1876 gross emigration per annum from Madura to Ceylon alone was 3·1 per cent of the 1871 population, and from Tinnevelly 1·2 per cent.[5] In 1895, emigration to Mauritius and Natal was largely from North Arcot and Chinglepet.[6] Generally speaking, the coastal districts of Andhra supplied emigrants to Burma, and the Tamil

[1] The Sanderson Committee reported in 1910 that 70 per cent of the agricultural immigrants from India to Ceylon returned to India; Sarkar, *The Demography of Ceylon*, p. 28.

[2] For instance, in the twentieth century it was found that where emigration to the estates was assisted, adult males formed 50 per cent of the emigration from India to Ceylon, whereas of the private emigrants only 10 per cent were women; *Census Report, 1931*, pp. 80, 90.

[3] Emigration to Ceylon:

from	*1860–1*	*1861–2*
Tanjore	1,699	708
Madura	26,883	32,326
Tinnevelly	15,253	12,691

(*Moral and Material Progress Report, 1861–62*, vol. I, p. 367.)

[4] Geogeghan, *Note on Emigration from India.*

[5] Total net emigration from 1st November 1869 to 1st November 1876:

	Emigration	*Immigration*	*Net*
Madura	432,372	296,916	135,456
Tinnevelly	127,698	110,498	17,200
Tanjore	66,198	48,764	17,425

Census Report, 1881, vol. III, p. 3.

[6] *Moral and Material Progress Report, 1895–96*, p. 167.

coastal districts, as well as South Arcot, to Ceylon. It is true that the figures were biased in that some emigrants from the inland districts would have registered themselves as residents of the district of departure, but this was probably not important.

Another qualification is that the emigrants came mainly from certain social and economic groups. In 1838 the Collector stated that emigrants to Mauritius from Godavari were discharged sepoys, weavers, agricultural labourers and 'inferior servants'.[1] Again, it was principally barbers, washermen, tailors and weavers who went to Burma from Rajahmundry in 1840. The Collector of Vizagapatam said in 1863 that there had been considerable emigration from his district to the French Colonies and Mauritius,[2] but the majority of the emigrants were weavers and there were no agricultural labourers.[3] Again, although it is true that nearly all emigrants to British Guiana were entered as 'agriculturists', their actual caste, as well as the quality of their labour, belied this.[4] In the twentieth century emigrants to Ceylon were mainly from the lowest castes,[5] including the agricultural labour castes; the presumption would be that this was also the case in the nineteenth century, and this is supported by the replies of some Collectors to the Board's enquiry of 1847. For instance, the Collector of Salem said that the migrants were not 'fixed cultivating ryots but field labourers who are in the habit of moving from district to district', and the reply of the Collector of Tanjore also implied that most of the emigrants were agricultural labourers or tenants.[6] On the whole, however, the evidence regarding the caste or class of the emigrants is too uncertain a basis for trying to estimate how many of them belonged to to each category.

Whatever the actual figures, the danger that emigration would reduce cultivation, and hence land revenues, exercised the Government as early as 1840, and similarly the danger that it would raise domestic wages worried employers throughout the nineteenth century and later.[7] Reply-

[1] Collector, Godavari to Chief Secretary, 28.8.1838; Godavari Records, vol. 4663, p. 274.

[2] Collector, Vizagapatam to Board of Revenue; P.B.R., 2.12.1863.

[3] *P.P.* 1841, XVI (427), *The Export of Hill Coolies*, p. 33.

[4] 'Had all the immigrants who come to this colony really been persons employed in agricultural pursuits in India, there would have been less discontent among them; the employers would have been spared a great deal of expense in hospital accommodation and would further have economised by getting the same quantity of labour done by a few good labourers. . . .'; *P.P.* 1871, XX (393) *Report of the Commissioners appointed to enquire into the Treatment of Immigrants in British Guiana*, p. 59.

[5] *Census Report, 1931*, pp. 88–90.

[6] P.B.R., 14.2.1848.

[7] P.B.R., 23.11.1843.

ing to a circular from the Board of Revenue expressing anxieties of this sort, the Collector of South Arcot wrote in 1843 that the emigration from his district (which seemingly amounted in all to twenty-eight emigrants to Mauritius) had not affected cultivation, and that therefore no measures were needed on the part of the Government 'to ameliorate the condition of the labouring classes so as to prevent their seeking for the means of subsistence out of their own country'.[1]

Once more in 1847 the Board of Revenue asked whether the population was not too small to permit emigration: 'Representations having been made by the Collectors of some districts regarding the injurious effects of encouraging emigration when there is no surplus population beyond what the wants of the country require for carrying out its cultivation, the Most Noble the Governor in Council desires that the Revenue Board will report if any bad effects are really produced in the Districts under this Presidency by the inducements to emigrate which are now held out to the Ryots.'[2] On the basis of the Collectors' replies the Board concluded that emigration had not taken place on such a scale as to harm the revenues by reducing cultivation. In Kurnool, Salem, Coimbatore and Bellary, where extensive lands were lying uncultivated, the Collectors usually concluded that emigration was harmful, even though they had to admit that it was not large enough to have been a cause of the reduction of cultivation. As a case in point, the Collector of Bellary admitted that the question was academic since no emigration had recently taken place from his district, but because thousands of acres of the best cotton land were still uncultivated he felt that the able-bodied should not be allowed to emigrate.[3] The Collector of Trichinopoly pointed out that after fifteen to twenty months the emigrants returned with Rs. 80 to 150 each and could buy a plot of land to cultivate on their own.[4] Emigrants from Salem were field labourers who moved from district to district so their temporary absence in Ceylon, the Collector felt, was not harmful. In Tanjore, in contrast, the Collector held that if facilities for emigration to Ceylon were extended, the loss of 'resident labourers' would be serious.[5]

There was further correspondence on this subject in 1850, though this

[1] P.B.R., 23.11.1843.

[2] Extract from Minutes of Consultation, 30.4.1847, sent to all Collectors; P.B.R., May 1847.

[3] P.B.R., 7.6.1847.

[4] P.B.R., 19.7.1847.

[5] The Collector's views were echoed sixty-five years later. In 1912 the *raiyats* of two taluks in Tanjore petitioned that the emigration of agricultural labourers should be restricted; their petition was of course refused: Proceedings of the Public Department, 8.1.1912, No. 24 (Mis.).

time the point at issue was whether or not the emigration was beneficial to the labourers. Most of the Collectors held that the labourers did benefit, though the Collectors of North Arcot[1] and of Chinglepet[2] reported that very few labourers had in fact emigrated from their districts. The Collector of South Arcot found that since wages in Ceylon were three times the agricultural wages in his district and the emigrants returned from Ceylon and Mauritius with Rs. 50 to Rs. 200, and sometimes as much as Rs. 500 in ready cash, this tended to raise wages in the district.[3] But home wages could not always be raised, since food prices were governed by other factors, such as imports, as the Collector of Trichinopoly pointed out.[4] The Collector of Tinnevelly also found that wages in Ceylon, though they had fallen, were higher than domestic wages, so that the labourers returned with some savings.[5] The only dissident note was struck by the Collector of Tanjore, according to whom the higher wages in Ceylon were offset by the high cost of living, the risk of disease and other factors which kept down emigration from his district,[6] in contrast to the fears of large-scale emigration expressed only three years earlier.

To the extent that land lay fallow because of lack of capital (which may itself have been caused by excessive taxation or high rents), emigration could lead to the extension of cultivation. The Collector of Kurnool said that he had been told in Mauritius in 1842 that Indians often saved £50 to £100 after a few years, and that this would enable them to 'stock a good-sized farm' in India.[7] For later years figures of the actual amounts brought back by returning emigrants are occasionally available.[8] Emigrants to Mauritius seem to have saved the least; in 1887 they brought back over Rs. 25 per head, but in 1888 their savings were less than Rs. 4 per head, in 1893–4 a little over Rs. 10, in 1894–5 less than Rs. 7, and in 1895 less than Rs. 11. Those who went to Natal did better. Although in 1888 they only brought back Rs. 16 each, in 1893–4 they returned with nearly Rs.

[1] P.B.R., 13.5.1850.
[2] P.B.R., 1.7.1850.
[3] P.B.R., 13.5.1850.
[4] P.B.R., 18.7.1850.
[5] P.B.R., 8.8.1850.
[6] P.B.R., 11.7.1850.
[7] P.B.R., 28.5.1847. The Collector of Salem pointed out that in Namakkal taluk there were 20,088 acres of dry arable land lying waste, but there was no need to give this to emigrants since they were only labourers; he probably implied that they had neither the capital nor the skill to undertake cultivation on their own; P.B.R., 17.6.1847.
[8] Unless otherwise stated, the data are taken from the *Moral and Material Progress Report* for the year.

140 per head, in 1894–5 with Rs. 224 and in 1895 with nearly Rs. 190. But with those amounts they could buy only an acre or less of wet land, or a few acres of dry land.[1]

Nevertheless, the amounts brought back by the emigrant did not represent his total savings, as the figures in Table 19 for remittances by money orders in the year 1900–1 show:

Table 19. *Remittances by Money Orders, 1900–1*

Country from which sent	No. of money orders	Total value (Rs.)
Ceylon	45,226	16,15,381
Straits Settlements	24,472	10,04,330
Mauritius	1,153	36,460
Natal	1,623	1,19,914
TOTAL	72,474	27,76,085

Source: Census Report, 1901, p. 209.

The average money order was for Rs. 38, but since the remittances were probably made several times a year, if not every month, *per capita* figures cannot be derived.

Emigration must also have increased social mobility in other ways; the emigrants would return with greater knowledge of agricultural techniques and less willingness to abide by caste restrictions. These effects of emigration would be particularly strong for the lower castes since they were the more immobile. 'The larger and more inclusive the territorial unit in which members of a caste can move, the higher the rank of that caste.'[2] Once they had overcome the restrictions on movement, the members of these castes would be more ready to disregard other restrictions, though it is not always clear where emigration was the cause and where the effect. But in this period these effects of emigration were, in the short term at least, marginal; its most important effect was probably to support wage levels or to mitigate the decline in them that would have taken place in

[1] For example, in Tanjore the average prices of wet land, as recorded in deeds of sale and mortages, rose from Rs. 12 per acre in 1823–4 to Rs. 39 in 1852–3 and to Rs. 245 per acre in 1878; in 1878 the dry land sold at Rs. 140 per acre and garden lands at Rs. 82 per acre (*Tanjore District Manual*, p. 321); and in 1899–1903 single crop wet lands sold at Rs. 63 to Rs. 458 per acre, double crop wet lands at Rs. 441 to Rs. 771 per acre and dry lands without wells from Rs. 64 to Rs. 233 per acre (Settlement Report for Tanjore, 1921). Since land prices varied so widely within the district and figures of yields per acre on land of different values are not available, it is not possible to be more precise about the value of the emigrants' savings.

[2] Miller, 'Caste and Territory in Malabar', p. 410, *et seq.*

the absence of this outlet for labour in the latter half of the nineteenth century.

In short, it is true that emigration from Madras was small compared to total population (or to European migrations in this period), but a net emigration of at least one-seventh to one-ninth of the annual growth of population, and a gross emigration at least four to six times as large again (these being the *recorded* figures for 1883–4 and 1892–1901), was not a totally negligible factor in reducing the pressure of population on land. Moreover, emigration may have reduced the natural rate of increase of population since the emigrants were in the most reproductive age groups;[1] but this is a factor of uncertain and probably minor significance.

[1] The Census Commissioner pointed out in 1931 that the birth-rate in Ramnad, Madura, Tanjore and Trichinopoly was much lower than in other districts and the death-rate only somewhat lower. One reason for the lower birth-rate was the continuing emigration from these districts, since the emigrants were at the most reproductive age and were drawn from the most reproductive classes; *Census Report, 1931*, pp. 32–3.

IX. WAGES

On the basis of the available date on land utilization and population alone it is not possible to say definitely whether or not the acreage under crops —taking into account not only the extension of cultivation to new lands but also more intensive cultivation of the old—increased at a faster rate than the growth in the numbers dependent on agriculture. Since direct evidence on the point is insufficient, recourse must be had to other evidence, of which the most important is wages. Changes in the land-labour ratio can be inferred to some extent from wage movements: a fall in wages would support the presumption that the land-labour ratio was decreasing, in other words that the extension of cultivation was insufficient to meet the growth of the labour force in agriculture. Over the first half of the nineteenth century population grew substantially, though probably not at the recorded rate of 130 per cent. It seems probable that there was hardly any significant extension of the area under cultivation over the same period—a drastic decline in cultivation up to 1825 or so being offset by substantial increases in the next two decades. Unfortunately, it is just for this period, when data on population and land utilization are most scanty, that wage data are also most defective: the few scattered wage quotations cannot be used to induce trends within the period, and can at best serve only as a basis for comparison with later wage quotations.

For the second half of the century, and particularly for the last quarter, the position is easier. From the figures of land under cultivation it would not appear that the extension of cultivation greatly exceeded the growth of the labour force in agriculture; it may well have fallen short of it if inferior lands were taken under cultivation. This latter presumption is strengthened by the wage data which show a falling trend: wages series for seven districts show that for all of them, except Tanjore, wages were lower at the end of the century than in 1873.

The wage data also throw light on the monetization of the economy. At the beginning of the nineteenth century it is clear that the wages of both attached and casual labourers were generally paid in grain, apart from perquisites in the form of clothes and money. With monetization the casual labourers were more frequently paid in cash, but this change proceeded very slowly over the century. In 1863 and 1864 wages were still paid in grain in most districts. In Godavari it was reported that agricultural labourers were invariably paid in kind, in Tinnevelly that there was no instance of payment in kind having given way to payment in money, and in Bellary that agricultural labourers were still, as in the past, paid very generally in kind.[1] But in Ganjam it was reported that in the last five or six years a few employers had begun to pay cash wages. Cash payments were made in Kurnool, but only for cultivation of special products such as cotton. And even for cotton, payments were sometimes made in kind, as a proportion of the crop picked. With the rise in cotton prices the employers of Kurnool tried to pay in cash, presumably since it was difficult to lower wages in kind. On plantations where there were foreign masters, immigrant labour and commercial crops, payment was made in cash. In the other areas, cash payments were made as a temporary arrangement during periods of scarcity, and the rates were 'regulated with reference to current market prices of grain'; this seems to imply that their real value was kept constant,[2] but as we shall see later this appears unlikely.

Farm labourers were paid in kind in most parts of Trichinopoly in 1878–9.[3] Even in 1892–3[4] grain wages were comman, except in the Godavari and Kistna[5] deltas, in two *taluks* of Coimbatore, and in the vicinity of the large towns. However, the wages of casual labourers were being more frequently paid in cash, particularly in districts where there were public works or railways being built, as in Godavari, or where non-food crops such as indigo were grown. But even for these crops wages were not invariably in money; in Madura, agricultural labourers who collected tamarind or picked cotton were paid a share of the produce. Both attached and casual workers would receive grain payments, though in Tinnevelly in 1893 the grain payments for cotton cultivation were giving way to money wages. But in some districts, including Bellary and Anantapur,[6] even casual labourers were paid almost always in grain except in periods of scarcity. Naturally harvest wages were frequently paid in grain, even when cash was paid at other seasons. While urbanization and the development of cash crops will have speeded up monetization, the extension of irrigation may have delayed it, since workers on wet lands were paid in kind to a larger extent than those on dry lands. In irrigated areas there would be a steady demand for labour, and a large part of the labour would be attached. What seems probable is that during the first half of the century, when wages were generally paid in kind, the rates in grain

[1] P.B.R., 29.1.1864.

[2] P.B.R., 24.6.1864.

[3] C. Benson, *Report of a Tour in Trichinopoly District* (Madras, 1879), p. 89.

[4] Except where otherwise stated, the material is from Appendix to Resolution 690, P.B.R., 29.10.1897.

[5] Government of Madras, *Statistical Atlas for Madras Presidency, 1908*, p. 139.

[6] See also evidence of the Collector of Anantapur, Government of India, *Report of the Indian Famine Commission, 1898*, vol. II, Appendices, p. 3.

were stable; one frequently comes across statements such as that made by the Collector of North Arcot as late as 1864; 'These wages in kind and rations never fluctuate; nor does the mode of payment ever change in consideration of bad seasons and high prices.'[1] But towards the end of the century, in those areas—probably still the minority—where cash wages had become habitual, when wages were paid in kind the grain payments may have fluctuated to keep money wages constant.[2] During the 1896–7 famine it was reported in Ganjam that labourers were generally paid in cash and not as usual in kind, and also that with the rise in prices the labourers did not get half the usual quantities of grain.[3] In Bellary too the landlords refused to raise cash wages when prices rose, and in fact the labourers would not leave the relief works till the *raiyats* began to pay them in grain.[4] Indeed it seems much more likely that the switch to money wages did not reflect the rise in prices since employers were in a stronger bargaining position than the workers. Another reason for the switch to cash payments may have been that in times of scarcity the smaller farmers had no grain stocks at the time of transplanting.[5] Thus the beginning of a trend towards the payment of money wages can be discerned, particularly for casual labourers and cash crops, but the pace of monetization was both slow and uneven. It would be interesting to trace the connection between monetization and changes in real wage rates, but for this far more data are required.

Apart from the wage series from 1873 onwards, which will be discussed later, the wage data are clustered around five points of time. First, in 1800–1 Buchanan quotes wage rates for several districts, then in 1863–4, 1872–3 and 1893–7, the Board of Revenue collected information about the modes of payment and movements of agricultural wages. Again, in 1884, on a resolution of the Government of India regarding measures for the relief of over-populated tracts, the Collectors were asked to comment on the Board's statement that:

'(1) The native labourer lives from hand to mouth and has little reserve upon which to fall to meet bad seasons or want of work.
(2) That in ordinary years he has sufficient food.'[6]

[1] P.B.R., 29.1.1864.
[2] See letter from Collector of Trichinopoly, P.B.R. (Settlement), 4.5.1891.
[3] *Report on the Famine in Madras Presidency during 1896 and 1897* (Madras, 1898), vol. II, p. 15.
[4] *Ibid.*, pp. 30 and 33.
[5] *Ibid.*, p. 41.
[6] The Board's circular and the replies of the Collectors are contained in P.B.R., 19.10.1888, Circular No. 96–F/6.

For the rest there are only odd quotations from the settlement reports, the reports on slavery, and other official papers.

Up to 1873 at least, the figures available are so widely scattered over time that only the broadest generalizations above movements in wages are possible. Difficulties of generalization arise not only from the scantiness of the wage data but also from the wide variety in modes of payment. Even at the end of the century there was 'a great diversity in the customs regulating agricultural wages, not only in different districts of the Presidency, but in different taluks in the same district and in different parts of one and the same taluk. For so vast an area as the Madras Presidency, it is well nigh impossible to make any safe generalization.'[1] Wages were paid either in cash or kind, and varied not only with the area but also with the status of the labourer. Casual labourers were generally paid more frequently in cash than attached labourers, and also at higher rates.

There were wide differences even in rates of payments in kind: payments in paddy wages in Palghat *taluk* (in Malabar) ranged from 1 to 3¾ *seers* per day in 1852–3.[2] These are the wages of the 'serfs'. In addition to the daily grain wages there were annual grain allowances at harvest time; the master also gave a few coconuts, some oil and clothes, but variations in these payments are unlikely to be large enough to account for the variations in daily wages. Such differences are naturally only to be expected in a society ruled by custom and where serfdom prevents the emergence of a proper labour market. Even wage figures for the same district therefore may not be perfectly comparable.

Secondly, in comparing any two sets of figures, the possibility that they may refer to different seasons and to different types of work must be taken into account. We have, for example, separate quotations for the daily wages for nine different types of work performed by agricultural labourers in Tinnevelly in 1864; two of these were made in cash and the rest in kind.[3] The seasonal differences are quite large, the highest rates being paid at harvest time—in Tinnevelly in 1864 the daily rates at harvest time were twice as high as other daily rates, such as those for irrigation, or even higher. But the difference was not always so great—in Viza-

[1] P.B.R., 29.10.1897, No. 690.

[2] Report of Collector, Malabar to Board of Revenue; P.B.R., 4.12.1863.

[3] The nine types of work were: fetching branches for manure; baling water and repairing bridges (cash payments were made for these two functions); removing weeds, fetching ashes and black clay for manure; removing nursery plants and threshing produce; transplanting; treading grain by cattle; irrigating; fetching cowdung and manure, and weeding; reaping and threshing. But the categories are not mutually exclusive, and the wage rates for some are the same. Collector, Tinnevelly to Board of Revenue; P.B.R., 7.1.1864.

gapatam in 1863 the daily wages were 7 *seers* at harvest time and 5½ *seers* before the harvest.[1]

Thirdly, when comparing grain wages the types of grain must be considered. It is interesting that payments in better quality grains did not necessarily involve smaller quantities; in fact it was frequently the other way round. Thus in Salem in 1864 payments in paddy were higher than those paid in coarse grains, such as *ragi*, *cholum*, or *cumbu*, whereas the latter (except for *ragi*) were likely to be the cheaper crops.[2] But this was not always the case. In Madras in 1863 the quantity of paddy given as daily wages was larger than the quantity of *ragi*, which was the more expensive crop. The differences in wage rates for different grains were related to but not identical with the differences between wages on wet lands and payments for labour on dry fields. These differences may have arisen partly from the differences in the farmers' profits (since labour was not completely mobile), partly from the differences in the nature of the labour itself, and partly because a far greater proportion of the labour on wet lands was attached labour, which was itself a consequence of the other factors.

In the fourth place, while daily wages might not change the wage rate per unit of work might alter. For example, in Vizagapatam the Collector reported in 1893 that although wage rates had on the whole been stable for the last thirty years, 'there has been a considerable alteration, but . . . it has taken the form of a reduction in the quality and quantity of work done for the same money'. This was partly because the better labourers worked on the construction of the East Coast Railway, so that the quality of the labourers remaining in agriculture declined.[3]

Fifthly, the wage would depend on the status of the labourer, but it is not always clear whether the figures relate to attached or casual labour. The differences between the wages of the two reflect not only differences in social status, but also in hours and conditions of work, perquisites and volume and stability of employment. Casual labourers generally worked shorter hours but were given less by way of perquisites. Attached labourers had more guaranteed employment though even for them, the

[1] Collector, Vizagapatam to Board of Revenue, P.B.R., 2.12.1863. The Agricultural Labour Enquiry shows that in 1951 wages for threshing were 24 per cent above the average wage rates; *Report on Intensive Survey of Agricultural Labour* (New Delhi, 1954), vol. VI, pp. 25–6.

[2] Reply of Collector, Salem; P.B.R., 9.3.1864.

[3] Collector, Vizagapatam to Settlement Department, 19.5.1893; P.B.R. (Revenue Settlement, Land Records and Agriculture), 15.6.1893. The reduction in hours of work was probably mainly the result of the poor quality of the labour and not of deliberate action, unlike the go-slow movement organized by the *pannaiyals* of Tanjore in recent years.

guarantee, it is true, was not absolute. Finally the wage sometimes also depended on the caste of the labourer and indeed even upon that of the employer. Even amongst the attached labourers or serfs those of the lowest castes were paid the lowest wages. As late as 1892–3 it was reported that the wages of the *pannaiyal* varied with his caste: 'The condition of panchama pannials is very little removed from that of slaves, as they get only so much as is required for their maintenance whereas the sudra pannials receive besides the payment in kind a number of advantages from their masters as well as gifts in money on certain occasions. Their material condition shows a distinct tendency to improve.'[1] Brahmin employers sometimes followed different customs of payment—the threshing fees for *agraharams*, or the Brahmin villages, are separately quoted for Ganjam in 1864.[2] Indeed all over India Brahmins paid lower fees for various village services than those paid by the other castes.[3]

Problems of comparability over time are greatest for attached labour, since over a long period a variety of customary perquisites would have been established.[4] The attached labourers were always paid at least partly in kind. The payments could be fixed either in absolute terms or as a percentage of the crop. But proportionate wages were probably paid only in the harvest season,[5] since it would be difficult to calculate the labourer's share at other times.[6] For reaping and threshing, the wages varied from 4 per cent to 12 per cent of the crop, and in addition a cooked meal would be provided. In some areas the supply of cooked food depended on whether the labourer was of a high enough caste to work in the house.[7] Labourers had the right to glean in the fields and the threshing floors after the harvest. In addition to grain payments and cooked meals the master might supply spices, coconuts and oil. One or two pieces of cloth a year were also provided, and the master gave cash or grain presents on festivals or for births, marriages and funerals. These payments would naturally vary much more than the daily grain wages.[8] In some areas the master

[1] P.B.R., 29.10.1897, No. 690. Panchamas are the untouchable castes.

[2] P.B.R., 4.4.1864.

[3] Thomas O. Beidelman, *A Comparative Analysis of the Jajmani System* (New York, 1959), p. 9.

[4] See, for example, reply of Collector, Arcot; P.B.R., 1.2.1864.

[5] Reply of Collector, Chinglepet; P.B.R., 24.6.1864.

[6] According to Kautilya, the classical Indian writer on political theory, if no remuneration were fixed the agricultural labourer and the cowherd could claim one-tenth of the product as wages; Kautilya, *Artha Shastra*, ed. Sama Sastry (5th edn. Mysore, 1956), Part III, ch. 13–40.

[7] P.B.R., 29.10.1897.

[8] 'The grains wage is very accurately fixed and varies very little from year to year. The money presents, however, no doubt, vary considerably according to the master's will'; reply of Collector, S. Arcot; P.B.R., 29.10.1897.

gave interest-free loans up to a narrow limit,[1] but doubtless adjustments for interest were in fact frequently made in the wage payments, another factor reducing comparability.

The agricultural labourer, like every other inhabitant of the village, was generally given rent-free land for his house on the village site, and his house, a mud and thatch hut which he built himself, would also be free. In 1928 it was stated that 'in the districts of South Arcot, Tanjore and Trichinopoly . . . a few high-caste persons called mirasidars claim, rightly or wrongly, to have a prior right over all the land in the village including unoccupied areas and including the house sites of the labourers. It is in villages of this type that emigration is most frequent as the low caste labourer has no chance of acquiring any land available, and is at the mercy of his master, being liable to be expelled from the only land available for the house-sites if he should offend him.'[2] But there are no other references in the literature to this position, and it may be that the landlords claimed these rights in the course of their battle with the Government over ownership rights, and only rarely attempted to assert them in practice. The labourer's house site would be in the low caste quarter of the village, and even if the village acknowledged the *mirasdar's* ownership of this area, which is doubtful, he could only use it to house another family of labourers. But it is occasionally mentioned that the employer paid the labourer's rent. On the other hand, 'in some districts, where the land-holders do not themselves cultivate, the farm servants are permitted to grow an after crop of their own account in remuneration for their services'.[3] In fact, in the Cudalur *taluk* of the Nilgiris, the farm servants were allowed every year the paddy crop on two of the best plots in the occupation of their masters, in addition to being paid daily wages.[4]

An important but not universal perquisite of attached employment was that the master was obliged to employ every male member of the labourer's family above a certain age.[5] But in practice this meant that when he had work available the master would first turn to the family of his 'serf'. This amounts to something less than guaranteed employment. After all, the attached labourer himself was not always automatically entitled to paid employment throughout the year. Even in Malabar in the early part of the century it was variously reported that the serf had to be paid a fixed wage all the year round, whether employed or not, and

[1] In Ganjam the limit was Rs. 10; P.B.R., 4.4.1864; in Madras city the limit was Rs. 35; P.B.R., 22.2.1864.
[2] *Report of the Royal Commission on Agriculture in India, 1928*, vol. 1, p. 315
[3] *Census Report, 1871*, p. 178.
[4] P.B.R., 29.10.1897.
[5] Reply of Collector, Ganjam; P.B.R., 4.4.1864.

that when not employed he was paid half the fixed customary wage or none at all.[1] But if he was not paid, he must have been permitted to work for other employers.[2]

The attached labourer was generally paid not by the day but by the month; deductions for days when the labourer was unemployed may have been made but were probably infrequent.[3] Even the monthly wages were sometimes paid for part of the year alone; during the harvest the labourer was given a proportion of the harvest. This harvest payment, furthermore, could be either in addition to or in lieu of the fixed monthly or daily wage, depending on their size. Thus in South Arcot in 1872[4] the harvest fees were in lieu of the monthly wages, whereas in Tinnevelly in 1897 the attached labourer on wet lands got 136–407 *seers* of paddy at the time of harvest, in addition to daily wages of 3·6 *seers* during the harvest and 1·8 *seers* at other times.[5]

The certainty of his obtaining some employment, and the fact that his master generally maintained the attached labourer in sickness and old age. were the main reasons (apart from perquisites and perhaps caste) why the daily wages of the attached labourer were almost invariably below the daily wages paid to casual labourers. In 1800 a male slave in South Canara got three-fourths the daily wage of the hired labourer.[6] In 1882 in Malabar it was remarked that the wages of the 'slaves' were lower than those of free labourers, even though the former worked much shorter hours. With loosening bonds the masters probably accepted fewer obligations towards the attached labourers, but even so the wage differential remained; there are not enough data to say in what direction and to what degree it changed.

For most of the century then, it is only these scattered wage quotations that are available. It is best to consider them district by district, to see if any trends are discernible. But before doing so, it must be remembered that even if the figures of the wage rates were correct,[7] the wage rates in

[1] *Select Committee Report, 1831–2*, Appendix K, p. 566.

[2] Reply of Collector, Malabar; P.B.R., 29.10.1897.

[3] Such deductions were reported in Andhra in 1948; Reddy, 'Transition in Caste Structure in Andhra Desh with Particular Reference to Depressed Castes', p. 135.

[4] P.B.R., 11.11.1872.

[5] P.B.R., 29.10.1897.

[6] Buchanan, *A Journey from Madras*, vol. II, p. 228.

[7] One of the major sources of error is the variety of measures used. Grain in Madras was measured in terms of volume, not weight, and by heaped, not struck, measures. It is not always clear what grain is being referred to, and the measures vary from period to period, from district to district, and indeed within each district. All these measures—*edangallis*, *mercals*, *tooms*, and so on—have been reduced to the standard Indian *seer*. A comprehensive, but not complete, description of the various

themselves would not be a complete guide to changes in the economic conditions of the agricultural labourer. As we have seen, even for attached labourers wages were paid only when the labourer was actually employed by the master, so that the volume of employment must be taken into account. For the period from 1875 onwards, when it appears likely that the pressure of population on the land increased, this would mean that a fall in wage rates would underestimate the deterioration in the condition of the labourer, since it is likely that there would also have been a fall in the number of days each labourer was employed.

Again, these figures would not reflect changes in perquisites, and these are likely to have fluctuated more sharply than the wage difference. Changes in status must also be taken into account. Thus it is very probable that the agricultural labourers were less subject to harsh physical treatment in the latter half of the century, but this may have been for social and legal, rather than economic reasons. A more important qualification is the type of grain consumed: there may have been some increase in welfare due to an improvement in the quality of the staple food. This was undoubtedly the case in the irrigated areas where paddy was grown instead of coarse grains.[1]

Of all the districts, Malabar has the largest number of wage rates quoted; it is also the district in which there is the most continuity in both modes and rates of payment. In 1801 Buchanan reported that both male and female serfs were given 2 *edangallis* of rice in the husk weekly, which would be equivalent to about 1·5 to 2 *seers*. This would, of course, be totally inadequate to support them 'but the serfs also got about 5 per cent of the gross produce, together with some cloth'.[2] It is not always explicitly stated that the labourer received a fixed proportion of the crop at harvest, but this seems likely. It is not always clear either whether this share of the crop supplemented or replaced the customary daily wages. This probably depended on the size of the share: 5 per cent would clearly have to supplement other payments. (In 1841 it was stated that the 'field slaves' were at harvest daily given 10 per cent of what they reaped.)[3] In addition to these payments, the labourer also got a certain proportion of the crop in return for guarding it; this was clearly additional to his other wages. In North Malabar the hired servants who belonged to the Tiya caste and worked

district measures is contained in the *Manual of Administration of the Madras Presidency*, vol. II, Appendix XC.

[1] Thus in Godavari with the extension of anicut irrigation after 1870, rice became the staple food grain instead of *ragi*; *Report on the Famine in Madras Presidency during 1896 and 1897* (Madras, 1898), vol. II, p. 96.

[2] Buchanan, *A Journey from Madras*, vol. II, p. 67.

[3] *Slavery Report, 1841*, p. 134.

only till noon got 2½ *edangallis* or about 1·8 to 2·5 *seers* per day,[1] whereas he Cherumans had to work till nightfall and sometimes watch the fields at night. In 1799 again, the overseer of the Government plantation wrote that he wanted to take on additional Pulaiyans and Tiyas to whom he would give Rs. 4 to Rs. 4.8.0 per month, together with three 'measures' of rice (or 4·8 *seers*) and one pice in cash per day;[2] he had apparently started off by paying Rs. 5 per month and had periodically reduced the wages till they came to Rs. 3 per month plus the daily allowance in 1801.[3] The modes and rates of payment did not change much in the second half of the century, except that one rather different method of calculating wages was reported of the village of Chevayur in 1866:

> It is said by the people that it is customary, when coolies are employed to do all the cultivation, to pay them for the whole work previous to harvest by giving them ordinarily the same quantity of paddy as the land which they cultivate can sow, and for the harvest about one-eighth of the produce harvested.[4]

In 1822 it was reported that the serfs got between 1½ to 1¾ *seers* per day while the casual labourers working shorter hours got 2 to 2¾ *seers* per day, or the equivalent in cash.[5] In addition to other perquisites such as cloth and a little cash, the serf was sometimes allowed to cultivate a little land on his own account.[6]

The average wage rate in 1852–3 was 2·1 *seers* per day, the actual wage ranging from ¾ to 3¾ *seers*. These wages were more or less unchanged ten years later, except for a rise in a few areas which took the average up to 2·3 *seers* per day.[7] In 1872 the Collector of Malabar reported that the great majority of the agricultural labourers were still attached, and were still slaves in all but name, and that they were paid for the most part 2·4 *seers* per day whether they worked or not. So there had been little perceptible improvement in their wages.[8] Twenty years later it was reported that the farm servants were paid for half the year in paddy at an average

[1] Buchanan, *op. cit.*, vol. II, p. 174.

[2] Letter of 16.7.1799, Malabar Records, vol. 1697. These are the rates for men; rates for women and children are also given.

[3] Malabar Records, vol. 2210, pp. 36–7.

[4] J. Cameron, *Report on the Village of Chevayur, 1866* (Calicut, 1868), pp. 6–9.

[5] Graeme, Report on Malabar, 14.1.1822, *Slavery Papers, 1828*, p. 922. The figures are given in 'Macleod *seers*' which seem to equal *endangallies*, and hence to be more or less (less rather than more) equal to ordinary *seers*.

[6] *P.P.* 1834 (128), *Slavery in India: Correspondence*, p. 9.

[7] Collector's reply to Board of Revenue; P.B.R., 4.12.1863. No distinction is made between the wages of attached and casual labour.

[8] P.B.R., 11.11.1872, No. 2179.

fixed rate of $2\frac{1}{4}$ *seers* per man and $1\frac{1}{2}$ *seers* per woman. At the harvest the labourers were paid from one-sixth to one-tenth of the gross produce. There had been, according to the Collector, some increase in both the grain and money wage rates for casual labour over the last twenty years.[1] Thus, almost throughout the century the attached labourer was paid a little more than 2 *seers* per day, with some small perquisites; the data available for the first half of the century show that the casual labourer was paid about a third more, and had also to work considerably shorter hours. This continuity is only to be expected in view of the fact that the Cheruman continued to be in a state of serfdom throughout the century.

In South Canara too, as one would expect, wages did not show any marked tendency to rise over the century. In 1801 Buchanan had reported that the hired labourer received about 1·3 *seers* of clean rice per day, and the male 'slave' got 0·9 *seers* per day ($1\frac{1}{2}$ *hanis*), both being given perquisites such as cloth and a little cash.[2] The rates for 'slaves' seem too low but are confirmed by the Collectors' reports. In the same year the male 'moondaul dherds' were each paid $1\frac{1}{2}$ *hanis* of rice per day together with 1 *mora* (28–29 *seers*) of rice and 2 cloths per annum; during the harvest they were given, instead of the daily allowance, one-eleventh of the crop.[3] In 1819 the Holeya was reported to get on the average $1\frac{1}{2}$ *seers* of coarse rice per diem and 2 pieces of cloth per annum, together with salt and spices, which were given at the discretion of the master.[4] These were more or less the wages paid in 1826 too.[5] Towards the end of the century it was reported that farm servants got 1 to 2 *seers* of clean rice per day, the average being $1\frac{1}{2}$ *seers*, as well as a midday meal and the usual perquisites, including an allotment of rent-free land of from one-eighth to one-third of an acre.[6] Thus in South Canara the wages of the serfs appear to have been a little lower than in Malabar, but here also wages remained remarkably stable throughout the century, though near the coast and the coffee plantations wages were somewhat higher than the average of 1·5 to 2 *seers* per day.[7]

The Tamil districts show a much greater variety in modes of payment, and there are also far more fluctuations in wage rates. For the first half of

[1] P.B.R., 29.10.1897, No. 690.
[2] Buchanan, *A Journey from Madras*, vol. II, pp. 227–8.
[3] P.B.R., 7.8.1801.
[4] *Slavery Papers, 1828*, p. 844.
[5] *Report on Slavery, 1841*, p. 47.
[6] *South Canara Manual*, vol. I, pp. 173–4.
[7] Resettlement Report for Kesargod and Mangalore, 30.3.1898, pp. 71–2. This report quotes wages, but per acre, not per labourer, e.g. 5 *seers* for each time 1 acre of paddy is ploughed, 11 per cent of the gross out-turn for reaping and threshing.

the century, data are available only for a few districts.[1] In Chinglepet, according to Place, the earnings of a *pannaiyal* amounted to around 105 *seers* per month, but from this the Board of Revenue estimated that there would have to be a small deduction for certain fees, so that the net wages would amount to 95 *seers* per month; very little was given by way of perquisites. In 1863 attached labourers were being paid fixed grain wages in the first six months only, while for the remaining six months they were given about 20 per cent of the harvest, together with the right to glean in the fields and certain other perquisites.[2] In 1884 the annual wages of a permanent farm servant were, according to an official, Rs. 56 or the equivalent of 840 *seers*, but according to a missionary, Rs. 24–30 per annum, or the equivalent of 360 to 450 *seers* of rice. It was generally agreed, however, that the labourer was very badly off, a fact partly attributed to the *mirasi* system, partly to the poverty of the soil.[3] In 1892–3 casual labourers were paid 3·7 to 4·9 *seers* per day which, according to the Collector, represented a decline of about 25 per cent in the grain wage for casual field labour over the twenty-year period; the money wage had gone up by 20 to 33 per cent. While the Sub-Collector felt that there had been a deterioration in the condition of the agricultural labourer, his superior officials did not agree with him—the wages of the permanent farm servant had remained unchanged for the last twenty years.[4] In fact, it was calculated that the total monthly earnings of the attached worker in 1892 would amount to more or less the quantity earned in 1801, that is, about 96 *seers*, including harvest perquisites.[5] But by 1900 the monthly wage in Conjeevaram *taluk* had fallen to around 64 *seers* of paddy, though it was calculated that the value of perquisites such as harvest gleanings, cloth and loans free of interest, would amount to more than this.[6]

In Salem around 1800 or so the daily labourer got the equivalent of 3·5 *seers* per day, and the ploughmen got in cash and kind the equivalent of 654 *seers* a year.[7] In 1863–4, wages ranged from 66 *seers* of rice per month, or 53 *seers* of *ragi* or other coarse grains, to 106 *seers* of rice

[1] Only districts where wage data are sufficient for comparisons over time are discussed.

[2] P.B.R., 24.6.1864.

[3] P.B.R., 7.10.1884, No. 9545.

[4] P.B.R., 29.10.1897, No. 690.

[5] Raghavaiyangar, *Progress of the Madras Presidency*, p. 146.

[6] P.B.R. (Settlement), 27.4.1900, No. 2068 (Misc.).

[7] In Kellamangalam the ploughmen got annually 20 bushels, worth 28 *fanams*, together with 16 fanams in cash and a hut. The daily labourer, male or female, got 0·356 bushels of rice per day, of which half was husk and has therefore been deducted; Buchanan, *A Journey from Madras*, vol. II, pp. 520–1. A bushel is roughly equivalent to 21·9 *seers* of coarse rice.

or 66 *seers* of other coarse grains, together with minor perquisites; these rates had remained unchanged for some time.[1] In 1872–3 the Collector reported that the *pannaiyal* was paid from 40 to 66 *seers* of either *ragi* or other grains together with an annual cash payment of Rs. 2 to 5; occasionally *pannaiyals* were paid in cash, Rs. 2½ to Rs. 4 per month. Casual labourers were paid 5 to 6·6 *seers* per day. The Collector felt that there had been some improvement in the condition of labourers, though this does not seem to be borne out by the figures.[2] In 1892–3 it was reported that the monthly wages of an adult labourer in Salem main division ranged from 63 to 84 *seers* per month, with a cash payment of Rs. 2½ to Rs. 3 at the end of the year. In another division of the district, rates were lower, from 46 to 62 *seers* per month, whereas in yet another division wages amounted to 112 *seers* per month.[3] In some parts of the district, then, there seems to have been a distinct improvement in wages, while in other areas wages tended to remain stable—between 1863 and 1893 at least.

In Coimbatore in 1801, according to Buchanan, the *padiyals* got in all, including their cash payment, the equivalent of 684 to 984 *seers* of paddy per annum in rough rice, of which half may have been husk; casual labourers got over 4 *seers* per day.[4] In 1819 the *padiyals* got one-eighth of the produce, and were sometimes given land for cultivation on their own.[5] Although it appeared that nominal wages had not risen for centuries, one official felt that real wages had in fact risen, if loans given for marriages or other purposes were included.[6] In 1863 the Collector reported that the payments which were generally in kind, except in times of scarcity, continued to be at the same rate as they had been for ten years or more.[7] In 1892–3 the wages of attached labourers ranged from 594 to 792 *seers* per annum, and were said to be the same rates as previously, while the wages for casual labourers amounted to 1·9 to 2·4 *seers* per day.[8] These figures are borne out in the statement in Robertson's Report on Coimba-

[1] Reply of Collector, Salem; P.B.R., 9.3.1864.

[2] P.B.R., 11.11.1872.

[3] Raghavaiyangar, *op. cit.*, p. 142.

[4] In Darapuram the farm servants got the equivalent of 31 bushels of rice in all, of which half was paddy. In Pollachi the *padiyal* got 29 bushels in grain, together with 10 fanams in cash, the whole amounting to 984 *seers*. In Bhavanikudal the *padiyal* was paid 13 bushels and 15–20 Gopal fanams per annum and was given a house. It is not stated whether this rice included husk or not, but it probably did; Buchanan, *A Journey from Madras*, vol. II, pp. 29, 32, 217–18.

[5] *Slavery Papers, 1828*, p. 837.

[6] Quoted in Mukherjee, *The Ryotwari System in Madras*, p. 298.

[7] P.B.R., 7.12.1863.

[8] P.B.R., 29.10.1897.

tore of 1881 that the wages of the attached labourers amounted to 768 *seers* per annum, and those of the casual labourers to 2·4 to 3·2 *seers* per day.[1] Thus, there seems to have been little change over the century in the wages of the attached or casual labourer in Coimbatore.

In South Arcot the Collector reported in 1863 that wages had remained unchanged for ten years at an average of 75 *seers* per month for the *padiyal*, together with one-twelfth of the harvest, a noonday meal, and other perquisites. He added that many *padiyals* had taken up land for cultivation on their own account.[2] In 1873 the Collector reported that the condition of the labourer had improved materially over the last twenty years, but this does not square with his own figures; the monthly wages of the attached labourer amounted to 18 *seers* of *ragi*, 74·25 *seers* of *varagu*, or occasionally as a substitute for the latter, 34 *seers* of paddy. These wages were paid from November to June; during the harvest season the labourers were paid 5 per cent of the harvest. Casual labourers were paid 3·3 *seers* per day, together with a midday meal. According to the Deputy Collector the labourers got 44·5 *seers* of paddy or *ragi* per month, and 7 to 8 per cent of the harvest, making 950 *seers* in all per annum, together with a midday meal.[3] By 1892–3 the wages of attached labourers had fallen further to 642 *seers* per annum; casual wages also declined to 1·6 to 1·9 *seers* per day.[4]

For the southern districts a fair amount of data are available only for Tanjore.[5] Tanjore was not a typical district, for the fertility of the soil, the extent of irrigation and the possibilities of emigration were here unusually great. Campbell's description of the Tamil serf in 1832—that while he received subsistence wages, he was much better fed and clothed than his counterpart on the West Coast—applied particularly to Tanjore.[6] In 1863 the attached labourer was paid 0·8 *seers* of grain per day for the period actually employed and was also given a small piece of land along with other perquisites; the casual labourer was paid 1·1 *seers* a day, but the use

[1] Robertson, W. R., *Reports on the Agricultural Conditions, Capabilities and Prospects of the Neilgherry and Coimbatore Districts* (Madras, 1881).

[2] P.B.R., 22.2.1864, No. 1146. The rates are given for each *taluk* and range from 66·25 to 118·8 *seers* per month.

[3] P.B.R., 11.11.1872.

[4] P.B.R., 29.10.1897.

[5] In 1801 the Board of Revenue wrote to the Collector, Tanjore, that they approved of the standards he had set for wages of over 9 per cent of gross production for wet cultivation and a little over 7 per cent for dry cultivation, but these may not have been the actual rates paid; P.B.R., 26.1.1801.

[6] *Select Committee Report, 1831–32.* One witness, Peter Gordon, said that the day labourers of Ramnad in Tanjore were miserably poor and much worse off even than the coolies in Calcutta, but this was disputed by an official from Tanjore.

of casual labour was extremely rare. The Collector reported that the increase in cash payments had kept pace with the increase in prices, and that even the grain rates in some districts had risen somewhat in response to the increased demand for labour; there had, therefore, been an improvement in the condition of the agricultural labourers. In 1872 the *pannaiyal*'s earnings were reported to be 1·6 *seers* of paddy a day for the period of employment (which would be about nine months in the year), in addition to harvest fees and some land free of assessment. His total yearly earnings, excluding those of other members of his family, were calculated at 1,346 *seers*, of which one-third would be the produce of the land given to him.[1] Around 1879 the wages of the *pannaiyal* were said to be a little under 2 *seers* per day.[2] In 1884 the *pannaiyal* was paid 2·24 *seers* a day by his employer, but he could earn higher wages in the slack season by working elsewhere.[3] In 1892–3 the Collector reported that wages had risen to 2·4 to 2·8 *seers* daily, and that the condition of the less degraded castes of labourers had tended to improve.[4] From these fragmentary data it would appear that there had been some improvement over the latter part of the century in Tanjore, if nowhere else.

For the Telugu districts there is much less information available for the first half of the nineteenth century. In Kistna in 1819 the Collector stated that the 'slaves' were paid 2 *seers* of paddy per day for six months; at the harvest they were given about 4 per cent of the gross produce, which constituted their means of subsistence during the rest of the year.[5] In 1863 the Collector mentioned that the old system of payment in kind to agricultural labourers still prevailed to a large extent, and that higher quantities of grain were given in spite of the increase in prices. In 1893 the daily wages of the farm labourers amounted to around 2·7 *seers* per day, together with 7·5 per cent of the gross produce at the time of harvest; in the upland districts labourers were paid about 3·2 *seers* of coarse grain per day. The casual labourer generally got higher wages, especially in the delta; his wages, if paid in kind, would amount to 3·2 to 4 *seers* per day of coarse grain.[6] On this scanty evidence there would seem to have been a rise in wages over the century in Kistna.

In Vizagapatam the Collector reported a fall in grain wages from 6½ to 8 *seers* per day, depending on the season, in 1854, to 5½ to 7 *seers* per day

[1] P.B.R., 11.11.1872, No. 2179.
[2] P.B.R., 23.1.1886, No. 622 (Misc.).
[3] P.B.R., 7.10.1884.
[4] P.B.R., 29.10.1897, No. 690.
[5] *Slavery Report, 1841*, p. 114.
[6] P.B.R., 29.10.1897.

in 1859;[1] however, even at the lower rate, these were very high wages by the standards of the rest of the region. But by 1892–3 real wages had fallen sharply to 0·8 to 1·7 *seers* per day for casual labour. This reflects the rise in food prices, since the cash wages do not show much change. One possibility of course is that the conversion may have been into different kinds of grain, so that the actual fall was not great; another possibility is that there was a reduction in the quality and quantity of the work done for the same period. The Collector also pointed out that as a general rule the grain wages of permanent farm servants had remained unaltered for a very long series of years.

In Ganjam the wage for permanent farm servants varied in 1863 from 90 to 100 *seers* per month in paddy, which would be equivalent to Rs. 18 to 24 per annum, excluding harvest fees, interest-free loans and other perquisites.[2] In 1895 it was reported that the casual labourer, whether male or female, got 6·5 to 13 *seers* of paddy during the harvest. In one part of the district, Goomsur, the farm servants got 96 *seers* per month excluding perquisites. The grain wages thus remained fairly steady over the thirty-year period; the Collector remarked, 'as the system of payment in kind has not been superseded to any appreciable extent by cash payments, there has apparently been little change in the condition of the bulk of the agricultural labourers'.[3]

Godavari, on the other hand, showed a distinct rise between 1872 and 1892. In 1863 the Collector gave no figures but only stated that the agricultural labourers were not paid in kind, and the rate at which they were paid was nearly double what it had been seven to eight years previously.[4] For later years figures are available: the permanent farm servants were given between 960 and 1,600 *seers* per annum in 1872, which rose in 1892–3 to between 1,600 and 2,400 *seers* per annum.[5]

In Nellore in 1872–3 the customary wage for farm labourers, which had prevailed for many years, ranged from 1,098 to 1,464 *seers* of paddy per annum, or 732 *seers* of *ragi* or *jonna*, together with a blanket, a pair of slippers and other perquisites.[6] In 1884 the average annual wage of the permanent farm servant had risen to 1,830 *seers*, according to the Collector.[7] Wages remained steady till 1892, when it was reported that the grain wages ranged from 1,098 to 1,830 *seers* per annum; the daily wage of the

[1] P.B.R., 2.12.1863.
[2] P.B.R., 4.4.1864.
[3] P.B.R., 29.10.1897, No. 690.
[4] P.B.R., 22.7.1863.
[5] P.B.R., 29.10.1897, No. 690.
[6] P.B.R., 11.11.1872, No. 2179.
[7] P.B.R., 7.10.1884, No. 9545.

casual labourer was on the average 3·5 *seers*.[1] In these Telugu districts, and particularly in Nellore, wages were fairly high in relation to the wages in the rest of the Presidency.

Wage levels were distinctly lower in Kurnool and Anantapur. Bellary too would probably fall into this low wage group, at least till 1880 or so, when the spread of cash crops and the introduction of cotton presses increased employment and wages. In Kurnool data are available only from 1888 onwards and they seem to show some decline in wages. In 1888–9 the wages of able-bodied agricultural labourers amounted to the equivalent of 570 *seers* per annum,[2] whereas in 1892–3 the permanent farm servants were given cash or grain wages varying from Rs. 4 to Rs. 50 per annum—depending on their age, skill, whether or not they were fed by the master and so on—the average being the equivalent of about 550 *seers* per annum. Casual labourers were paid 2 to 3 *seers* of *cholum* per day. The Collector added that in times of distress the grain wages were occasionally reduced by 25 to 50 per cent, though they reverted to the customary rates after the period of distress was over.[3] In 1896–7 the grain wage had fallen further to 356 to 475 *seers* per annum, perhaps as a result of the famine.[4] Wages in Anantapur, which is one of the less fertile districts, were significantly lower than in the other Telugu districts; in 1897–8 the Deputy Collector of the Gooty Division reported that in ordinary seasons the agricultural labourer earned from 244 to 391 *seers* of *cholum* per annum and even these low rates would fall at the time of famine.[5]

On the basis of the Collectors' reports, the examination of about 7,000 service agreements for both agricultural and non-agricultural labourers, and his own personal enquiries, Raghavaiyangar concluded in 1892 that 'there has been nowhere any reduction in the customary wages paid for agricultural labour . . . the grain wages given for casual labour, e.g. additional labour employed during harvest, appear to have generally increased, and in some cases doubled. The tendency towards increase in the rates of daily grain wages allowed to field hands permanently employed is less marked, though there are a number of instances in which there has been an increase even as regards these. This shows that custom is gradually

[1] P.B.R., 29.10.1897, No. 690. All these wages are reported in *tooms*, and have been converted at 61 *seers* to the *toom*, the rate given by the Collector in both 1872 and 1892. According to the *Manual of Administration for Madras Presidency*, however, the standard *toom* in Nellore equalled 56 *seers*. At this rate the grain wages would have ranged from 1,008 to 1,680 *seers* per annum.

[2] P.B.R. (Settlement), 8.8.1889, No. 3067. The monthly wage as well as food prices are given for each *taluk*, from which average wages have been arrived at.

[3] P.B.R., 29.10.1897, No. 690.

[4] *Report of the Indian Famine Commission, 1898*, Appendices, vol. II, p. 143.

[5] *Ibid.*, pp. 25–6.

giving way to competition, and that the tendency on the whole is towards an increase in the earnings of labourers as estimated in food grains.'[1] The Board of Revenue agreed, as it well might, with this conclusion.[2] Yet most of the data support the view that wages tended to be stationary in real terms, although in some districts wages rose slightly towards the end of the century as compared with the beginning. But the quotations are far too scattered over time and space to warrant any firm generalizations of this type, although it seems probable that in most districts for much of the time wages were near the subsistence line.[3] The agricultural labourer generally earned just enough to feed himself and his family. If he earned enough to save, these savings would be wiped out in a period of famine or crop failure, when real wages were sharply cut. The data do show clearly that the wages of attached labour, being paid in kind and being regulated by custom, remained stable over a long period, and showed the greatest stability in Malabar, where the conditions of serfdom were most stringent. As against this stability in the rates of payments in kind, the price of rice from 1896 to 1900 was around 140 per cent more than the average in 1809 to 1813.[4]

For the century as a whole it is therefore impossible to arrive at any firm conclusions about the movements in wages. But this is not the case for the last quarter of the century. From 1873 onwards there is a regular wage series for which the data were collected every six months, and from which it is possible to draw much firmer conclusions than from random quotations taken from widely different sources. It is true that this series is also subject to a number of shortcomings, but even so it can yield useful, and in the light of the Board's observations, surprising conclusions. From 1873 onwards the Government collected figures of average monthly agricultural and other wages for a number of districts (seven in Madras) every six months. The official statistical agency itself pointed out that:

> The record obtained entirely fails to give a reliable indication of the remuneration of the labourers. This result is due to the inherent difficulties of the problem, and the practical impossibility of getting the untrained reporting agency to make the

[1] Raghavaiyangar, *Progress of the Madras Presidency*, p. 157,

[2] P.B.R., 29.10.1897. The Board added, however, that the famine of 1896–7 would lead to the substitution of money for grain wages, and to a fall in real wages.

[3] The agricultural worker would eat from about 24–30 oz. of rice per day, together with meat very occasionally, and some vegetable oils and spices. A wage of 2 *seers* or just over 4 lb. a day, would, if supplemented by the earnings of his wife and children, just suffice to maintain a family of five. In fact, of course deficiency diseases and malnutrition were very common; *Report of the Royal Commission on Agriculture*, New Delhi, 1928, vol. III, pp. 732 and 746.

[4] See Table 6, p. 91.

necessary allowances for the varying conditions of employment. Payment in kind is commonly practised, either for the entire wage, or as a supplement to cash wages, and the supplements vary according to the season and the nature of the employment. The regularity of employment also varies greatly, and employment is practically nowhere continuous through the year. The most common expedient for avoiding these, and other difficulties, is to return cash wages for labourers employed in towns or their neighbourhood, which are in no way typical of the rates prevailing throughout the district.[1]

But this statement applies to the all-India figures, and for Madras at least it would appear from the records that the 'common expedient' of returning cash wages for labourers employed in towns was not adopted. The Collectors sent in figures separately for towns and 'rural tracts', and the figures for urban wages are almost always higher. The village officials collected the wages rates in grain and converted them into cash at the local prices, but the statements do not mention the types of grain and their prices, or the perquisites included, all three of which varied widely. In addition, the villages taken into account sometimes changed; there were frequent inconsistencies in the figures, and discrepancies arose which even the Collectors could not explain. So these figures[2] must be used with caution.

Tables 20 and 21 set out the series in monetary and real terms for the seven districts for which the data have been collected, namely, Ganjam, Vizagapatam, Bellary, Tanjore, Tinnevelly, Salem and Coimbatore. There was a marked rise in prices over the last quarter of the century; the average annual retail price of common rice for the Presidency went up from Rs. 2·466 for 40 *seers* in 1873 to Rs. 4·297 in 1900. Overlying the long-term trend, there were short-term fluctuations, particularly in famine years, such as 1876–8, when prices shot up.[3] The graphs show sharp fluctuations in real wages; since in most of these districts wages were actually paid for the most part in kind, this would imply that the actual wage rates did fluctuate sharply. But it may be that conversions into money rates were made at conventional and not actual prices, since the

[1] Government of India (Director-General of Commercial Intelligence and Statistics), *Prices and Wages in India, 1907*.

[2] Summary figures are contained in *Prices and Wages in India, 1907*; detailed figures as well as details regarding the collection of the figures are available in P.B.R. (Settlement), e.g. No. 3067 of 8.8.1889; No. 1514 (Misc.) of 14.4.1890 and No. 3736 of 11.9.1890; No. 349 of 16.8.1893; No. 6691 (Misc.) of 24.11.1893; No. 994 (Misc.) of 21.2.1895; No. 228 of 26.7.1895; No. 1696 (Misc.) of 1.4.1896. In 1898 the Board explained that the wages reports should be obtained every month from three or four 'representative' villages, the wages of adult males should be given, payments in kind and perquisites should be converted into cash and any differences between adjacent districts should be explained; P.B.R. (Settlement), 7.12.1898, No. 446.

[3] *Prices and Wages in India, 1915*, p. 78.

Table 20. *Average Monthly Wages of Agricultural Labourers in Seven Districts at the end of Each Year, 1873–1900*
(Rupees per month)

Year	Ganjam	Vizagapatam	Bellary	Tanjore	Tinnevelly	Salem	Coimbatore
1873	3	3·75	4	2·95	6·25	2·5	5
1874	3	4·5	4	2·95	6·25	2·5	5
1875	3	4·5	4	2·48	6·25	2·5	5·5
1876	3	5	4	6·2	6·25	2·5	5
1877	3	5	6	4·28	6·25	2·5	5·62
1878	4	5	4	4·96	6·25	2·5	5
1879	3·75	5	4	2·95	6·25	3	5·62
1880	3	3·19	4	2·82	6·25	2·5	3·75
1881	3·75	3	4	2·3	6·25	2·25	5·62
1882	3·75	3·5	4	2·3	6·25	2·25	7·5
1883	3·75	3·5	4·18	2·14	6·25	2	7·5
1884	3·5	5	4·27	3·44	6·25	2·33	7·5
1885	3·5	5	4	2·95	6	2·67	7·5
1886	3·5	5	4	2·82	4·5	2·33	7·5
1887	4·69	3 to 6	5 to 5·62	4·06	4·5 to 6	3 to 5	3 to 7·5
1888	4·75	4·5	5·31	5·08	5·25	4	4·8
1889	3·75	4·5	5·31	6·09	5·25	3·67	5
1890	4·12	3·12	3·95	4·22	3·81	2·62	4·8
1891	4·19	3·57	4·12	4·77	4·09	2·62	5
1892	4·12	3·34	4·31	5·33	4·11	2·92	5·1
1893	4·31	3·17	4·31	5·06	4·11	3·06	5·07
1894	4·45	3·21	4·56	4·82	4·11	3·06	5·07
1895	4·5	3·27	4·56	4·88	4·11	3·21	4·5
1896	4·44	3·37	4·56	5·01	4·11	3·32	4·28
1897	4·5	3·31	4·5	5·19	4·12	3·37	4·56
1898	4·31	3·44	4·56	5·12	3·81	3·31	4·19
1899	4·12	3·44	4·69	5·06	4·62	3·31	3·81
1900	4·06	3·37	4·69	5·06	4·75	3·44	4·19

Sources: Government of India: Director-General of Commercial Intelligence and Statistics, *Prices and Wages in India, 1898*, for figures from 1873 to 1883; later figures from *Prices and Wages in India, 1905*.

local officials collected data on the payments in kind and then converted these into money rates. Alternatively, the local officials may have used the price prevailing in the village for which the wage rate was quoted, whereas of necessity the average price of the district has been used here. It is possible therefore that the real wage rates did not fluctuate to the extent

Table 21. *Annual Wages in Grain of Agricultural Labour in Seven Districts, 1873–1900*
(in *seers* of common rice)

Year	Ganjam	Vizagapatam	Bellary	Tanjore	Tinnevelly	Salem	Coimbatore
1873	1081	820	626	735	993	506	826
1874	878	808	659	464	759	425	676
1875	873	780	697	406	963	485	853
1876	818	820	538	838	827	376	651
1877	458	515	513	460	588	209	520
1878	413	404	351	613	642	251	509
1879	570	302	528	483	779	371	711
1880	611	575	669	561	1047	376	584
1881	873	518	648	500	998	423	1122
1882	833	487	643	566	1260	421	1368
1883	909	496	667	514	1350	384	1413
1884	689	780	681	665	1005	408	1296
1885	584	654	600	524	871	394	1179
1886	580	618	595	602	767	386	1242
1887	878	367–734	822–924	799	697–929	529–882	522–1305
1888	859	582	870	1052	827	683	824
1889	483	576	849	1056	788	589	803
1890	622	428	606	674	470	404	702
1891	745	500	556	634	520	338	668
1892	553	374	477	684	486	340	614
1893	604	394	546	622	414	369	628
1894	655	402	590	781	572	429	723
1895	855	470	594	775	556	462	637
1896	775	478	567	880	623	510	602
1897	468	323	451	702	515	431	537
1898	560	428	499	662	445	378	472
1899	580	450	608	834	663	468	520
1900	512	383	472	572	521	383	450

Sources: Government of India: Director-General of Commercial Intelligence and Statistics: *Prices and Wages in India, 1898* and *1905*.

shown by the graphs (Figure 1).[1] An additional point is that there may be

[1] In Tanjore, for instance, it would appear that a fixed rate of grain wages was converted at fluctuating prices between 1873 and 1885, although our graphs show fluctuations; however, even the money wages quoted in the letter from the Collector differ from those printed in the series; P.B.R., 23.1.1886, No. 622 (Misc.). See also P.B.R. (Settlement) 12.1.1900, No. 94 (Misc.) where the Collector explains that the variations in money rates between 3 *taluks* is caused by the fact that a higher commutation rate is used in Shiyali where the big landlords store paddy for export to Ceylon.

differences in the grains for which prices were taken, since all money rates have been deflated by the prices of common rice. But this is not likely to be a serious source of error, at least as regards trends in wages, since on the whole, the prices of the different grains tended to move rather closely together, as Table 22 shows.

Table 22. *Quinquennial Averages of Food Grain Prices in Madras Presidency, 1871–96*
(1871–5 base)

Year	Rice	Jawar or Cholum	Bajra or Cambu	Ragi
1871–5	100	100	100	100
1876–80	143	170	152	166
1881–5	107	99	97	102
1886–90	117	111	109	114
1891–5	140	142	139	142
1896–1900	148	160	151	165

Source: Prices and Wages in India, 1906; Tables 23, 26 and 27.

Some of the short-term fluctuations do, of course, reflect events. The fall in wages in 1878 in Bellary, Ganjam and Vizagapatam obviously records the effects of the famine of 1876–8; famine too would be the cause of the fall in wages around 1898 shown in all the seven districts. Indeed, it is likely that nearly all the more serious fluctuations reflect crop failures, though some of the short-term rises may be due to temporary increases in employment, such as the construction of the railways or road building. In Tinnevelly and Tanjore emigration may also have brought about short-term fluctuations in wages, though it is more likely perhaps to have influenced the longer-term trends. Again, the rise in wages in Vizagapatam in 1888 was attributed by the Collector to emigration to Godavari district.[1] In spite of all these rapid and short-term fluctuations, the significant long-term feature of the wage movements is the marked trend downwards.

For the seven districts it is only in one, Tanjore, that real wages were higher in 1900 than in 1873. For the remaining six districts wages were substantially lower in 1900 than in 1873, and if, to even out temporary fluctuations, the averages of the first and the last three years are taken, there was still a fall. Taking averages of the years 1873–5 (before the

[1] P.B.R., 11.5.1889, No. 1853, (Misc.).

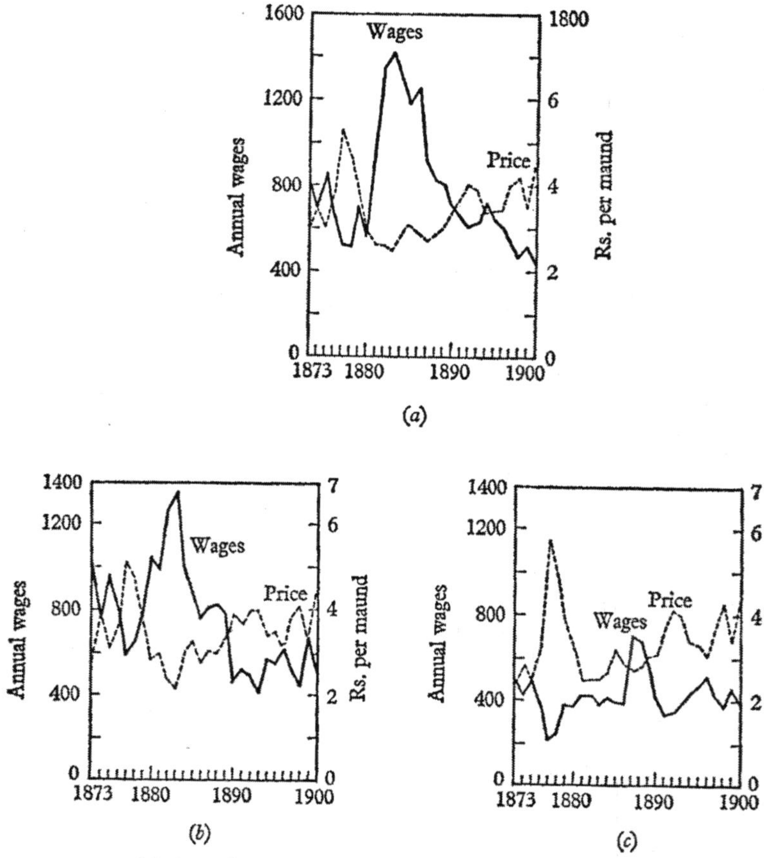

(*a*) Coimbatore (*b*) Tinnevelly (*c*) Salem

Fig. 1. Real wages (in *seers* of common rice) and prices of common rice (per *maund*).

1876–8 famine) and 1898–1900,[1] the decline in real wages amounted to 42 per cent in Ganjam, 48 per cent in Vizagapatam, 20 per cent in Bellary, 41 per cent in Tinnevelly, 13 per cent in Salem, and 39 per cent in Coimbatore. The only exception was Tanjore where there was an increase in wages of 29 per cent. It is striking that for two of the districts, namely Vizagapatam and Coimbatore, there was actually a fall even in the money

[1] It is true that there was a famine in 1896–7 also, but wages continued to be low, with minor fluctuations, in the first decade of the twentieth century.

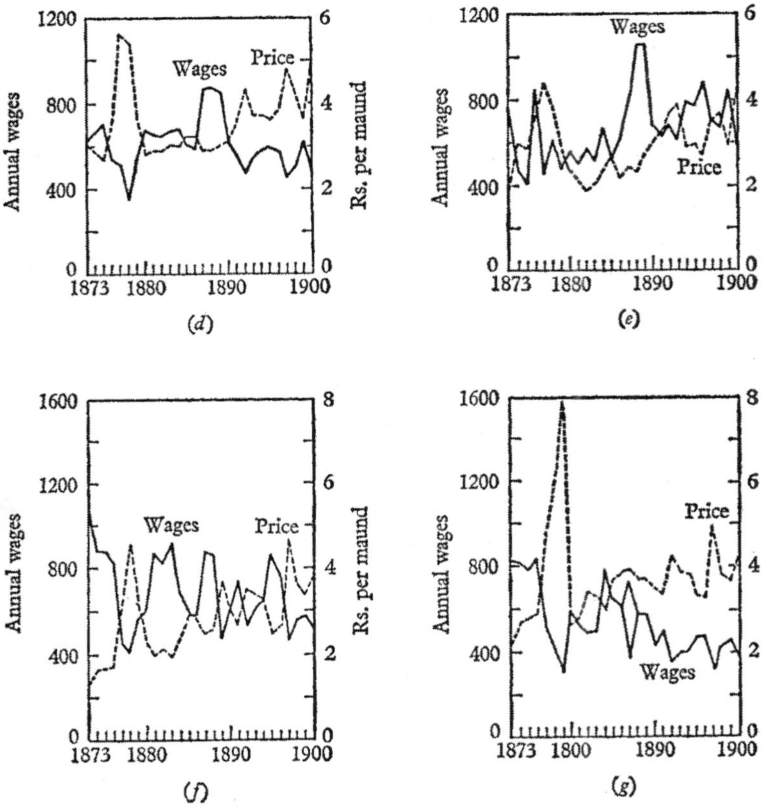

(*d*) Bellary (*e*) Tanjore (*f*) Ganjam (*g*) Vizagapatam

wages, although there was a sharp rise in the prices of food grains throughout the Presidency over the period. These seven districts are not atypical, except for Tanjore, where it is likely that wages would have followed a different course than for most of the rest of the Presidency. It thus seems fairly certain that throughout the Presidency there was a tendency for wages to decline in real terms from 1875 onwards. This conclusion is all the more likely since it reinforces our findings that it was in this period that the pressure of population on the land began to be felt in certain districts of the Presidency.

X. THE GROWTH OF AGRICULTURAL LABOUR FROM 1871 TO 1901

It was argued in Chapter IV that at the beginning of the nineteenth century the great majority of traditional agricultural labour castes in most of the Tamil districts, Malabar and South Canara were in fact agricultural labourers, owning little or no land, and deriving the major part of their income from agricultural labour. If this hypothesis is correct then at least 10–15 per cent of the *total* population in these districts would have been agricultural labourers; and there are no indications that the proportion of agricultural labourers in the other districts was widely different. The data on which this argument is based relate to the first forty years or so of the century, after which there is no information on the strength of agricultural labour till 1871. Details of occupation are given in the decennial censuses from 1871 onwards so that it is possible to make a rough estimate of the growth of this class over the century; and for the last thirty years of the century one can relate movements in agricultural labour to changes in the strength of landowners and tenants.

The Censuses[1] are, of course, very much more satisfactory than the sources available for the earlier period, but even so they are not perfectly comparable with each other. Apart from the difficulties of definition and classification inherent in the facts, there are several problems raised by the changes in the system of classification made in each Census. (These changes are set out in Appendix I to this chapter. The only changes relevant here are, first, that while from 1881 onwards separate figures are given for the two 'orders', agriculture and pasture, in 1871 the two orders are combined. Naturally each Census improves on its predecessors as regards detail. In 1871 the group 'agriculture' merely covers 'cultivators'; agricultural labourers are excluded,[2] and no breakdown between landlords and tenants is available. From 1881 onwards it is possible to sub-

[1] The term 'Censuses' by itself in this chapter refers to the decennial censuses taken from 1871 onwards for Madras Presidency. Earlier censuses are referred to with date. Each census was presented in three main volumes; vol. I contained the Census Report and is hereafter referred to as *Census Report* with date; vol. II (or Part II) contained the so-called 'Imperial Tables', which are what concern us, and vol. III contained the Provincial Tables.

[2] On the other hand, those following other occupations but with interests in land are included, but it is not clear from which source they derived the major part of their income. In any case, as the Census Commissioner himself remarked, their numbers are severely underestimated; *Census Report, 1871*, p. 168.

divide 'agriculture' into the three broad groups of landholders, tenants and labourers, and in 1891 and 1901 these can be further subdivided into cultivating/non-cultivating landholders/tenants, and 'farm servants' and 'field labourers'.

Apart from these classificatory changes, there were changes in the universe classified in each Census. In 1871, occupational figures are given for the male population alone; in 1881 a breakdown of the working population, male and female, is given; in 1891 the entire population is classified according to means of subsistence, in other words no distinction is made between workers and dependants; while in 1901 separate figures are available for workers and dependants. But with certain rough adjustments the figures can be made reasonably comparable. Even if occupational figures for women were available in 1871 they would have to be ignored, since occupational figures for women in India are notoriously unreliable,[1] partly because of the frequently sporadic nature of their employment. A further adjustment must be made for 1891, when separate figures for workers are not available.

But the crucial difficulties in the use of the census data arise from ambiguities in the terms used, or from changes in their meaning, and unfortunately most of these difficulties are encountered in the field of agriculture. None of the terms used—landlord, tenant, cultivator, labourer—is clear-cut. Broadly, *zamindars*, *inamdars*, or *raiyatwari* holders of land are classified as landowners; but the treatment of occupancy tenants, particularly those under *zamindars*, varied. Occupancy tenants were excluded from the term 'landholder' in 1881,[2] whereas in 1891 they were included in theory, though not always in practice:

> A fairly common entry was 'cultivation', without the addition of any word to show connection with the land. These persons were assumed to be cultivating tenants, but many of them had occupancy rights, for the occupancy tenant or peasant proprietor and the mere tenant-at-will both alike usually describe their occupations as cultivation.[3]

Another ambiguous distinction is that drawn in the 1891 and 1901 Censuses between cultivating and non-cultivating landowners or tenants. In theory the distinction is a useful one. Changes in the total number of cultivating landholders and tenants could affect the demand for agricultural labourers; the figures would also serve to prove or disprove the

[1] In 1881, for example, 'wife' was a separate occupation, but women were sometimes classified under the occupation of their husbands, and sometimes as 'unemployed'; *Census Report, 1881*, p. 135.

[2] *Ibid.* pp. 149–50.

[3] *Census Report, 1891*, p. 330.

thesis that ownership was being increasingly concentrated in the hands of large absentee or non-cultivating landlords. But in practice the distinction is almost impossible to draw. The difficulties of defining 'cultivation' are illustrated in the recent literature on the subject;[1] many of them arise from the fact that with land reforms, no landowner is willing to admit that he is not personally engaged in cultivation. There was nòt this incentive to deliberate misinformation in the nineteenth century, and the Censuses seem to assume that the meaning of the term is self-evident, but it is very unlikely that in fact the term was given a uniform meaning.

Similarly the share-cropper, who is nominally a tenant paying as rent a share of the crop, may frequently have been an agricultural labourer in type of work and level of income—in fact in all but name and perhaps caste. Even in as rich an area as Tanjore, the Collector stated in 1885 that on a farm of ten acres the net produce was only Rs. 140/-, and the *parakudi* after paying the rent and land revenue was in a state of abject poverty. The *parakudis*, who were practically labourers, were in a state of debt bondage (a point on which the Board of Revenue disagreed).[2] Again, in Kurnool there were *palanikam* cultivators who were nominally crop-sharing tenants but actually agricultural labourers, getting around 25 per cent of the crop for their labour.[3] An enquiry made in Malabar in 1881 revealed that the bulk of the tenants had become *verumpattamdars* with no occupancy rights, but the customary share of the *verumpattamdar* had declined well below one-third of the net produce, and he lived in conditions of near-starvation: this was in spite of the fact that considerable lands—about five acres per man in the agricultural classes—remained to be taken up.[4] The status of the share-croppers has already been discussed in Chapter II; here it is only necessary to note that it is not clear how these ambiguities would affect the census data. While one would presume that most share-croppers would be classified as tenants rather than as labourers, it should be noted that in Tinnevelly, according to the *Gazetteer*, some of those who called themselves field labourers should have been classified as cultivating tenants.[5]

Another problem is that a person might move frequently from labourer to tenant or owner, and relapse into labourer again—so that how he was

[1] See, e.g., Daniel Thorner, 'India's Agrarian Revolution by Census Re-definition', *Indian Economic Review* (August 1956), pp. 1–21.

[2] P.B.R., 11.2.1886; P.B.R., 19.10.1885; Proceedings of the Revenue Department, 23.11.1885.

[3] Government of Madras, *Report on the Famine in Madras Presidency, 1896 and 1897*, vol. II, p. 143.

[4] *Malabar Manual*, vol. II, p. 583.

[5] *Tinnevelly Gazetteer*, p. 194.

classified would depend on when the Census was taken. The Census figures may therefore show only temporary changes in economic status. This was made possible by the *raiyatwari* system, under which any one prepared to pay land revenue could take up waste lands: 'In many individual cases, men who have not sufficient capital take up waste lands when seasons and prices are auspicious, and then are driven to ruin by a fall in prices, or an unfavourable season.'[1]

Again, in Malabar 'almost anyone who can hold a plough and guide the cattle can rent grain lands, for he can borrow the seed and the implements, if he has none of his own, but to farm and maintain a garden requires the exercise of the best qualities of mind and body.'[2]

A more significant difficulty is that the roles of owner, tenant, and labourer were frequently played simultaneously. As the 1901 Census Commissioner remarked, 'The chief difficulty, no doubt [in collecting agricultural statistics] was that the small agriculturist is frequently a cultivating and non-cultivating landowner, a tenant, a farm servant, and a field labourer all rolled into one; owning land which he partly cultivates and partly lets out for rent, hiring other land from someone else, and eking out his earnings by working on the land of others in between whiles.' He adds, 'Probably, however, the errors due to this cause correct one another,'[3] but this is not so clear. For example, in 1890, out of the total 2,854,087 *raiyatwari pattas*[4] held by 4,687,281 *raiyats*, the land revenue was under Rs. 10 on 1,870,694 *pattas*, or over 65 per cent of the total, held by 2,728,808 *raiyats*. The average assessment was Rs. 3.13.6 which would roughly have been payable on a little over three acres of dry land, or less than one acre of irrigated land;[5] this implies that these holdings were far too small to support a family. Even if allowance is made for the fact that several *pattas* could be held by the same person, it is still clear that a large proportion of landowners could not support their families by cultivating their own holdings alone, and would therefore rent more land or hire themselves out as labourers. In the 1890's about three-fourths of the *raiyats* of Ramnad had to work as labourers, either in India or Ceylon

[1] *Moral and Material Progress Report for India, 1874–5*, p. 27.

[2] *Report of the Malabar Special Commission, 1881–82* (Madras, 1882), vol. I, para. 139.

[3] *Census Report, 1901*, p. 191.

[4] The *patta* is the document registering ownership of each separate field, or part of the field if its ownership is split up.

[5] Raghavaiyangar, *Progress of the Madras Presidency*, pp. cxxxviii (no. of *pattas*) and cci (average rates of assessment per acre). While the rates of assessment varied widely, the average for the Presidency was Rs. 1.1.3 per acre of dry land occupied and Rs. 4.11.8 per acre of wet land occupied.

in addition to cultivating their own lands.[1] In Anantapur it was calculated in 1891–2 that two-thirds of the *pattas* were for plots which would yield 120 *seers* of grain, or three months' food for one man.[2] Such persons should be classified according to the source from which the bulk of their income is derived, a rule which was in fact laid down in the Censuses,[3] but it was of course difficult to ensure that the rule was followed.

A further source of error is the difficulty of differentiating between agricultural and other forms of labour. This is an easy distinction to draw in theory but not in practice, since agricultural labourers would, particularly in lean years, supplement their earnings by working on roads and irrigation schemes, as porters, gatherers of firewood, and on other unskilled jobs. And it is not easy to see which way the figures are biased. On the one hand, one might assume that agricultural labour would be overestimated at the expense of general labour, partly as a result of the prestige of agriculture, and partly because agricultural labour, as the traditional occupation, would be regarded as his permanent occupation even by a labourer who for some period had been forced to accept other forms of work. On the other hand, the enumerators may have regarded 'general labour' as a catch-all category; the 1891 figures for general labour included a large number of agricultural labourers, according to the Census Commissioners in both 1891 and 1901. In 1881 too the Census Commissioner remarked of general labourers that 'these are more often than not identical with the agricultural labourers . . . and both at times qualify for inclusion under Order 15, Sub-Order 3, as earth-diggers'. It is therefore not clear whether the very small number of general labourers in 1901, in comparison not only with 1891 but also with earlier years, is itself an underestimate, or a sign of improvement in classification, or of increased numbers employed in agriculture.

Table 23. *Occupational Breakdown of Male Population, 1871–1901*

	1871	1881	1891	1901
1. Total Male Population	15,874,235	15,421,043	17,619,395	18,836,313
2. Working Force	10,026,056	10,325,300	10,572,910	12,063,298
2:1	63·2%	67·0%	60·0%	64·0%
3. Agricultural Working Force	6,500,687	6,124,927	6,265,741	8,114,273
3:2	64·8%	59·3%	59·3%	67·2%

[1] *Ramnad Manual*, p. 78.

[2] *Report of the Indian Famine Commission, 1896–97*, vol. II, p. 310.

[3] Thus in 1871 enumerators were instructed, in the case of a person with more than one occupation, to enter that 'which is the most important to him'. *Census Report, 1871*, p. 24.

4. Landholders		2,185,066	3,405,312	4,503,361
4:3	4,938,385	35·7%	54·3%	55·5%
5. Tenants	76·0%	2,279,770	1,712,382	1,419,350
5:3		37·2%	27·3%	17·4%
6. Agricultural Labour	1,562,302	1,660,091	1,148,047	2,191,362
6:3	24·0%	27·1%	18·4%	27·1%
6:2	15·6%	16·1%	10·9%	18·1%
7. General Labour	520,768	541,364	661,890	135,874
6+7	2,083,070	2,201,455	1,809,937	2,327,436
(6+7):3	32·0%	35·9%	28·9%	28·7%
(6+7):2	20·8%	21·3%	17·1%	19·3%

Sources: Census, 1871, vol. II, Table 17.
Census 1881, vol. II, Table 12.
Census 1891, Part II, Table 17.
Census, 1901, Part II, Table 15.

Notes to Table 23

A. All figures relate to total British territory; the feudatory states are excluded.

B. *Working Force*

1. The term 'Working Force' for all years includes beggars, prisoners, pensioners, inmates of asylums, etc. In 1901 only beggars connected with a religious order are classified, but in a religion as loosely organized as Hinduism the distinction is not important.
2. 1881: Order XVIII, 'Persons of no specified occupation' have been excluded from the total of occupied males.
3. For 1891 the working force is defined as consisting of men over the age of 15; similarly all the other occupational figures refer to this age group.

C. *Agricultural Working Force*

1. 1871—The figure includes, besides the figure for 'cultivators' given in the census, the workers transferred from general to agricultural labour.
2. 1881—Census figures for Order VIII 'agriculture', excluding 'arboricultural' and 'horticultural' population and herdsmen and shepherds.
3. 1891 and 1901—Excluding 'growers of special products, etc.'

D. *Tenants*

1. 1891—Includes 'lessees, etc.' as well as cultivating and non-cultivating tenants and sharers.

E. *Agricultural Labour*

1. For 1881, the figures for 'herdsmen' and shepherds have been deducted from total agricultural labour.

F. *General Labour*

1. 1871—Of 2,083,070 'labourers for hire', three-fourths have been attributed to agricultural labour.
2. 1901—'General Labour'. The other group included in 'labour, indefinite' consists of earthwork, etc. and comprises 124,634, i.e. almost as many labourers as 'general labour'.

Table 23 shows the movements in the agricultural population from 1871 to 1901 as shown by the four Censuses. For reasons already discussed, only the male working force is taken into account. And for 1891 the means of subsistence of the adult male population (those aged 15 and above) have been taken to be equivalent to their occupation; in other words, the working force includes a small percentage of the population who were in fact without an occupation. It is interesting that nevertheless the working force in 1891 is a smaller proportion of the total population than in the other years; apparently the number of workers under 15 who are excluded is larger than the numbers of unemployed of 15 and over who are included.

For 1871 the class 'Agriculture' contains just one sub-division: 'cultivators', which has been taken to cover both landholders and tenants. There was no separate entry for agricultural labourers, but the Census Commissioner himself felt that 'probably three-fourths [of the general labourers] find employment in connection with the land. They represent in some degree the classes of the community who were formerly predial slaves, bound to labour for their master, and renumerated for the most part, even to this day, by payment in kind'.[1] Three-fourths of the 'general labourers' have therefore been reclassified as agricultural labourers, thereby increasing the size of the total agricultural working force.

But the 1871 figure includes those engaged in pasture, as well as in arboriculture and horticulture, all categories which, being separately enumerated, have been excluded from the later years. These latter categories amounted to some 3 per cent of the total in 1891 and to 7 per cent in 1901. The precise categories covered in Table 23 are shown in Appendix I. One further adjustment has been made for 1881 in Table 23. Although there is a separate category for 'those engaged about animals', the entries under 'those engaged about the land' include shepherds and herdsmen, both of whom are included under 'pasture' in later years. These figures have therefore been deducted from the agricultural working force in 1881.

But this group is a possible source of error even in later years; the Census Commissioner of 1901 felt that many of the cowherds and shepherds, collectors of firewood, grass-cutters, personal servants of landlords, etc., should have rightly been shown as agricultural labourers, since they depended mainly on the land.[2] Of these the largest group were the cowherds

[1] *Census Report, 1871*, p. 171.

[2] *Census Report, 1901*, p. 197. There is no way of checking these even from Table 17 of the Census of 1891 which gives a breakdown of 'partial agriculturists' into owners, tenants and labourers: out of the 505,109 males who derived a subsidiary income from the land, only 11,233 did so as agricultural labourers; *Census, 1891*, Part II, p. 691.

(492,578 in 1881, 104,581 in 1891 and 229,393 in 1901),[1] and the second largest the shepherds (162,286 in 1881, 94,100 in 1891 and 118,600 in 1901), and these groups are large enough for mistakes in classification to affect significantly the totals of agricultural labourers and agricultural working force. Thus if two-thirds of these groups are included in the agricultural population in 1881 (when they were much larger than in later years) they raise the agricultural working force to 63 per cent of the total working force, and agricultural labour to 30 per cent of the agricultural working force in that year. Incidentally, it is worth noting that cowherds and shepherds traditionally are Idaiyans, Kurumbas and Gollas, that is, not of the agricultural labour castes.

Table 23 seems to show an increasing dependence on agriculture over the last thirty years of the century, but this may be misleading. If one bears in mind that the 1871 proportion of the agricultural to the total working force, 64·8 per cent, may well be some 3 to 4 percentage points too high, since those engaged in pasture, arboriculture and horticulture are included in that year, the table would seem to show a definite increase in the agricultural working force in 1901. On the other hand, the 1871, 1881 and 1891 proportions in agriculture may all be too low because of the wrong classification of herdsmen, general labour, and so on. If general labour had grown by as much as the total adult male population between 1881 and 1901,[2] and the difference between that figure and the actual figure in the 1901 Census were deducted from the figure for agricultural labour, then the agricultural working force would have been only around 63 per cent of the total working force in 1901. It is difficult to tell, therefore, from the Census figures alone whether or not the proportions engaged in agriculture increased. There is the further possibility that an increasing dependence on agriculture may be shown in the increasing numbers who derived subsidiary income from the land; between 1891 and 1901 at least, the population of those who were 'partial agriculturists' remained at around 7 per cent of the working force[3] *outside* agriculture, or about 2·8 per cent of the total working force: this is so small that it is unimportant.

In fact, the line of demarcation between general labour and agricultural labour is so vague that it is useful to consider them together, as has been done in the last two rows of Table 23, as well as separately. Agricultural

[1] These are the figures for those of 15 and over, like all others in this chapter for 1891; but since this is particularly an occupation for boys, those between 5–15 years (for cowherds 184,033 and 43,158 for shepherds) should also be included.

[2] In fact, between 1881 and 1891 general labour grew at a faster rate than adult male population.

[3] *Census, 1891*, Part II, Table 17; *Census, 1901*, Part II, Table 15.

labour alone formed 24 per cent of the agricultural population in 1871, 27 per cent in 1881, 18 per cent in 1891 and 27 per cent in 1901. If agricultural and general labour are considered together, the range of variation is much smaller: together they amounted to 17–20 per cent of the total working force and 29–36 per cent of the agricultural working force. To what extent can movements in agricultural labour be related to movements in the other two classes—landholders and tenants? Do the figures support the thesis that there was a growing tendency for landowners to be turned into tenants, and tenants into agricultural labourers?

A preliminary point to be noted is that population increases in themselves would lead to a small fall in the proportion of landowners to total population, and an increase in the proportion of agricultural labourers. Only a very small minority followed the laws of primogeniture.[1] The equal division of property meant that other things being equal, the proportion of landholders to total agricultural population would depend upon the relative natural rate of increase of the group (ignoring changes in the sex ratio). And the landowners, being richer and of higher caste, probably had a slightly lower rate of increase than the rest of the population.[2]

But, of course, the economic changes making for greater or less concentration of holdings were far more important than the demographic factors. The Census figures show that the percentage of landholders to total

[1] Broadly, amongst most Hindus all sons have equal right to property, but in a joint family, although all sons would have equal rights to the fruits of the property, the ownership may be registered either in the name of the head of the family, or of all the male members. The *Shariat* Law of the Muslims prescribes the shares in which the property must be divided amongst the heirs. Malabar, as usual, has more complex systems of inheritance (some castes follow a matrilineal system of inheritance) and of joint families. Amongst the Nambudris only the eldest son might marry; the younger sons had children by Nair women who became part of their mother's family. See Shea, 'The Land Tenure Structure of Malabar and its Influence Upon Capital Formation in Agriculture', pp. 62–93.

Apparently the larger *zamindars* followed the law of primogeniture. The revenue statistics showed that in 1900–1, 16 out of the 25 *zamindars* paying a land revenue of over Rs. 50,000, 50 out of the 170 paying from Rs. 5,000 to 50,000 and 110 out of the 1,245 paying from Rs. 100 to Rs. 5,000, were under the law of primogeniture. *Agricultural Statistics of British India for the years 1896–97 to 1900–01*, p. 316. If the younger sons were permitted to live off the estate, they might be classified either as landholders or as dependants; primogeniture would make a difference to the Census figures only in the latter case.

[2] On an analysis of the 1931 Census data, Dr. Kingsley Davis found that the fertility of owners and tenants was much lower than that of field labourers. One reason was that the owners and tenants belonged to higher castes, which taboo widow remarriage; Davis, *Population of India and Pakistan*, pp. 73–5.

There is no discussion of differentials in death-rates for different castes and classes, but these are unlikely to be as large as the differences in fertility, as is indirectly seen from the fact that the Brahmins have steadily diminished as a proportion of the total Hindu population over the census period.

agricultural population went up from 35·7 per cent in 1881 to 54·3 per cent in 1891 and 55·5 per cent in 1901 for male workers alone, and from around 25 per cent in 1881 to 50 per cent in 1901 for male and female workers together. But it is almost certain that the number of landholders was underestimated in 1881 and overestimated in 1901. Some check on the Census figures is provided by the land revenue statistics:

	Owners: Land revenue statistics*	Owners: Census†
1881	4,217,829	2,726,442
1901	6,837,980	7,254,637

* The land revenue statistics relate to 1880–1 and 1900–1, respectively. The 1880–1 figures are taken from the *Census Report, 1881*, pp. 149–50. The 1900–01 figures are from *Agricultural Statistics of British India for the years 1896–97 to 1900–01*, p. 316.

† Census figures of 'actual workers'.

These figures are only very roughly comparable for two reasons: first, the land revenue statistics would have to be deflated for those landowners who held land in different villages, and inflated for those cases where the land was held jointly by several people, but registered only in the name of one.[1] Secondly, over 60 per cent of the *raiyatwari* landholders (who numbered 5,900,520 in all in 1901) were probably unable to support themselves on their own land, whereas the Census figures in theory relate only to those who derived the major part of their income from holdings—landholders following other pursuits are omitted. The importance of this omission may be judged from the fact that over 410,000 workers in 1901 were partially occupied in agriculture, whether as landlords, tenants, or field labourers.[2] Separate figures for landlords in the group 'partial agriculturists' are not available, but it is obvious that this factor increases the degree of overestimation of landowners in 1901. If the land revenue figures for landowners are substituted for the Census figures in Table 23, the proportion of landowners to working force in agriculture would be 39 per cent in 1881 and 47 per cent in 1901 (if allowance were made for partial agriculturists the proportions would be somewhat lower) instead of 35·7 per cent and 55·5 per cent; in other words, there would still be a significant increase in the proportion of landowners, though it would be less than one-third the increase shown by the Census figures.

The Census figures in themselves can throw little light on the concentration of holdings: so long as no landholder was evicted from all of his

[1] Where all the names were registered, this would show in the figures since they refer to 'landholders and shareholders'.

[2] *Census, 1901*, Part II, p. 357.

lands,[1] changes in the pattern of ownership within the group of landowners will not show in the Census returns, although in fact many former landowners may have had to work on the land of others for the major part of their income. But some information is available from other sources. In 1878–9 the Famine Commission collected reports from the Collectors on the amount of land which had fallen into the hands of non-agricultural landlords, particularly money-lenders. In Madura it was reported that 10 per cent of the land had been alienated (including mortgages) to non-agriculturists; in Tanjore 10 per cent; in South Canara 50 per cent; in Coimbatore 5 per cent; in Chinglepet at least 40 per cent;[2] and in Salem 25 per cent of the dry lands and 75 per cent of the wet lands. In nearly all the remaining districts the Collectors reported that alienation had not taken place to any appreciable extent. Probably this represents the temporary effects of famine.

A very different picture emerges from the review of sales and mortgages made around 1890 by the Government of India:

> The Local Government [i.e., of Madras] considers that there is nothing to suggest any general or permanent impoverishment of small landholders as a consequence of the continued unfavourable seasons. It is believed also that, at any rate in the more advanced districts, the ryots are less dependent than formerly upon professional money-lenders, and that the ownership of land is not passing from the agricultural to the non-agricultural classes to any injurious extent.[3]

This conclusion was strengthened when a detailed analysis was made of the sales and mortgages of land between 1893 and 1896. It was found that only 3·4 per cent of the total area held under *raiyatwari* was mortgaged and only 1 per cent was mortgaged to non-agriculturists, one-tenth of which was mortgaged with possession. The net area passing from agriculturists to non-agriculturists in a year was 15,935 acres, which was 4 per cent of the total area sold, or 0·08 per cent of the total occupied area. Madura was the one district where a good deal of land was going into the

[1] Strictly, the landholder should retain enough land to provide him with the major part of his livelihood, but, since the Census enumerators are unlikely to have followed this rule rigidly, even the ownership of a tiny plot would put its owner in the group 'landowners'.

[2] One reason why the alienation was so great (if indeed it was) in Chinglepet may have been the existence of a number of *mirasdars* with preferential rights to waste land. Many of these were absentee landlords, since the district is so near Madras City, and let their lands to *payakaris* with insecure tenancy rights. As a result the lands tended to be inefficiently cultivated. See, e.g., P.B.R., 13.4.1876, and *Statistical Atlas for Madras Presidency*, 1908.

[3] Quoted in Government of India, *Note on Land Transfer and Agricultural Indebtedness in India* (date unspecified); pp. 64 and 65. All the figures in this paragraph are from this document.

hands of non-agriculturists, and in South Canara, Salem, Chinglepet, Tanjore and Tinnevelly the figures showed a considerable change from 1878 to 1897 in that not much land was being sold to non-agriculturists. Indeed in Salem the difference was astonishing: here the net transfer of land was in the reverse direction.[1] Thus there seems to have been no large-scale dispossession of the peasantry by money-lenders and traders.

Now, at last, we can turn to our second question: what were the changes within the agricultural group itself? The Census figures show that the proportion of landowners to agricultural population actually *grew* between 1881 and 1901. This rather surprising conclusion may be partly accounted for by the extension of cultivation: the new lands may well have had a larger ratio of landowners to tenants or labourers than the old. (The average holdings on the new lands may also have been larger than on the old, and the process by which the landowner declined into a tenant or labourer delayed. For example, in Madura the considerable extension of cultivation, particularly on irrigated lands between 1905–6 and 1910–11, was accompanied by an increase of 8·9 per cent in the number of *pattas* on which the land revenue was over Rs. 30/-, whereas those paying less increased at less than half the rate.[2] It is true that the average rate of land revenue per acre also rose, since so much of the new cultivation was on irrigated land, so that the size-pattern of holdings may not have been altered significantly, but in terms of yield the average holding had probably increased.) Towards the end of the century some missionaries and Collectors also tried to settle Paraiyans and Panchamas, generally agricultural labourers, on the new lands as farmers, but these settlements are unlikely to have made much difference to the total situation, especially since the Government policy seems to have been to give only those lands which could not be sold to the villagers.[3] This attempt to turn agricultural labourers into landowners was trifling. Also, the growth in landowners

[1] Proceedings of the Revenue Department, 14.5.1900; G.O. Nos. 461, 461A.

[2] Resettlement Report for Madura, 8.1.1916.

[3] See, for example, the correspondence between the Collector, Kistna and Government on this question. In 1892–3 the Collector had allotted 3,192 acres to 669 Paraiyan families of agricultural labourers. The Government felt that his scheme was not well-considered but allowed the experiment on the following conditions:

(*a*) Lands should first be set aside for the villagers and the remainder auctioned for a price of over Rs. 10/- per acre.

(*b*) Only the unsold lands could be assigned in small plots to Paraiyans and others, the grantee 'being regarded merely as a tenant from year to year'.

(*c*) If the grantee held and cultivated the land for 10 years he could then apply to the Government for the lands; the Government could give it as a free gift or at a price not exceeding Rs. 10/- per acre.

Proceedings of the Revenue Department, 17.10.1894. In later years a number of applications from missionaries for similar purposes are recorded.

shown by the Censuses—which may be mainly statistical—was at the expense of the tenants. The proportion of agricultural labourers remained more or less steady between 1881 and 1901, even as the figures stand, and would have fallen, if possible errors in classification are taken into account.

Incidentally, the 1891 and 1901 Censuses give some information on institutional forms of agricultural labour: both Censuses give separate figures for 'farm servants'—those employed on a yearly or even more permanent basis, and 'field labourers'—those employed by the day or month or season. The Census Commissioners themselves pointed out that the figures should be used with caution.[1] The figures have been set out, for what they are worth, in Table 24. They show that even in 1891 about

Table 24. *Types of Agricultural Labourers, 1891 and 1901*

	1891 (15 and over)	1901 (actual workers only)
1. Total Agricultural Labourers	2,597,788	5,031,644
1(a) Male	1,148,047	2,191,562
2. Farm Servants: Total	560,155	662,531
2·1 (%)	21·6	13·2
2(a) Male	329,240	500,977
2(a): 1(a) (%)	28·7	22·9
3. Field Labourers and Crop-watchers Total	2,037,633	4,369,113
3:1 (%)	78·4	86·8
3(a) Male	818,807	1,690,585
3(a): 1(a) (%)	71·3	77·1

Sources: Madras Census, 1891, Part II, 'Imperial Tables', p. 414.
Madras Census, 1901, Part II, 'Imperial Tables', pp. 232–3.

30 per cent of the male agricultural labourers were attached labourers, and the decline to 22 per cent in 1901 may be exaggerated.[2] It is, of course, only to be expected that the proportion of attached labourers would be lower for female workers, but the figures for 1901, when separate figures for actual workers are available, show that the absolute number of

[1] 'The statistics should be accepted with reserve as far as the distinction between farm-servants and field labourers goes'; *Census Report, 1891*, p. 332.

[2] In 1901 the Census Commissioner pointed out that in Malabar only 1,359 persons were returned as farm servants although nearly all the 245,000 Cherumans in the district were in fact farm servants; *Census Report, 1901*, p. 193.

female day labourers was much larger than the number of male day labourers.[1]

What light do the later Census figures throw on changes in the dependence on agriculture—and hence in the proportion of agricultural labour to the agricultural population over the century? In Chapter IV we had estimated the numbers of agricultural labourers at the beginning of the nineteenth century as at least 10 to 15 per cent of the *total* population (as compared to 15 to 20 per cent in the period 1871–1901), but in some ways it is more significant to study the change in the proportion of agricultural labour to the *agricultural* working force. This is, however, more difficult because of the lack of information for the earlier part of the century.

In 1901 the proportion of agricultural population, including women and children, to total population was about 69 per cent. In 1852, the only year previous to 1871 for which separate figures for agricultural population are available, the proportion was about 63 per cent.[2] This figure is very rough, but if correct it means that over the second half of the century there was an increase in the proportion of the total population dependent on agriculture, a rise which would reflect, at least in part, the decay of domestic industry.[3] At what rate had these industries already declined in the first half of the century? That they did decline seems probable: after an initial period in which the Company encouraged local industries for the sake of the 'investment', British goods flooded the market. But the extent to which employment actually declined in the textile, iron and other industries affected has not yet been, and perhaps cannot be, measured.

In any case the argument that agricultural labour was not unusual at the beginning of the nineteenth century is not weakened by this consideration. Indeed, if the period 1800–50 did see a considerable fall in employment outside agriculture, then the agricultural population would have been less than 60 per cent of the total population in 1800. If the agricultural population was 60 per cent of the total population in 1800, then agricultural labour (which was, as we have seen, probably around 10–15 per cent of the total population) would have formed 17–25 per cent of the agricultural population. But agricultural labour would have formed an even

[1] 'The extent to which women are employed in field labour may to some extent be taken as a measure of the standard of living in the district'; Raghavaiyangar, *Memorandum on the Progress of the Madras Presidency*, p. cc.

[2] P.B.R., 19.7.1852, and P.B.R., 18.10.1852. The figures for agricultural population (14,192,941) are very rough; the total includes an estimate of 720,000 for Madras city which was later changed to 450,000.

[3] See, for example, Raman Rao, *Economic Development of Andhra Pradesh, 1766–1957*, pp. 172–87; D. R. Gadgil, *The Industrial Evolution of India*, 4th ed. (Calcutta, 1942), pp. 31–44.

higher percentage of agricultural population, if the latter were less than 60 per cent of the total population. On either hypothesis, the fact that agricultural labour amounted to 27–29 per cent of the agricultural population in 1901 could hardly be regarded as a radical transformation of the agrarian economy.

Appendix—Classification of Census Data

Year	Class	Order	Group or Sub-order	Sub-Group	Universe
1871	6 Classes of which				
	IV. Agriculture	A. *Cultivators*			Adult male population, i.e. those over 12 years
	VI. Indefinite	A. *Labourers for hire* B. Proprietors C. Unproductive D. Others			
1881	6 Classes of which				
	IV. Agriculture	A. Those engaged about the land	A: a. *Agricultural*	a: i. Land holders ii. Tenants iii. Labourers	Working population; male and female figures separately given
			b. Arboricultural c. Horticultural		
		B. Those engaged about animals			
	VI. Indefinite and unproductive	A. Persons of rank or proprietors			
		B. Labourers and others	B: a. *General labourers*	a: i. General labourers ii. Watchmen	
			b. Others		
		C. No specified occupation			

Appendix—Classification of Census Data

Year	Class	Order	Group	Sub-Group	Universe
1891	7 Classes of which				Entire population, i.e. 'occupation' is equivalent to 'means of subsistence'
	II. Pasture and Agriculture	A. Agriculture	A. a. *Landowners and farmers*	a. i. Non-cultivating occupants	
				ii. Cultivating occupants	
				iii. Lessees, etc.	
				iv. Non-cultivating tenants and sharers	
				v. Cultivating tenants and sharers	
			b. *Agricultural labourers*	b. i. Farm servants	
				ii. Field labourers	
			c. Growers of special products		
		B. Livestock	d. Agricultural training and supervision		
	VII. Indefinite and independent	A. Indefinite			
		B. Independent of work (excluding landed proprietors)	A. a. Unskilled labour	a. i. Special branches	
				ii. *General labour*	
			b. Undefined and disreputable		

Appendix—Classification of Census Data

Year	Class	Order	Sub-Order	Sub-Group	Universe
1901	8 Classes of which			i. Cultivating landowners	Entire population. Separate figures for workers and dependants
				ii. Non-cultivating landowners	
	II. Pasture and Agriculture	A. Agriculture	A: a. *Landholders and tenants*	a: iii. Cultivating tenants	
				iv. Non-cultivating tenants	
			b. *Labourers*		
			i. Farm servants		
			ii. Field labourers		
			c. Growers of special products		
			d. Agricultural training, etc.		
		B. Livestock			
	VII. Unskilled labour, not agricultural	A. Earthwork and general labour	A: a. Earthwork		
			b. *General labour*		
		B. Indefinite—disreputable occupations			

Note: Italicized classes are included in whole or in part in Table 23.

XI. CONCLUSION

The lack of data on the numbers of agricultural labourers in India before the era of the all-India Censuses has encouraged the belief that this class was small in size on the eve of British rule. And this assumption is connected with the belief that before the British seized power the typical Indian village was composed in the main of small peasants tilling their own land. Thus:

> ... there is a consensus of opinion that in pre-nineteenth-century India, there was no noticeably large class of agricultural labourers.... That in the course of about a hundred years, the whole social basis of a traditional society which had outlived so many previous invaders, could be so completely smashed by a handful of adventurers from an island in the far-off Atlantic and by a few of their native allies, in a country divided from the place of their birth by half the globe; that of its cultivators and artisans one-third could be turned into landless labourers and one-half into petty cultivators, tenants-at-will and share-croppers, are accomplishments for which one would look in vain for a parallel in the whole history of mankind.[1]

This is the picture of the self-sufficient village first drawn by Metcalfe and Maine, and then taken over by Marx,[2] who went on to show that the destruction of this system—a destruction he regarded as necessary—had been brought about by British imperialism. 'England has broken down the whole framework of Indian society without any symptoms of reconstruction yet appearing.'[3] Marx's assumptions that native institutions could not survive the coming of the British, and that none of the changes in them had been self-generated, were shared by the imperialists them-

[1] S. J. Patel, *Agricultural Labourers in Modern India and Pakistan* (Bombay, 1952), pp. 32, 63. See also R. Mukherjee, *The Dynamics of a Rural Society* (Berlin, 1957); A. R. Desai, *The Social Background of Indian Nationalism* (Bombay, 1948); R. Palme Dutt, *India Today* (2nd ed. Bombay, 1949); Tara Chand, *History of the Freedom Movement in India*, vol. 1 (New Delhi, 1960). Some version of this view is expressed with varying degrees of caution or competence by almost all modern Indian historians, e.g. S. C. Bartarya, *The Indian Nationalist Movement* (Allahabad, 1958), pp. 13–16. Indeed this view underlies the analysis of most economists concerned with agrarian India today. See, e.g. K. N. Raj, *Employment Aspects of Planning in Underdeveloped Countries* (Cairo, 1957), p. 14.

[2] For Marx's description of the unchanging Indian village, see K. Marx, *Capital* (English translation, London, 1883), vol. 1, Chapter XIV, Section 4.

[3] Marx, 'The British Rule in India', *New York Daily Tribune*, 25.6.1853; quoted in Marx, *On Colonialism* (Moscow, n.d.), pp. 31–7.

selves, who justified their rule by claiming to be the active agents of change in stagnant societies.[1] But Marx's picture of the stagnant village community has been touched up and transformed into this idyllic view:

> The village community was mainly composed of peasants. The village committee, representing the village community which was the *de facto* owner of the village land, distributed this land among the peasant families in the form of holdings. Each holding was cultivated by the collective labour of its members. . . . The peasant family enjoyed a traditional right to possess and cultivate its holding from generation to generation.[2]

These Golden Age descriptions correspond to the accounts current a hundred years ago of village life among the earlier European communities, descriptions which Victorian writers sometimes guessed might have applied to India as well.[3] In contrast with those heroically simple pictures of the Indian village before and after British rule, the process of transformation is left in mystery; here the village would seem the exact opposite of sentient beings, 'whose beginnings are not manifest, whose ends are not manifest, only the interval between birth and death is manifest'.[4]

By 1900 British paramountcy over most of India was already a hundred years old; and it seems clear that the fuses which led to the dynamiting of rural society must have been laid during this time. But the structural changes in nineteenth-century Indian agriculture have received so little attention hitherto that this process has been left unexamined. Older historians such as the British administrators and R. C. Dutt, the classical critic of their rule, had much to say about the problems of land, but their main concern was with issues of the Government policy—land revenue, the 'drain' and the like—rather than with such analytical questions as changes in the size of social and economic classes.[5] More modern writers, such as Dr Anstey and Professor D. R. Gadgil, have chiefly been con-

[1] E.g. *The Legislative Minutes of Lord Macaulay*, ed. C. D. Dharker (Madras, 1946) *passim*.

[2] Desai, *The Social Background of Indian Nationalism*, pp. 1–2.

[3] E.g., H. S. Maine, *Village Communities, East and West* (6th ed. London, 1890); F. Seebohm, *The English Village Community* (Cambridge, 1926); K. Marx, *Capital*, vol. 1, Chapter 14, section 4; M. Kovalevsky, *Obshchinnoye Zhemlevlabyenie, Prichini Khod i Posled' styiya evo Razlozhyeniya* (Communal Landholding: the causes, the course and the results of its disintegration) (Moscow, 1879), esp. pp. 156–96. (I am grateful to Professor D. Thorner for drawing my attention to this book, and for providing me with a translation of part of it by Dr L. Lister.)

[4] *Bhagavad Gita*, Chapter II, verse 28.

[5] Dutt mentions the farm labourer and his wages, it is true, but these references are only in passing, and the subject is not even included in the index; R. C. Dutt, *The Economic History of India Under Early British Rule* (London, 1906).

cerned with the history of India after the first half of the century; in any case, their main emphasis was on the problems of an industrial reserve army made up of agricultural labourers, landless and under-employed.[1]

An important exception to the general tendency to neglect the agricultural labourer is W. H. Moreland. Arguing that the *Report on Slavery* of 1841 and other official reports are sufficient evidence that 'a servile labouring class was a normal element in the rural population up to the introduction of British rule', he infers that this servile class must have existed at least as early as the sixteenth century, since there is no evidence of a social revolution which could have created the class in the intervening years.[2]

Nevertheless, the most popular view of recent Indian economic history, in India at least, remains one that can be crudely summarized thus: British rule and the flooding of India with foreign manufactures, destroyed domestic industries, and so drove the artisan on to the land. The British introduced in certain areas a system under which land revenue was assessed at high rates and was payable in cash, and which held individuals responsible for payments. This led to the destruction of the old village communities. The British brought about changes in the law which made it possible to sell land; the monetization of the economy, the stagnation of agriculture, and the pressure of population on resources increased the propensity to do so. The peasant was forced to sell land; it went either to the State for non-payment of taxes, or to the money-lender for non-payment of debt. This turned the peasant into a landless labourer. Supporters of this theory concede that there were some landless labourers before the British took power, but their numbers, so it is held, were insignificant.[3]

Indeed the assertion that agricultural labourers were few is crucial to the whole theory. Using the start of British paramountcy (say, 1800) as a

[1] Although Dr Anstey has chapters on agricultural problems and the land system, her reference to agricultural labour is very brief, and occurs in the chapter, 'The Prosperity of the People'; V. Anstey, *The Economic Development of India*, 4th ed. (London, 1952). Prof. Gadgil deals at somewhat greater length with agricultural labour, but about the growth of the class he has only the following *obiter dictum*: 'The creation of such a class is one of the results of famines; it also results from the steady movement towards the dispossession of old peasant proprietors which has gone on in India now for nearly fifty years'; Gadgil, *The Industrial Evolution of India*, 4th edn., Calcutta, 1942), p. 138.

[2] W. H. Moreland, *India at the Death of Akbar* (London, 1920), pp. 111–15.

[3] 'In pre-nineteenth century India there were domestic and menial servants; but their numbers were small, and they did not form a definite group. . . . The large class of agricultural labourers represents a new form of social relationships that emerged during the late nineteenth and early twentieth centuries in India'; Patel, *Agricultural Labourers in Modern India and Pakistan*, p. 32.

base, it sets up what purports to be a mark against which the later changes in the social structure can be measured.[1]

There are two closely related but separate points at issue here. First, is it true that the agricultural labourer of today is the descendant of the pre-British peasant proprietor who cultivated the land with the assistance of his own family? Secondly, even if there was a distinct group of labourers in the pre-British period, were they not in fact very different from the rural proletariat of today?

To rephrase the first point: is it true that in the agrarian society of pre-nineteenth century India 'there was no room for the existence of an independent and distinct class of agricultural labourers whose main source of livelihood was work on the land of others, for which they received compensation in kind or cash'.[2] This implied view of the self-sufficient village composed of peasant proprietors and artisans is, of course, an absurd over-simplification; whether such villages were ever typical is doubtful, and it is certain that the actual villages of the eighteenth and early nineteenth centuries were very different. Unfortunately there has been very little detailed study yet of the way the land was in fact owned, leased out, and cultivated. But the administrative reports do show that even at the beginning of the nineteenth century in South India there was a sizeable number of farmers with holdings too large to be cultivated by family labour alone. While the very large estate cultivated by several hundred labourers was practically unknown, there were many holdings which required two or three families of labourers, and in Tanjore at least, some holdings were considerably larger. What is more important, there was the group of Brahmin landowners, forbidden most types of

[1] Mr Palme Dutt (*India Today*, pp. 222–3), for example, has the following statement which is taken over by Dr Patel: 'The growth, at the other end of the scale, of the landless labourers is even more significant than the growth of non-cultivating rent receivers. In 1842 Sir Thomas Munro, as Census Commissioner, reported that there were no landless peasants in India (an undoubtedly incorrect picture, but indicating that the numbers were not considered to require statistical measures). In 1882 the census estimated 7½ million "landless day labourers" in agriculture. The 1921 census returned a total of 21 million, or one-fifth of those engaged in agriculture. Since then the proportion is nearer one-half.' It does not strengthen one's confidence in this view to recall that there was no all-India census until 1871, that there was no Madras census in 1842, that Sir Thomas Munro was never Census Commissioner, and that in 1842 he was dead. Moreover, the assertion that now 'the proportion is nearer one-half' is tendentious. It is based on the census data of 1931, which merely showed that agricultural labourers were 32 per cent of the agricultural population. To this Mr Dutt has added the entire figure for 'unspecified labour' to arrive at a percentage of about 37–8. The 1941 census does not contain details of occupation, and the 1951 census, which does, appeared after the second edition of his book had been published.

[2] Patel, *Agricultural Labourers in Modern India and Pakistan*, p. 9.

manual labour by the rules of their caste, who were letting their lands to tenants or employing hired labourers to do the tasks they might not do themselves. From this evidence regarding the structure of South Indian society, it is clear that there was a need for agricultural labourers even before the impact of the British was felt.

And in this, after all, the South Indian agrarian economy was not so different from the economies of other Asian societies in similar stages of development. The *pannaiyal* and *padiyal* of Tamilnad, for example, can be compared with the *fudai* and *genin* of seventeenth-century Japan.[1] But it was peculiar to Indian society that agricultural servitude was a function of caste; only members of certain castes could be made serfs or 'slaves'; and what is more, it appears likely that at the beginning of the nineteenth century the bulk of the agricultural labour castes were following their traditional occupation.

There are a number of difficulties in using the caste figures, but none of them is insuperable; and it is useful to extrapolate from caste figures in the Censuses of the late nineteenth century. Even in 1901 93·5 per cent of the Cherumans of Malabar, 65·7 per cent of the Holeyas of Canara, 75·5 per cent of the Teluga Malas and 64·2 per cent of the Tamil Paraiyans were agricultural workers, and there is a great deal of evidence that caste and occupation were at least as closely correlated one hundred years earlier.

If one assumes that agricultural labour castes grew at roughly the same rate as the rest of the population during the nineteenth century, then at the beginning of this period these castes would have formed 12 to 20 per cent of the total population; if one assumes that there was a close connection between caste and occupation, then the proportion of agricultural labourers would have been, let us say, at least about 10 to 15 per cent of the total population. This deduction would, of course, hold good chiefly for districts where serfdom was still widespread at the beginning of the nineteenth century, and particularly for South Malabar and South Canara where there were hardly any agricultural labourers apart from the 'slaves'. In certain Tamil districts, particularly in the irrigated areas where there was naturally a greater demand for labour, caste and occupation appear to have been fairly closely correlated. In the other districts hired labourers, who may or may not have belonged to these castes, were more widely used. This chain of reasoning backwards from the Census figures has admittedly a number of weak links, but it is supported by the scattered

[1] The *genin* were servants bound to serve for long periods; the *fudai* were hereditary servants; Thomas C. Smith, *The Agrarian Origins of Modern Japan* (Stanford, 1959), pp. 8–9. It is interesting that Prof. Smith estimates that the *genin* formed 10 per cent of the peasant population of seventeenth-century Japan.

evidence of the Collectors in the early nineteenth century. From their reports it is clear that a large segment of the population then belonged to the agricultural labour castes, that most members of these castes worked on the land of others, and that they could not, for economic or social reasons, hold land of their own.

The growth in the number of agricultural labourers must of course be related to the size of the agricultural population as a whole, since it is possible that the labourers were recruited not only from former landowners, but also from village artisans and others outside agriculture. In 1901 the proportion of those engaged in agriculture to total population was about 70 per cent; male agricultural labourers formed about 27 to 29 per cent of the total male working force in agriculture. In 1852 the agricultural population formed about 60 per cent of the total, and this would also have been the case at the beginning of the nineteenth century, if one assumes that the increasing dependence on agriculture, resulting *inter alia* from the destruction of village industries, was chiefly a phenomenon of the second half of the century. Since agricultural labour formed about 10 to 15 per cent of the total population around 1800, on this assumption it would have formed 17 to 25 per cent of the agricultural population at that time. What is more, if the growing dependence on agriculture took place from the beginning of the nineteenth century, so that agriculturists in 1800 were a smaller component of the total population than in 1852, then it follows that agricultural labourers in 1800 would have formed an even larger proportion of the agricultural population, given the estimate that they formed 10 to 15 per cent of the total population.

But here the second problem referred to earlier arises. Even if it is established that there was a large group of agricultural labourers who were in some senses distinct from the landowners at the beginning of the nineteenth century, were they not in a very different position from the landless labourer of today? Did not the dependent status of the earlier serf imply a right to cultivate the land and to share in the crop, in contrast to the complete insecurity of employment of the wage labourer of today?

As we have seen, these rights were not invariably granted. The tied agricultural labourer did not always, or even generally, have the right to work on a particular plot of land, but he would be sold, of course, only to another landowner who could employ him; in this sense his livelihood was always secure. It is more important that he did not always have the right to work and earn; if his master could not employ him, he need not always pay him but could let him try to get some employment as a casual labourer. The issue would be raised presumably only when there was a failure of the crops, and it would be precisely at times like these, when his rights were most needed, that they were most insecure. Certainly in the famines in the early part of the century the agricultural labourers suffered the most, though within the group the casual labourers may have been the worst hit.

On the actual changes in the volume of employment, as well as in the level of wages in the first half of the nineteenth century, there is unfortunately very little information. But there seems to be no discernible trend towards a deterioration in wages up to 1860 at least; wages fluctuated around subsistence level, falling below it in times of famine.

Changes in the land-labour ratio were obviously far more important than changes in social status (and may well have led to the latter). Between 1802 and 1901 the population of Madras Presidency rose by over 300 per cent, and on the assumptions made here the numbers of agricultural labourers must have increased by 400 to 700 per cent. To what extent were these increases matched by the growth of land under cultivation? Although the population increased fairly steadily throughout the first half of the century, the acreage under cultivation fell during the first quarter at least; over the first fifty years as a whole, there does not appear to have been any significant increase in the area under cultivation. In the second half of the century, and particularly towards the end of the period, the reduction in the rates of land revenue and the rise in agricultural prices, together with the pressure of population, did lead to an extension of the land under cultivation. But it would seem that this increase barely kept pace with the growing population in the last fifteen years of the century. In this period the total area cropped went up by 15–16 per cent, while the population increased by 16–17 per cent. And it may be that the inferior lands brought under cultivation depressed average yields, and that this was insufficiently counteracted by the extension of irrigation and by changes in crop patterns.

To some extent, the pressure on land was reduced by emigration. During the last quarter of the century, recorded net emigration was running at about one-seventh to one-ninth of the annual growth of population, and gross emigration (which is in some ways a more significant measure of the reduction in the domestic supply of labour) was four to six times as large again. Emigration also increased social mobility, since those who returned had frequently both the means and the will to escape from caste restrictions on the ownership of land. It was not, of course, the only factor increasing social mobility; the various measures taken by the British also loosened the social bonds of the agricultural labourers. Indeed the small cultivator of the second half of the nineteenth century was not always the descendant of wealthier ancestors whose holdings had been reduced by economic and demographic pressures, or an artisan whose craft had been destroyed by the machine or by foreign trade; he was also, though admittedly far less frequently, a former landless labourer turned tenant or landowner.

Further evidence regarding the decline in the land–labour ratio is supplied by the movements in wages. It seems quite clear that real wages were generally falling from 1873 onwards—apart from temporary fluctuations —and in districts such as Coimbatore and Tinnevelly the decline is marked from the middle of the eighteen-eighties. This reinforces the conclusion that in the fourth quarter of the nineteenth century the extension of cultivation failed to keep pace with the increase in population and the growth in the agricultural labour force.

Thus it was not the case that a class of landless agricultural labourers was wholly created during the British period by the impoverishment of the peasant proprietor and the village craftsman. Even before British rule, there was a sizeable group of landless labourers at the lowest rung, both economically and socially, of the village hierarchy. Whether the economic conditions of this group deteriorated over the nineteenth century is still uncertain, and when the facts themselves are so uncertain causal relationships can hardly be established.

SELECT GLOSSARY

Terms which occur only once or twice in the text are not included. Only brief definitions are given; for fuller definitions of terms see text. No uniform system of spelling Indian words has been used, though in general modern conventions are followed. Many words occur in all four South Indian languages, for example *grama*, but only the original language, or the language relevant in the text, is cited. For all words deriving from Persian, Arabic, Urdu or Hindustani, following H. H. Wilson's *Glossary of Judicial and Revenue Terms of British India* (reprinted Calcutta, 1940), Hindustani (H) is cited.

adima (Malayalam) *adimai* (Tamil)	Slave, bondsman
agraharam (Tamil)	A village occupied by Brahmins and assessed at reduced rates or none
al (Tamil, Malayalam) *alu* (Canarese)	Man, labourer, slave
anicut (Tamil)	A dam
ardhachandrarkam (Sanskrit) *arudikarei* (Tamil)	*Mirasi* village held in severalty
Bakuda	Same as Mundala, sub-caste of Holeyas
bajra (H)	A kind of millet
Boya	Telugu caste
cambu (Tamil)	Same as *bajra*
chaligeni (Canarese)	Tenancy-at-will
Cheruman	Agricultural labour caste in Malabar
cholam (Tamil)	A kind of millet
Dhed	Agricultural labour caste, usually found in the Deccan and North Canara
ekabhogam (Sanskrit) *ijamana gramam* (Tamil)	Village held by one person
Fanam	A coin
grama (Sanskrit)	Village
gulamu (Telugu, from H)	Slave
Hasala	Canarese caste
haveli (H)	Crown lands
Holeya	Canarese agricultural labour caste
huttalu (Canarese)	Serf; from *hutta*: birth; *alu*: servant
inam (H)	A gift; grant of land free of land revenue
inamdar (H)	One who holds an *inam*
inamdari (H)	System of land tenure under which lands are held wholly or partially free of land revenue

jagir (H)	Assignment of land
Jaghire (H)	The old name for Chinglepet District which was originally granted as a *jagir* by the Nawab of Carnatic
janmi (Malayalam)	Landlord
janman (Malayalam)	Literally birth-right, used in Malabar to denote a superior form of land tenure
jawar (H)	A kind of millet
jonna	Same as *cholam*
kadim (Telugu)	Telugu equivalent of *mirasdar*
kanam (Malayalam)	Literally property or possession, used to denote a quasi-mortgage form of land tenure in Malabar
kanamdar, kanakkar (Malayalam)	Person holding land under the *kanam* tenure
kareiyedu (Tamil)	Form of communal land holding with rotation of shares
kasalu (Telugu)	Personal servant
khadim (H)	Servant
kuthugai (Tamil)	Rent fixed in cash
kuzhikanam (Malayalam)	Form of *kanam* tenure
kaul (H)	Agreement, contract
Kusa	Caste name
Madiga	Telugu caste
Mala	Telugu caste
mannalu (Canarese)	Serf, from *mannu*: earth; *alu*: labourer
manyam (Sanskrit)	Revenue-free grant
Mappilla	Muslim community in Malabar
Mari	Sub-group of the Holeyas
maund	A measure; the standard Indian *maund* is 82·2858 lb.
Meri	Sub-group of the Holeyas
miras (H)	Hereditary right
mirasi, *mirasdari*	Hereditary land tenure in the Tamil districts
Mogeru	Fisherman caste in Canara
mulada (Canarese)	Serf
mulawarga (Canarese)	Ancestral estate
mulawargadar (Canarese)	Holder of an ancestral estate
mulgeni (Canarese)	Hereditary occupancy right
Mundala	Sub-group of the Holeyas
naik	Chieftain
Nair	Malayali caste
Nambudri	A Brahmin sub-caste
otti (Malayalam)	Form of mortgage
padi (Tamil)	Fixed daily allowance

padiyal (Tamil)	Hired farm servant receiving wages in kind
pagoda	A coin, usually equivalent to 3½ rupees
palalu, paleru (Telugu)	Hired labourer
Pallan	Tamil agricultural labour caste
Palli or Vanniyan	Tamil caste
pannai (Tamil)	Field, farm
pannaiyal (Tamil)	Farm labourer, serf
parakudi (Tamil)	Tenant not residing in the village
Paraiyan	Tamil agricultural labour caste
pasankarei (Tamil)	Earliest and strongest form of communal land holding
patta (H)	Document given to occupants of land showing the terms of the lease, area held, etc.
pattadar	Holder of a *patta*
pattamdar (Malayalam)	Tenant
payakari (Tamil, Telugu)	Tenant; share-cropper
peramboke (Tamil)	Waste land
peshkash (H)	Land revenue paid by *zamindars*
phalabhogam (Sanskrit)	Same as *arudikarei*
poligar (Telugu)	Military chieftain
Pulaiyan	Tamil caste
ragi	A kind of millet
raiyat (H)	Peasant, cultivator
raiyatwari system	A system of land tenure under which assessments are made directly on individual land holdings
Relli	Agricultural labour caste found in Orissa
salada (Canarese)	Debt slave, from *sala*, debt
samudayam (Tamil)	Identical with *pasankarei*
sarkar, sarkari (H)	Government, governmental
seer	Measure; the standard Indian *seer*=2·057 lb.
taluk (H)	Sub-division of a district
Tiyan	Malayali caste
ulkudi (Tamil)	Resident tenant
Urali	Caste name
vaidageni (Canarese)	Lease for a term of years
Vanniyan or Palli	Tamil caste
varagu (Tamil)	A kind of millet
varam (Tamil)	Share
Vettuvan	Tamil caste
visabadi (Tamil, Telugu)	Form of communal land holding with rotation of shares
zamindar (H)	Landholder; from *zamin*: land
zamindari settlement	A system of land settlement under which the estate of the *zamindar* was assessed as a whole

SELECT BIBLIOGRAPHY

A. PRIMARY SOURCES

I. UNPUBLISHED

The archives of the Madras Presidency, which are kept mainly in the Madras Record Office, fall into two main categories, the Public and the Revenue Records. Of these, the former are of little relevance to the present study since they are confined to political matters, all documents dealing with economic matters having been separately classified since the end of the eighteenth century. Hence nearly all material bearing on revenue, agriculture, and the affairs of rural society generally, whether its provenance be London, Madras or the Collectorates in the districts, is grouped under the Revenue Records.

Most of the unpublished sources for this book have come from these records. They are in five main categories:

(a) *Proceedings of the Board of Revenue, Madras*

These contain correspondence between the Board and the Governor-in-Council and between the Board and the Collectors in the districts. The latter includes the annual settlement reports for each district, together with special *ad hoc* reports by the local officers. Nearly all the Proceedings are in manuscript until 1 April 1860; after this date, some items are still in manuscript. Generally we have referred to extracts from the Proceedings with the date of the Proceeding, for example, P.B.R., 3.11.1863. But for settlement reports and special reports, such as L. Place's 'Report on the Jaghire', we have omitted the P.B.R. date as being unnecessary for identification. Some of these reports were also published in *Parliamentary Papers* and in various selections from the records; but documents consulted in the original are generally referred to in the original.

(b) *Proceedings of the Department of Revenue*

These documents overlap with (a), and also contain reports and memoranda and copies of despatches from London on certain revenue topics.

(c) *Revenue Despatches to London*

At the opening of the nineteenth century these included reports on revenue matters sent every few months. But later they became annual general abstracts, which are usually of little value.

(d) *Despatches from the President, Board of Control (after 1858, the Secretary of State for India to Madras)*

These tend to be recapitulations of the material in (c). But they are of interest during the early years of late *raiyatwari* and during the famine period of the 1870's, when London and Madras came into occasional disagreement.

(e) *District Records*

These contain the correspondence, etc., which passed through the office of the Collector of each district. Settlement reports (apart from the annual reports) are usually bound separately, but other documents are bound according to date, not according to subject. Nearly all of them are in manuscript, and some are available only in the Collector's offices in the districts. There is a good deal of overlapping with (a). For each district the records are calendared in *Guide to the Records of —— District.*

II. PUBLISHED

1. *Parliamentary Papers*

The following have been referred to in the text:

P.P. 1812, VII (377)—*Fifth Report of the Select Committee on the Affairs of the East India Company* (reprinted Calcutta, 1917).

P.P. 1828, XXIV (125)—*Slavery in India: Correspondence and Abstracts of Regulations and Proceedings.*

P.P. 1831–2 (XI–XII)—*Report from the Select Committee on the Affairs of the East India Company: Minutes of Evidence, Appendix and Index.*

P.P. 1834 (128)—*Slavery in India: Correspondence.*

P.P. 1837–8, LI (697)—*Slave Trade: Correspondence, Orders and Regulations and Proceedings taken thereon, 1829–36.*

P.P. 1841, III (54)—*Slavery: Letter from the Government of India, and Minute of the Governor General.*

P.P. 1841, XVI (427)—*Export of Hill Coolies.*

P.P. 1841, XXVIII (238)—*Slavery: Correspondence in Continuation of H. of C. Paper 697 of 1837–8.*

P.P. 1841, XXVIII (262)—*Slavery: Letter from the Government of India, dated 8th February, 1841, with Report of Indian Law Commissioners.*

P.P. 1843, LVIII (525)—*Slavery: Despatch from Government of India, 1843.*

P.P. 1854–5, XL—*Report of the Madras Torture Commission.*

P.P. 1871, XX (393)—*Report of the Commissioner appointed to enquire into the Treatment of immigrant Coolies in British Guiana.*

2. *Selections from Records*

J. Long—*Selections from the Unpublished Records of Government for the years 1748–1767*, Calcutta, 1869.

Selections of Papers from the Records at the East-India House, Relating to the Revenue, Police and Civil and Criminal Justice under the Company's Governments in India, London, 1820

3. *General*

(a) The annual series *Statement Exhibiting the Moral and Material Progress and*

Condition of India (Moral and Material Progress Reports), which were presented to Parliament are also published separately.

(b) Government of Madras: *Manual of Administration of Madras Presidency* (C. D. Macleane) 3 vols., 1885.

(c) Government of Madras: *Standing Information on the Administration of Madras Presidency*, 1877.

(d) For each district, there is a *District Manual*, giving administrative details, and a *Gazetteer*, which also gives more general information on its history, etc. The following *Gazetteers* were found particularly useful:

Gazetteer for Tinnevelly, by H. R. Pate, 1916, 2 vols.
Gazetteer for Madura, W. Francis, 1906.
Gazetteer for Trichinopoly, F. R. Hemingway, 1907, 2 vols.
Gazetteer for Malabar and Anjengo, C. A. Innes, 1908.
Gazetteer for Cuddapah, C. F. Brackenbury, 1915.
Gazetteer for Vizagapatam, W. Francis, 1907.
Gazetteer for South Arcot, W. Francis, 1906.
Gazetteer for Bellary, W. Francis, 1904.
Gazetteer for Anantapur, W. Francis, 1905.

Of the District Manuals, W. Logan: *Malabar* (1887, reprinted Madras, 1951), was found most useful.

4. *Statistics*

Government of India: Census of India for 1871, 1881, 1891 and 1901. For each province there was a *Report*, followed by a volume containing 'Imperial Tables' where the smallest geographical unit is the district, and further volumes containing 'Provincial Tables', that is, details for villages, etc. Only the two main volumes, that is, the *Census Report* and *Imperial Tables* (herein referred to as vol. II of the Census of that year) have been used.

Government of India, Revenue and Agricultural Department: *Agricultural Statistics of British India*, vol. I (British India) for 1884–85 to 1901–02.

Director-General of Statistics, Government of India: *Prices and Wages in India*. The volumes for 1898 and 1908 have been used.

Government of Madras: *Statistical Atlas for Madras Presidency* for 1895, 1900–1, 1908 and 1913. These volumes contain details of cultivated area, land revenue and prices.

5. *Official Reports, etc.*

i. Land Tenure and Land Revenue

Government of India: *Papers regarding Cultivable Waste Lands at the Disposal of Government*, no date, probably 1859.

Government of India: *Memorandum on the Resolution of the Power to Alienate Interests in Land*, 1895.

Government of India: *Note on Land Transfer and Agricultural Indebtedness in India*, no date, probably 1895.

Government of India: *Papers Regarding Land Revenue System of British India*, no date.

Government of India: *Extracts from the Records showing Land Revenue Systems prevailing in India in pre-British Days and Contemporary Practice in Native States*, no date.

Government of Madras: *Memorandum on the Duration of Assessment*, no date.

Government of Madras: *Papers Relative to the Introduction of the Field Assessment*, no date, but the latest paper is dated 1832.

Government of Madras: *Minute on Inams*, 13.5.1859 (by Sir Charles Trevelyan).

Government of Madras: *Memorandum on the Share of the Produce to be taken by the State*, no date, but the latest paper is dated 1861.

Government of Madras: *Correspondence on the Moplah Outrages in Malabar*, 1863.

Government of Madras: *Report on Entire Operations of the Inam Commission*, 30.10.1869 (by W. T. Blair).

Government of Madras: *Report of the Malabar Special Commission, 1881–82*, 1882.

Government of Madras: *Malabar Land Tenures*, 1885.

Government of Madras: *Report with Appendices of the Malabar Land Tenures Committee*, 1887.

Government of Madras: *A Collection of Papers Relating to the Value of Land in the Early Years of the Nineteenth Century*, 1916.

Government of Madras: *Extracts from Papers Relating to Tenancy Rights in Inams*, 1935.

Government of Madras: *Collection of Papers Relating to the Inam Settlement in Madras Presidency*, reprinted 1948.

ii. Famine

Government of India: *Report of the Indian Famine Commission, 1880*.

Government of India: *Report of the Indian Famine Commission, 1898*.

Government of India: *Report of the Indian Famine Commission, 1901*.

Government of Madras: *Report on the Famine in Madras Presidency During 1896 and 1897*, 2 vols., 1898.

iii. Labour and Emigration

Government of India: *Report of the Committee on the Emigration of Labour into Assam*, 1881.

Government of India: *Report of the Assam Labour Enquiry Committee*, 1906–7.

Government of India, Ministry of Labour: First Agricultural Labour Enquiry: *Rural Manpower and Occupational Structure*, 1954; *Report on an Intensive Survey of Agricultural Labour*, 1954, Vol. I: All India, and vol. VI: *South India*. *Report on the Second Agricultural Labour Enquiry*, 1960, vol. I.

iv. Agriculture

Government of Madras: *Report of the Agricultural Committee*, 1880.
Government of India: *Report of the Royal Commission on Agriculture*, 1928.
Government of India: Ministry of Agriculture: *Studies in the Economics of Farm Management in Madras, 1954–55*; 1957.

v. Reports by individual officials and other contemporary writers:

Arbuthnot, A. J., ed.: *Sir Thomas Munro: Selections from his Minutes and other official writings*, 2 vols., London, 1881.
Baird Smith, R.: *The Cauvery, Kistnah and Godavary, being a Report on the Works Constructed on these Rivers for the Irrigation of the Provinces of Tanjore, Guntoor, Masulipatam and Rajahmundry in the Presidency of Madras*, 1856.
Barbosa, Duarte: *A Description of the Coasts of East Africa and Malabar*, English edition, London, 1866.
Bayley, W. H. and Hudleston, W., eds.: *Papers on Mirasi Right*, Madras, 1892.
Benson, C.: *Report of a Tour in Trichinopoly District*, Madras, 1879.
Benson, C.: *Report of a Tour in Cuddapah and North Arcot made in August, 1879*, Madras, 1879.
Buchanan, Francis: *A Journey from Madras through the Countries of Mysore, Canara and Malabar*, 1801, 2nd ed., 2 vols., Madras, 1870.
Cameron, J.: *Report on the Village of Chevayur, 1866*, Calicut, 1868.
Digby, William: *The Famine Campaign in South India, 1876–1878*, 2 vols, London, 1878.
Dykes, J. W. B.: *Salem: An Indian Collectorate*, London, 1853.
Dykes, J. W. B.: *The Ryotwari Tenure*, Madras, 1858.
Gleig, G. R.: *Life and Correspondence of Major-General Sir Thomas Munro*, 3 vols., London, 1830.
Naidu, Ramakrishnan: 'Remarks on the Revenue System and Landed Tenures of the Provinces under the Presidency of Fort St. George', Part I, *Journal of the Royal Asiatic Society*, 1834.
Norton, J. B.: *Letter to Robert Lowe, Esq., on the conditions and requirements of the Madras Presidency*, Madras, 1854.
Phillips, H. A. D.: *A Blacker Pamphlet, or an Attempt to Explain the Severity of the Last Famine and the Poverty of the Madras Ryot*, Madras, 1878.
Robertson, W. R.: *Reports on the Agricultural Conditions, Capabilities and Prospects of the Neilgherry and Coimbatore Districts*, Madras, 1881.
Smollett, J. B.: *Madras, Its Civil Administration, being rough notes from personal observation written in 1855 and 1856*, London, 1858.
Strachey, J.: *A Report on the Northern Division of Malabar, 1801*, Calicut, 1908.
Sullivan, J.: *Report on the Provinces of Malabar and Canara, 1841*, Calicut, 1916.
Walker, A.: *The Land Tenures of Malabar*, Madras, 1801, reprinted Cochin, 1879.
Warden, T.: *Report on the Land Tenures in Malabar, 1815*, Calicut, 1916.
Warden, T.: *Report on the Condition of the Palghaut, Congaad, Mannoor, Eddatenah, Konilparah, and Narattum Divisions, 1801*, Madras, 1867.

Wye, J. W.: *Report on the Southern Division of Malabar, 1801*, Calicut, 1907.

B. SECONDARY SOURCES

Adam, William: *The Law and Custom of Slavery in British India*, London, 1840.
Anstey, Vera: *The Economic Development of India*, 4th edn., London, 1952.
Appadorai, A.: *Economic Conditions in South India, 1000–1500 A.D.*, Madras, 1936.
Baden-Powell, B. H.: *Land Systems of British India*, Oxford, 1892, 3 vols.
Baden-Powell, B. H.: *The Indian Village Community*, reprinted New Haven, 1957.
Baines, Sir Athelstane: *Ethnography (Castes and Tribes)*, Strasbourg, 1912.
Banaji, D. R.: *Slavery in British India*, Bombay, 1933.
Bartarya, S. C.: *The Indian Nationalist Movement*, Allahabad, 1958.
Beidelman, Thomas O.: *A Comparative Analysis of the Jajmani System*, New York, 1959.
Bell, K. and Morrell, W. P.: *British Colonial Policy, 1830–1860*, Oxford, 1928.
Bernadelli, H.: 'New Zealand and Asiatic Migration', *Population Studies*, July, 1952.
Bhatia, B. M.: *Famines in India, 1850–1945*, Bombay, 1963.
Bloch, Marc: *Feudal Society*, English edition, London, 1961.
Buchanan, D. H.: *Development of Capitalist Enterprise in India*, New York, 1934.
Burn, W. L.: *Emancipation and Apprenticeship in the British West Indies*, London, 1937.
Burnell, A. C.: *South Indian Paleography from the Fourth to the Seventeenth Century A.D.*, 2nd edn. London, 1878.
Caldwell, R.: *A Political and General History of the District of Tinnevelly in the Presidency of Madras from the Earliest Period to its Cession to the British Government in A.D. 1801*, Madras, 1881.
Cambridge History of India, vol. v and vol. vi, Indian reprint, New Delhi, 1958 and 1963.
Cobden Club: *Systems of Land Tenure in various Countries*, London, 1870.
Comins, D. W. D.: *Notes on Emigration from India to British Guiana*, Georgetown, 1894.
Cumpston, I. M.: *Indians Overseas in British Territories, 1834–1854*, London, 1953.
Dalyell, R. A.: *Memorandum on the Madras Famine of 1876.*
Davis, Kingsley: *The Population of India and Pakistan*, Princeton, 1951.
Desai, A. R.: *The Social Background of Indian Nationalism*, Bombay, 1948.
Dharker, C. D., ed.: *Lord Macaulay's Legislative Minutes*, Madras, 1946.
Dodwell, H.: *Report on the Madras Records*, Madras, no date.
Dutt, R. C.: *The Economic History of India Under Early British Rule*, London, 1902.
Dutt, R. C.: *The Economic History of India in the Victorian Age*, London, 1904.
Dutt, R. Palme: *India Today*, 2nd Indian edition, Bombay, 1949.
Furber, H.: *John Company at Work*, Cambridge, Massachussetts, 1957.
Gadgil, D. R.: *The Industrial Evolution of India*, 4th edn., Calcutta, 1942.
Geoghegan, J.: *Note on Emigration from India*, Calcutta, 1873.

Gover, Charles E.: *The Folk Songs of Southern India*, 1871 (Reprinted, Madras, 1957).

Habib, Irfan M.: *The Agrarian System of Mughal India*, Bombay, 1963.

Hewitt, J. F.: 'Communal Origin of Indian Land Tenures', *Journal of the Royal Asiatic Society*, new series, vol. XXIX, 1897, pp. 628–41.

Hjejle, Benedicte: The Social Policy of the East India Company with reference to Sati, Slavery, Thagi and Infanticide, 1872–1858. Unpublished thesis presented for the D.Phil. degree, Oxford, 1958.

Hutton, J.: *Caste in India*, 2nd edn., London, 1951.

Kautilya: *Artha Shastra*, ed. Sama Sastry, 5th edn., Mysore, 1956.

Kondapi, C.: *Indians Overseas, 1839–1949*, New Delhi, 1951.

Kovalevsky, M.: *Obschinnoye Zhemlevlabyenie, Prichini Khod i Posled' styiya evo Razlozhysniya* (Communal Land Holding, the causes, the course and the results of its disintegration), Moscow, 1879.

Krishnan, V.: The Thambraparni Ryot. Unpublished thesis presented for the Ph.D. degree, Madras University, 1931.

Leach, E. R., ed.: *Aspects of Caste in South India, Ceylon and North-West Pakistan*, Cambridge, 1960.

Maine, H. S.: *Village Communities, East and West*, 6th edn., London, 1890.

Macnaghten, W. H.: *Principles and Precepts of Hindu Law*, 2 vols., Calcutta, 1828–9.

Marx, Karl: *Capital*, vol. 1, English trans., London, 1883.

Marx, Karl: *On Colonialism*, Moscow, n.d.

Mayer, Adrian C.: *Land and Society in Malabar*, London, 1952.

Mendis, G. C.: *Ceylon Under the British*, 2nd edn., Colombo, 1952.

Menon, K. P. Padmanabha: *History of Kerala*, 4 vols., Ernakulam, 1924.

Miller, Eric J.: 'Caste and Territory in Malabar', *American Anthropologist*, June, 1954.

Moreland, W. H.: *The Agrarian System of Moslem India*, Cambridge, 1929, reprinted Allahabad, n.d.

Moreland, W. H.: *From Akbar to Aurangzeb, A Study in Indian Economic History*, London, 1923.

Moreland. W. H.: *India at the Death of Akbar*, London, 1920.

Mukherji, Nilmani: *The Ryotwari System in Madras*, Calcutta, 1962.

Mukherjee, Ramakrishna: *The Dynamics of a Rural Society: A Study of the Economic Structure in a Bengal Village*, Berlin, 1957.

Patel, Surendra J.: *Agricultural Labourers in Modern India and Pakistan*, Bombay, 1952.

Raghavaiyangar, S. Srinivasa: *Memorandum on the Progress of the Madras Presidency During the Last Forty Years of British Administration*, Madras, 1893.

Raj, K. N.: *Employment Aspects of Planning in Underdeveloped Countries*, Cairo, 1957.

Raju, A. Sarada: *Economic Conditions in Madras Presidency, 1800–50*, Madras, 1941.

Raman Rao, A. V.: *Economic Development of Andhra Pradesh, 1766–1957*, Bombay, 1958.

Reddy, N. S.: Transition in Caste Structure in Andhra Desh with Particular Reference to Depressed Castes. Unpublished thesis for the Ph.D. degree, Lucknow University, 1952.

Sarkar, N. K.; *The Demography of Ceylon*, Colombo, 1957.

Sastri, K. A. Nilakanta: *The Colas*, Madras, 1955.

Sastri, K. A. Nilakanta: *The History of South India*, Madras, 1955.

Seebohm, F.: *The English Village Community*, Cambridge, 1926.

Shea, Thomas W., Jr.: The Land Tenure Structure of Malabar and its influence upon capital formation in Agriculture. Unpublished thesis presented for the Ph.D. degree, University of Pennsylvania, 1959.

Smith, Thomas C.: *The Agrarian Origins of Modern Japan*, Stanford, 1959.

Srinivasachari, C. S.: 'Poligar System in the Tamil Country: Its Origin and Growth', *Proceedings of the Indian Historical Records Commission, 1928*, pp. 100–106.

Stokes, Eric: *The English Utilitarians and India*, Oxford, 1959.

Sundaraja Iyengar, S.: *Land Tenures in Madras Presidency*, Madras, 1916.

Tara Chand: *History of the Freedom Movement in India*, New Delhi, 1960.

Thomas, P. J. and Natarajan, B.: 'Economic Depression in the Madras Presidency, 1820–54', *Economic History Review*, November 1936, pp. 67–75.

Thomas, P. J. and Ramakrishnan, K. C.: *Some South Indian Villages: A Re-Survey*, Madras, 1940.

Thorner, Daniel: 'India's Agrarian Revolution by Census Redefinition', *Indian Economic Review*, August 1956, pp. 1–21.

Thurston, E.: *Castes and Tribes of Southern India*, 7 vols., Madras, 1909.

Thurston, E.: *Ethnographical Notes on South India*, Madras, 1906.

United Nations: *The Determinants and Consequences of Population Growth*, New York, 1953.

Wilson, H. H.: *A Glossary of Judicial and Revenue Terms of British India* (reprinted, Calcutta, 1940).

Wright, H. R. C.: 'Some Aspects of the Permanent Settlement in Bengal', *Economic History Review*, 1954, Second Series, vol. VII, No. 2, pp. 204–15.

INDEX